IN/EQUALITY

AN ALTERNATIVE ANTHROPOLOGY

Fourth Edition

PEM DAVIDSON BUCK

CP CAT PUBLISHING

ISBN: 978-1-56226-680-6 © 2016, 2013, 2010, 2009, CAT Publishing Inc. Palo Cedro, CA

Table of Contents

ACKNOWLEDGEMENTS

First and foremost I thank my students. Without them this book would not exist, both in the obvious sense that without them there would be no point in writing it, but more importantly in the sense that they made me *want* to write it and have left their footprints all over it. This book takes the shape it does because it reflects what I have found to work in helping them see the world through a new pair of glasses. It reflects equally what I have learned from them over the last twenty-five years about the world in which they and I live. And, of course, it reflects their boredom with the variety of big glossy texts I initially felt obliged to subject them to. Their (relatively!) passive resistance led me to write the initial little booklet from which this book grew.

Secondly, my own teachers have left their footprints all over this book. Faye V. Harrison, Fred Hicks, and Ed Segal introduced me at the University of Louisville to a form of cultural anthropology that I found fascinating—not the rather functionalist and androcentric version to which I had been exposed as an undergraduate. Their influence made me as impatient with the glossy texts as were my students. Faye Harrison then shepherded me through the initial years of my career as an anthropologist, and has been an enduring source of support ever since.

My thanks go also to the Association of Black Anthropologists, which over many years has provided me with an intellectual home and has been the source of tremendous stimulation. In particular, the several 'Teaching as Praxis' sessions held irregularly over the years at annual meetings of the American Anthropological Association, often sponsored or co-sponsored by the Association of Black Anthropologists, provided me both as organizer and as participant with the opportunity to work with others on some of the knottier issues of teaching about inequality in its various forms.

Irma McClaurin, many years ago, gave me a much needed validation of the original booklet that I had written specifically for my own classes. Many years later she was seconded by Walter Matherly, who accidentally spent some time in my college's bookstore while he was traveling around the country tracing his genealogical roots; he picked up and read that booklet, and encouraged me to take it seriously, as more than just a booklet for my own classes.

I owe particular thanks to people who read and commented on earlier drafts of the book: James Gardiner, Derrick Hodge, Ann Kingsolver, Vin Lyon-Callo, Enoch Page, Naomi Palagi, and several anonymous reviewers. The book underwent many changes as a result of their insights. For the second edition I owe a special debt of gratitude to Derrick Hodge, Ann Kingsolver, and Yvonne Jones. And for the third edition, my thanks to Boone Shear, Faye V. Harrison, Antoinette Jackson, and Arthur Spears. My thanks also in this fourth edition to David Aliaga for his helpful comments and suggestions, and to Warren Perry for his advice and support—and for the support and intellectual stimulation I continue to receive from the scholars I mentioned for earlier editions.

Janet Henderson was a wonderfully resourceful work study student, particularly in her ability to locate web materials—and she did a lot of typing, despite being bored to tears by the job! Joella Spataro, secretary for the Social and Behavioral Science Division, of which I am a member, did the original formatting of the booklet and presided over several of its revisions. Elizabethtown Community and Technical College granted a sabbatical for the 2006-2007 academic year, during which the major portion of the first edition was written. Leslie and James Golden, at CAT Publishing, have been truly supportive, as well as being a pleasure to work with through the whole editing and publishing process.

And finally, there is David Buck, an excellent critic and editor, always ready for a good discussion of the issues I was grappling with as I wrote, and an indefatigable advocate for my work when I hit those discouraging moments when I no longer believe in it. There would be no book without him.

To the Instructor

A major change in this 4th edition of *In/Equality* is the provision of links in the margins of many pages to online materials related to the issues being discussed in the text. Materials in the links include news items, brief articles, and websites of organizations. Some video material is also included, but given the uncertainly of online copyright issues, most are simply suggested, without a direct link. *In/Equality* is available as an online digital book, which enables students to click on the links to go directly to these sites. It continues to be available in hard copy as well. Students who have the hard copy version can go to http://www.catpublishing.com/pdf/links.pdf on the CAT Publishing website, where there is a downloadable PDF file containing the links, making it possible for them to click on the links, rather than having to type out the URLs. It is hoped that students will ignore ads and other pop-ups that are associated with some of these sites. Although materials have been chosen with the likelihood of their longevity in mind, unfortunately, given the ephemeral nature of some online material, there can be no guarantee that all links will still be available by the time students try to access them. It is hoped that instructors will find that these online materials provide greater flexibility and depth to the use of the text.

As an online book *In/Equality* is accessible to students for six months through the internet. During that time it is also fully printable, should the student so desire. Individual students may choose to purchase the online version through RedShelf at http://www.redshelf.com.

As did the 3rd edition of *In/Equality*, the 4th edition provides another form of flexibility to the instructor. Each chapter is written so that it can stand alone or, with the exception of the first, be taught in any order. CAT Publishing will bind individual chapters or combination of chapters to meet the instructor's requirements; syllabi can also be included. For more details on this possibility please use this link to the CAT Publishing website: http://www.catpublishing.com/chapters.cfm.

CHAPTER 1
A NEW PAIR OF GLASSES

Anthropology[1]
The study of humans, past and present. Cultural anthropology focuses on how people in various parts of the world organize and govern themselves, and the meanings they create as they deal with the world they live in.

• **Want more?** Try exploring *American Anthropological Association* http:// www.americananthro.org /

Note to the student: You are encouraged to download a PDF document that contains active links to the websites referenced in this textbook and to visit the websites as a part of your studies for this course. To download the PDF document go to: www.catpublishing.com/ pdf/links.pdf

The object of this book is to give you a framework for thinking and learning about other societies and about your own—about learning to see in a very new way, through a different, and I hope clearer, pair of glasses. It is about an anthropological understanding of the world, particularly the world of societies like our own, where some people have far more power and wealth than others. It is not a standard textbook: it does not try to introduce you to anthropology as an academic subject with a certain body of knowledge about certain topics, which anyone who has 'taken' **anthropology** 'ought' to know. Instead it uses anthropology to introduce you to that new pair of glasses.

The glasses this book constructs are those of a particular tradition within anthropology, growing out of the recurring arguments anthropologists have had about what anthropology is, what its purpose is, and even about whom anthropologists should study. Sometime during the 1980s some of us began to discuss the ways in which anthropology should be 'decolonized.' More recently, a number of anthropologists have been talking about 'engaged' anthropology. This book grows out of these traditions. It uses the glasses of those traditions in trying to see what is important about how social structures work, for ourselves and for people all around the world.

Bear in mind that not all anthropologists take this approach, although some have always done so. This approach has gained greater acceptance over the past twenty or so years, however. More anthropologists are taking a critical look not only at anthropology itself, but also at the way many human societies, including our own, are organized to produce inequality both at home and in their relationships with other societies. Also bear in mind that what you see as you begin to look at the world through this new pair of glasses may frequently contradict, or at least give a different perspective on, what you are told on the evening news or on news channels. This is because a decolonized or engaged anthropology takes seriously the views and knowledge of people experiencing exploitation and is often written by members of such groups. That is why we can't assume that the people we 'study' know less about the system in which they live than we do. In fact, we can't even assume we really understand our own system. Ideally we have different areas of knowledge and expertise and ways of understanding and by working together our types of knowl-

---

1. Words in bold are defined in the glossary. There is more about the glossary and the words anthropologists use in the section "Consoling Advice" starting on page 26

edge complement each other. Together we can understand more than we do separately. In fact, a few anthropological organizations bring anthropologists from all over the world together to share insights and work collaboratively—a huge change from the days when most people with degrees in anthropology couldn't imagine seeing the people they studied as equals, even if they did care deeply about them.

Anthropologists from the *Global South*[2] are studying and writing about their own societies and about the *Global North,* and developing theories about how the differences came to exist and continue to exist even as the world becomes more interconnected. All these approaches, decolonized, engaged, collaborative, assume that people who are being exploited or who are members of societies that have been colonized have something to say that people in all parts of the world need to hear and learn from. Anthropological knowledge is more valid as a result, and consequently it will be of greater use to people fighting oppression.

HOW DO YOU KNOW IF IT'S ANTHROPOLOGY?

But first, some basics about anthropology. Almost anything about being human is fair game, in one way or another, for anthropology. Anthropology tries to understand how and why people live as they do all over the world.

According to one 'joke,' anthropologists study dark-skinned people and sociologists study light-skinned people. There has been some truth to that joke. However, it is more accurate to say that most cultural anthropology, the subject of this book, has studied the societies of people who have been colonized or exploited, while sociology most often focuses on the people who live in the colonizing countries but are exploited by the *elites* of their own country. Both sociology and anthropology connect with history, and all three are concerned with related historical processes. Recent changes in the three disciplines have brought them closer in method and content.

Holism has been one of the major differences between cultural anthropology and the other social sciences, including most sociology. It is the goal of much anthropology, even though it is actually impossible to achieve, to understand a society or a particular group within a larger society by looking at *all* aspects of the society. In attempting to be holistic your goal is to study the society as a whole, rather than just particular aspects of it, such as its economy. You are placing the particular issues that interest you in a broad context. Some history and sociology is also holistic, although until recently this was a less consistent approach than it has been in anthropology.

Global South
A term which is used in place of terms such as third World, which has negative implications.*

Global North
A term which is used in place of terms such as First World, which has positive implications.*

Elite
In a system of relationships based on inequality, the elite are the people who directly benefit from inequality and control the lives and labor of those who suffer from inequality.*

Holism
An important aspect of anthropological method and perspective. In a holistic approach the anthropologist is attempting to understand the society as a whole, rather than just particular aspects of it, such as its economy.*

---

2. When there is an asterisk at the end of a margin definition, as there is with this and other terms, see the glossary for the full definition.

Gender
The learned behavior and attitudes associated with a particular sex in a particular society.

Ethnography
A book, article, or film that makes an anthropological description or analysis of a particular culture.

Participant observation
An anthropological research method in which researchers live among the people whose culture they are studying.*

Ethnocentrism (ethnocentric)
Judging the members of another culture or subculture by the standards of one's own culture, with the assumption that one's own culture is best and that it is the way all rational people would naturally choose to live.

Culture
The learned and shared behavior patterns of a group of people; includes all that the society produces, ideas as well as things.*

> *Anthropology works on the assumption that you can't understand one aspect of a society without seeing how all aspects are interwoven and influence each other.*

For instance, you can't understand why doctors in our society frequently use their patients' first names, while patients rarely use their doctor's first names, without also holistically understanding our patterns of class, race, and **gender** inequality and our system of profit-making based on illness. So, ultimately, a 'simple' little question about who uses whose first name leads into a study of our entire social structure. You may find this aspect of anthropology frustrating. You may feel that everything you want to say about the **ethnographic** literature you are reading along with this book is connected to five or six other issues that need to be explained, making it hard for you to organize your thoughts. There is no easy fix for this problem, other than to go ahead and do a lot of explaining.

As part of the holistic approach, many anthropologists have depended on **participant observation**. In participant observation, the anthropologist

> *By participating, the anthropologist hopes to gain a much deeper understanding than could be achieved by merely observing, or by asking questions and administering surveys.*

lives with the people he or she wants to learn about and learn from. The anthropologist observes and participates in their daily activities.

For instance, if you want to know why coal miners go on strike when employers threaten to reduce health care benefits, you could gain a gut-level understanding by working for a year or two in a coal mine, or by working in a community where coal miners you know and grow to care about are slowly dying of black lung. Or if you want to know why families in India are willing to spend a great deal of money on jewelry as part of their daughter's dowry, you could learn an Indian language and then go to live with a family that has several marriageable daughters. As much as possible, you would become like a member of the family. You would listen to family discussions about arranging the marriages, sit in on negotiation sessions, visit with family friends and neighbors, attend weddings, meet prospective bridegrooms, see or hear about what happens when a family can't provide adequate jewelry, and follow up whatever opportunities came your way. You would probably eventually conclude that families had good reason to be concerned about dowries and about arranging suitable marriages. You might also conclude that your original reactions to the idea of arranged marriages and dowries were actually quite **ethnocentric**—you were judging them by the standards of your own **culture**. Participant observation would have given you a new way of looking at a culture different from your own.

Traditionally, this immersion in other people's lives and culture has been done far from home. It was, and sometimes still is, expected that anthropologists have to work in a very different place and culture from their own in order to be 'objective.' This 'very different place' is called 'the field,' and the whole process is referred to as *fieldwork*. The information gathered is then analyzed and pulled together and written up in an ethnography like the articles or books you may be reading along with this one. More recently various forms of multi-sited fieldwork have become common, with anthropologists following their topic as it shifts from site to site. Other anthropologists do much of their work on the internet, perhaps studying aspects of popular culture or analyzing what the Far Right has to say about the political process in the U.S., for instance. Some are engaged in cultural critique, analyzing the causes and effects of patterns within our own culture, usually ones the anthropologist sees as damaging. Some study the effects of the wars in Iraq and Afghanistan; others critically examine the policies that have created an unprecedented rate of imprisonment in the US. Still others study how people in the areas most affected by climate change are dealing with their changing environment or with the loss of homes and community; others interested in climate change seek to learn why so many people in the US don't think it is real or caused by humans. Some are engaged in policy analysis for government agencies or work in non-profit organizations in the US and around the world.

Many anthropologists have theoretical questions that they are attempting to answer, trying to explain connections between various cultural patterns. For instance, is there some underlying factor which has lead to the growing influence of fundamentalism in Christianity, Islam, and Hinduism? Or, is there any connection between the use of dowries and a particular organization of women's and men's roles in a *society*? Do particular types of economies or *inequality* systems tend to be associated with dowry systems? Does everyone in a society with the dowry system actually use it? If it is limited to particular groups, what causes that difference? Do societies using the dowry system have similar kinds of religious explanations for men's and women's roles? Do dowry systems change as a result of colonization? What effect have World Bank policies had on marriage patterns? How do bridewealth and dowry relate to the financial arrangements made around marriage in societies that lack these systems?

Fieldwork
The process of studying the way of life of a particular group of people or of people in a particular situation by living with them.*

• **Want more?** Try Anthropology Now http://anthronow.com/ Or try Huffington Post Anthropology Association Blog http://www.huffingtonpost.com/american-anthropological-association/

Society
Groups of people who are relatively separated from surrounding populations, occupy a specific territory, and share a common culture.*

Inequality
A system whereby certain individuals can gain more power, prestige, influence, or wealth than others.*

> *Anthropologists interested in engaged or decolonized anthropology have made it clear that there are other ways of doing anthropology, and their views have played a part in the shifts that have occurred recently in the discipline as a whole.*

Some anthropologists, particularly those who practice engaged anthropology, reject the notion that anthropology is valid only if it is far from home. Instead, they may practice anthropology 'in their own backyard.' This is no threat to objectivity. It is now generally understood that totally objective fieldwork is an impossibility. It took a long time for us to realize that people, including anthropologists, are always influenced by their own culture, and even by their position in their own culture—by their class, race, and gender, by their religion, by their political opinions, and many other factors. To do as accurate a job as possible of understanding other people's lives, anthropologists try to understand themselves and the biases they are carrying from their own culture and their own lives. Knowing how these are likely to influence you helps you avoid being ethnocentric—you can discount some of your initial reactions. Many anthropologists now also make clear to their readers where they are coming from so that the reader can factor in the biases and understand the perspective of the anthropologist. Anthropologists who do this are acknowledging that all humans have a perspective. We are not truly detached scientific observers. We bring human emotions with us; we learn to love or hate some of the people with whom we work. We have political opinions, whether they are conservative, middle of the road, or radical, that influence how we interpret what we see. We care about what happens to the people we learn about, and we care about the effects on people's lives of decisions made by government, corporations, religious institutions, local elites, various helping organizations, the World Bank and International Monetary Fund. All of this influences how anthropologists interpret the facts and situations they encounter.

Engaged and decolonizing anthropologists have a second concern about anthropology as it has traditionally been practiced. The emphasis on 'the field' as disconnected from home has had some unfortunate consequences in their eyes. It has discouraged anthropologists from studying their own societies, and it has encouraged ethnography readers, and to some extent anthropologists themselves, to see themselves and their communities as having very little in common with the people studied in 'the field.' A 'we/they' attitude may thus be fostered, helping to perpetuate beliefs about other people that make *exploitation* easier. The emphasis on studying far away people has also meant that most anthropologists—with some notable exceptions—until recently did not apply the skills and knowledge of their discipline to understanding or combating issues such as exploitation and inequality in their own society.

Exploitation
Using other people or their resources for your own benefit, without ensuring equal benefits to the people being exploited; possible only in situations of inequality.

SOME THOUGHTS ABOUT BEING HUMAN

We humans do not simply act as we wish.

> *To a large extent our behavior is dictated to us by our culture. Or perhaps a better way to put it would be that the options we see as reasonable, the ones we choose between, are ones set up by our culture.*

Cultural determination
The way in which human behavior is heavily influenced and to some degree controlled by the culture of the particular group in which a person lives.

Class marker
Behavior, consumption patterns, and/or display of objects that identify someone as being a member of a particular class. See also status marker.

Often those options are different for various groups within our society, so, for instance, the options set up for women may be different from those set up for men. People do sometimes step outside those options, but they frequently pay a heavy price for doing so. This process of setting options is referred to as *cultural determination*. So, for instance, all people everywhere have to eat. But your culture 'tells' you what kinds of food are acceptable; you are unlikely to think foods taste good if they are not part of your society's definition of acceptable. If broccoli is on your society's list of acceptable food, you may or may not personally like broccoli, but you don't vomit at the thought of eating it. The foods you do like will all, like broccoli, be on your culture's list—your culture is presenting you with a set of options to choose among. You are very unlikely to choose to like grubs, marshmallows, pawpaws, raw oysters, pig, horse, sheep eyes, beef, or dog if they are not on your culture's acceptable list. Within your culture, if you are in a complex and stratified society, there will be groups with slightly different lists. Raw oysters and raw fish eggs are standard good food in some societies, but in the U.S. eating them acts as a bit of a *class marker*. So does eating pork rinds or pinto beans. You are pretty unlikely to find people who think both pinto beans and raw fish eggs are truly acceptable forms of food.

And, in addition, your society will also present you with options about the possible ways to get food. This book will describe some of the different methods people have followed in various cultures. You will also see that these methods can change.

For instance, many people in the U.S. now work to get money to buy meals at fast food places—which means there are now many more such places than there were, and many more people working in them. This is partly because our culture has changed significantly in the last fifty or so years. There are now many more people buying fast food because there are now so many more women working outside the home or farm. Exhaustion due to working two jobs, one for pay and the other housekeeping for free, makes fast food an attractive option if you can afford it. There are also many more people living alone, making cooking feel like it is not worth the effort, and often not economical. The kind of fast food you eat is also part of your culture. Lots of people eat fast food in India, too, but beef is never used in mainstream society: most Indians feel that is irreligious. The idea of eating a hamburger makes many Indians feel sick to their stomachs.

Means of production
The resources used in the process of production (tools, land, raw materials, etc.).*

Unless you are in the class that owns resources in the U.S. and in much of the rest of the world, your strategy for eating will involve getting a job—selling your labor and using your wages to buy food that has been produced and processed by people working in industrial agriculture. This process of buying and selling labor and goods is part of our market economy. You need the job because in our culture the **means of production** are not available to most people. Land, machinery, factories, tools, capital—all are privately owned by comparatively few people. If you are hungry, you can't just find an empty piece of ground and grow a garden. You are denied that right. That is called trespassing and can get you time in jail. And you aren't part of a lineage or clan that conveys to you the right to use land just because you are a member or married to a member. So you are going to have to sell your labor and buy food. But there are, and used to be many, societies where this was not the case. If you were a member of one of the traditional Papua New Guinean societies, for instance, you wouldn't be in that fix. Like everyone else, you would have the right to garden somewhere.

In addition, our culture, like most others today, has different patterns for different groups of people. If you are Black, for instance, and get a restaurant job, in many parts of the U.S. your job is less likely to involve direct customer contact than if you are White. Cultural patterns associated with gender are also likely to affect fast food jobs. Women are far more likely than men to be dependent for long periods of time on low-paying, dead-end service jobs of this type.

Another concept closely related to cultural determination is the **social construction of reality**. People's behavior makes what is real in our world.

Social construction of reality
A way of understanding the world and human life which recognizes that people make what is real in our world.*

> *The Thomas Theorem explains the social construction of reality by stating that if enough people believe something is real, it can have real consequences. Those consequences can occur even if what people believe is a flat out lie.*

For example if people in your society believe that ghosts inhabit graveyards at night, that belief has real consequences on people's behavior: they stay out of graveyards at night. Or if your society believes that the forest is inhabited by evil spirits, people stay out of the forest. If being skinny is defined as beautiful, then lots of people will struggle to eat less than is healthy, and some will even die of malnutrition. And skinny people will have an easier time getting jobs, finding spouses, and gaining respect.

Even the birth of a baby is subject to the social construction of reality. If birth is defined as a medical emergency rather than as a natural process, then surgical procedures and the use of drugs increase. More babies are born in a drugged condition, sometimes creating a real medical emergency. And if adequate nutrition and prenatal care are fairly inaccessible to women with little money, then their babies are more likely to be born prematurely, and the mothers are more likely to have serious health problems, creating more medical emergencies. In other words, how people with policy-making *power* perceive birth, pregnancy, and the right to health care and food has real effects. Even the physiological processes of pregnancy and birth are influenced by the social construction of reality, shaped by people and their culture.

Power
The ability to get other people to do as you want, even in the absence of their consent.

> *The social construction of reality is basic to the social organization of all societies.*

For instance, a group of people may be defined as inferior and treated as if they actually were inferior. If this happens then their supposed inferiority leads others to mistreat them, and the resulting inequality makes them appear to be actually inferior. These consequences are real, and have real effects on people's lives even though the beliefs they are based on are false. People who are treated as inferior really do have fewer chances at decent jobs, have higher *infant mortality rates*, die younger, are treated unfairly in courts.

The effects of hurricane Katrina in 2005 made these consequences dramatically clear. Most of those who were left stranded in New Orleans were poor and many were Black. Years of *discrimination* meant that they were the people most likely to have neither a car nor the money to leave; and apparently those in power had not considered it important to make evacuation plans for those who couldn't leave on their own. So it was mostly the poor, mostly Black people, who died from neglect, from the denial of rights, not from inferiority, not even from the hurricane itself. They died of the consequences of being defined as inferior and unworthy of the effort needed to evacuate them; they died of a lie. Did fewer people die in hurricane Sandy in 2012 partly because fewer in the affected areas were poor and Black? As you go through this book you will see many more examples of the consequences of living in a society that is designed to deny rights to people.

Infant mortality rate
The number of children per thousand births who die before one year of age. A high rate means lots of children die.

Discrimination
Action that treats someone, usually based on their identity, differently from how a similarly qualified person of another group would be treated. Distinguish from prejudice, which has to do with attitudes, not actions.

• **Want more?** Try
Race an Issue in Katrina Response http://
www.cbsnews.com/
news/race-an-issue-in-katrina-response/

> *All culture is learned behavior, and all people are equally able to learn any culture. In other words, 'race' is meaningless for understanding culture.*

A baby born to a small town or rural or urban White family would act exactly like a Kawelka of Papua New Guinea or a Mbuti of the African Ituri forest or an Iraqi, if the child were adopted as an infant and raised in one of those cultures. A baby from one of those cultures adopted by an American family would be indistinguishable from other Americans. The only possible difference would be if the people in the adopting group discriminated against the child or treated the child differently in some way. The same is true of various groups in the U.S.: race or ethnic group does not determine behavior biologically. Having red hair and Irish ancestors does not make you biologically bad tempered. But suppose people around you think you can't help your temper and tolerate your tantrums because they believe your red hair means a bad temper is in your genes. In that case you may never learn to control your temper, and grow up to be a bad-tempered adult. You have learned to have a bad temper to go with your culturally defined red hair. This is also another example of the social construction of reality: defining you as red haired and therefore bad tempered had the real consequence of making you into a bad-tempered person.

> *All people have exactly the same inborn biological and emotional needs. How these are met varies from culture to culture.*

Cultural universal
All cultures have elements that meet universal basic human needs.*

Language
The communication system that consists primarily of vocal sounds used as symbols to stand for ideas and objects & the rules about how to organize those sounds into statements that are meaningful to other speakers of the same language.*

Cultural variation
Different cultures meet basic human universal needs in different ways.*

Cultural universals are the elements in all cultures that deal with these universal needs, like child care, getting food, having fun, and rules about sex. *Language* is another cultural universal. As children growing up we all learn to speak the language that is spoken around us. If different groups have different versions of the language, as often happens in relation to class, gender, race, or geographical location, we learn our own group's version. As people change groups or move back and forth between groups, they often change how they speak the language. Although few English-speakers in the US have done this, around the world many people have learned three or four languages as a matter of course. What language we speak, how we speak it, and how many we think it is normal to speak is an example of cultural variation.

Cultural variation refers to the various ways societies carry out the universals. In one society children may be cared for mainly by mothers and in another by a large group of male and female relatives, and in yet another, once children are weaned, fathers take over as the main care-takers. In others they are often put in large groups where they are cared for by just a few adults (day care centers). Or women who aren't their mothers can be forced or paid to nurse and care for the babies of the elite. This pattern depends on having a majority of people devalue the children of the women who are exploited as mammies, nannies, and wet nurses, believing they don't need or deserve the kind of care given to elite children. Perhaps the same can be said of a day care worker's children also, since their parent is paid so little that the child will of necessity be deprived of much that is given to elite children. These are all examples of cultural variation in fulfilling the cultural universal of child care.

ANOTHER THOUGHT ABOUT CULTURE

So far what I have said about culture may have left you with the feeling that people have no choices, that everyone has to act the same way, that everyone in a society thinks the same things, and that culture is cast in concrete and never changes. If you think about our own society, you will see that this isn't true: yes, we all know broccoli is an OK form of food, but we don't all like it. And yes, we all agree that getting a job is a reasonable thing to do, but, as you will see later in the chapter, a fast food worker, the manager, and the owner are likely to have very different attitudes toward jobs and toward the people who hold them. Some people used to believe that slavery was part of God's plan, while others, sometimes in the same family, thought it was evil and slave owners were sinners. However, given the culture of the time, even most White abolitionists couldn't imagine a world in which Blacks and Whites were truly equal—the culture they lived in determined to a significant extent the way they thought about ending slavery. Black abolitionists, and many people who were enslaved, saw things quite differently. Some who were enslaved bought into the idea of their own inferiority, but many others did not. Like many people in a subordinate position in an unequal society, they didn't buy into the ideas of the dominant group. Instead, they rejected much of the dominant culture. And our culture did change. Legal slavery is no longer with us. Illegal slavery, however, is still alive and well, though operating in the shadows. And coercion and mistreatment are common, while human trafficking for both labor and sexual purposes continues to be an issue in the U.S. and around the world.

All cultures change; in all societies there are individuals and groups who contest certain cultural patterns. They may reject the meanings assigned to them or to certain behaviors. Their rejection may remain muted, or it may form a parallel understanding of the world. If anthropologists talk only to members of one group in a society, they may never become aware of the underground or parallel understandings held by others. Consequently, their description of a culture may make it appear far more unified than it actually is. The contest between these differing views may ultimately lead to changes in the culture, as may many other situations. A 'traditional culture' may in reality be only a few generations old, as was the teepee-dwelling, horse-riding, buffalo-dependent culture of the Plains Indians when European settlers began to invade the plains.

• **Want more?** Try *Working in the Shadows* http://www.usnews.com/opinion/articles/2014/04/24/denise-brennan-examines-americas-labor-trafficking-problem

HOW DO YOU KNOW IF WHAT YOU ARE READING IS TRUE?

Anthropology, like other areas of life, is, as you can see from the preceding sections, riddled with issues about perspective.

> *What appears to be 'true' varies immensely with the position and interests of the person who is speaking.*

Let's take two people in very different positions. First, suppose you work at a fast food place for low wages, no benefits, aren't allowed to work full time, and have to adjust your schedule at a moment's notice to fit your employer's needs. Second, suppose you are the manager of that fast-food joint. From your point of view as manager, your employees are a real problem. You say they don't care about their jobs; they quit at the drop of a hat and call in sick needlessly. They grumble about going the extra mile and have no team spirit. You agree there are a few loyal and hard workers among them, but mainly you think you have to go through a tremendous number of bad apples to find them. You may well decide that welfare is to blame, saying that if people didn't have handouts to fall back on they would be willing to work harder and be more dependable because they would really need the job.

Now take the position of the employees at the fast-food joint. You say all the manager cares about is getting as much work as possible out of you for as little as possible. You may feel that your life is very insecure, that you teeter from one crisis to the next, that there is risk involved in whatever course you choose for you and your family, that you may unpredictably encounter a cliff to fall over (a situation anthropologists call *precarity*—you feel your life is precarious). The manager doesn't make allowances for sick kids and will fire you if you miss much. The manager won't hire enough workers and therefore is always having emergencies and expecting you to forget all the other obligations in your life to come in and rescue the situation. The manager pays wages so low you need food stamps to feed your kids, and then complains about the lazy people on welfare while refusing to let you work full-time so as to avoid the cost of benefits. You may also resent people getting welfare or other forms of help. You say you are busting a gut and think it is unfair that lazy people are getting handouts paid for with your tax money when you don't get any help. You think those taxes are what makes your take-home check small and blame people on welfare rather than the fast-food joint that pays such low wages. You agree some managers are nice people, and you agree that the manager is under pressure from higher-ups to make a good profit, but you are still going to quit the minute you have a better option, and you'll say you're sick if you really have to in order to find it—or to take care of sick kids.

Precarity
A worker's perception that the conditions under which he/she is living are unpredictable, insecure, and full of risk.

• **Want more?**
Try playing Spent   http://playspent.org/

On the other hand, you may get angry when someone else gets 'employee of the month.'

What is the 'truth' here? If you reread, you will see that although the tone of voice and attitude of the speakers in the two positions is very different, the *facts* they describe are actually very much the same. The manager and the worker have very different explanations for these facts, however. If you were an anthropologist working in a fast food joint, you would be learning about all the people there—about their lives, their work, and their attitudes.

You would keep track of the number of times people really call in sick. You might well find that the manager is unconsciously exaggerating or stereotyping all employees because one or two call in a lot. You might also find out why those people call in, and decide that you would also call in if you were in their shoes. Or you might end up thinking the manager has a point with those particular employees. You might also conclude that higher wages might make it easier for people to pay for child care and that insurance would mean better health care for themselves and their kids, and therefore employees might miss fewer days. You would learn people's reasons for quitting and probably have to argue yourself out of quitting too. You would also learn that the workers almost all hate the idea of being on welfare; those who have been on welfare struggled to get off it, and everyone they know who has been on welfare wanted a job. You might find that many who had *not* been on welfare were convinced that people like being on welfare.

You would also be sure to learn about the manager's working conditions. You might well find the manager is getting ulcers putting in a sixty to eighty hour workweek without overtime pay. You might find that company policy, which the manager can't control, does not allow hiring more full-time workers. And you might find that company policy doesn't let the manager raise wages. If the manager decides to improve working conditions enough that workers have some reason to develop loyalty to the job, getting fired is a real possibility.

So the 'truth' becomes a rather complicated item.

Neither group is lying; however, managers can be blinded by their higher status to the ways in which their situation is similar to that of the workers, despite (usually) better pay.

The manager is being used by the owners as their **collaborator,** expected to extract as much work from the workers as possible, and as much money from customers as possible, all for the owner's enrichment. The manager is expected to work for long hours under intense pressure so the owners don't have to lose profits by hiring adequate help. In other words, both manager and worker are being exploited, although the manager earns enough to keep food on the table and might even be able to support a family.

Collaborator
A member of a subordinate group who cooperates with the dominant group in maintaining control and/or extracting profits from the subordinate group.

Ideology
Belief systems that
rationalize and legitimize
the distribution of power.*

Blaming the victim
Claiming a bad situation is
the result of the victim's
own actions, thus avoiding
the need to look for the
social forces which might
be causing the situation.

• **Want more?** Try
*I Work in Fast Food and I'm
not a Teenager.* http://
money.cnn.com/2014/05/
30/news/economy/fast-
food-educated-older/
?iid=EL

Class bias (classist)
The assumption that how
one's own class sees the
world and acts is the only
natural, correct, and moral
way; particularly the
assumption that classes
more exploited than one's
own are irrational or
stupid if they behave
differently.*

Racism
The belief that members of
another race are inferior
and that unequal treatment
is therefore justified and
natural.*

Sexism
The assumption that the
way one's own sex lives
and works and thinks is
the natural and correct
way, and that members of
the other sex are actually
inferior, so that unequal
treatment is justified.*

The manager has bought into the *ideology*—the beliefs that make the distribution of power in a society seem natural—that helps to keep this exploitation going. This ideology gets the manager to accept the owners' explanation of the problems on the job, blaming his or her problems on the employees, rather than on the exploitative policies of corporate management. *Blaming the victim* this way keeps the manager from challenging company policy and banding together with the other workers to improve things for all of them. Strangely enough, praising victims—calling victims heroes—has a similar effect in taking attention off the cause of their problems. So for instance, while a woman who somehow manages to raise successful children on fast food wages certainly deserves our respect, focusing on how strong she is in her struggle lets us avoid questioning why she should have to struggle so hard in the first place.

In focusing their complaints on welfare recipients both manager and employees are blaming the victim, rather than the actual source of their problems. In reality, getting rid of welfare won't make any difference for either group, so their anger is directed at the wrong people. The manager will still have trouble getting devoted workers for minimum or near minimum wages with no benefits and only part-time work available. The workers' take-home checks will still be low because their wages are low, but not because of the tiny percentage of their check that goes to pay for welfare. Welfare reform, removing many people from the welfare roles, has not increased anyone's take-home check. And if you are working in fast food, you may be a paycheck away from needing welfare yourself. Welfare reform has merely made it harder for people to get the help they need and has forced many into working for even less than minimum wage. And for the workers, blaming the manager really won't help either. The manager doesn't set policy. By blaming each other, no one is noticing that the CEO and other corporate administrators are making more in a year than the workers will make in several lifetimes, and that the owners are making millions—all from the work you do, paying you so little that you qualify for food stamps even if you are allowed to work full time.

In fact, the belief that people with less than you are the cause of your problems, like blaming welfare recipients, is a piece of ideology.

Unknowingly you are helping to maintain the system of exploitation that hurts both workers and manager. The *class bias, racist,* and *sexist* beliefs on which this ideology is based make it seem natural that some people have less than enough to live on, or have to put together several part-time jobs in order to make it. The idea that some people actually deserve less—deserve to be exploited—makes your own small wages seem reasonable. It serves as a smokescreen, keeping us from seeing that the wealth of the owners is based on exploitation. And it keeps you from seeing the way you yourself depend on the exploited labor of people all over the world, like those who made the shoes you wear or picked the lettuce in the salad you eat.

If you could interview the corporate executives who hire fast food managers, you might well find that they have complaints, just like the managers do, about finding decent employees to be managers. They might say it is hard to get dedicated and skillful managers who are willing to go the extra mile for the company without complaint (that is, who are willing to ignore their other obligations in life to increase corporate profits).

> *In other words, as you go up the corporate ladder, each group finds fault with the people below them.*

WHERE DO THESE CONFLICTS OVER THE 'TRUTH' COME FROM?

Conflicts like this tend to come from differences in perspective caused by the fact that people are looking at the world from their very different and unequal positions in our social structure. The different perspectives in the example above were based on differences between the owner, the manager, and the workers in relation to the unequal factors of class positions, gender, and in many cases also race.

Class
A group of people who have the same relationship to the means of production.*

People's *class* depends on whether or not they own a business or productive resources such as a mine or farm land. Such people are in a different class from the people who work for them. People who don't own resources themselves make up a second class, selling their labor to those who do.

> *So there are two basic classes, those who own resources and those who provide labor.*

In this fast food case, the manager and the other employees are all in the same basic class, all working for the owner. But the manager is in a different position from the other members of this class. This position is often referred to as the *professional/managerial class.* The manager is much better paid because the owner depends on the manager to get as much work out of the other workers as possible, so that the owner will make a good profit. The owner also depends on the manager to keep the other workers under control and to deal with the workers' complaints, so that the owner doesn't have to deal with all the unpleasantness caused by low wages and other company policies.

Professional/managerial class
In a capitalist economy, the section of the working class that performs professional services and/or managerial services for the capitalist class by managing, training, and controlling the rest of the working class.*

The ideological perspective, based on class bias, that accompanies this conflict between manager and workers, makes many people inclined to believe that the manager's perspective about workers is the only true one. This is particularly true of other people in the professional/managerial class and the people they associate with, other 'middle class' people who are also workers but often identify more with the owners and their needs than with low-wage workers. They, and also many low-wage workers themselves, tend to believe that the way the middle class behaves is the only normal way to act. This ideology says that if you act 'right,' then you will have a job, or a husband with a job, with a wage that is big enough to support a family, especially if both spouses work. If you really do it right, you will be in the well-paid part of the professional/managerial class, and you will make sure your children get an education that will let them follow in your footsteps. The flip side of this ideology is the belief that if you are poor, working for close to minimum wage, it must be your own fault: you didn't act right. In addition, there is an ideological tendency to believe that the higher a person's class the more likely they are to know what is really going on. Notice television news reporting: poorer people are sometimes interviewed for simple descriptions of an event or situation, or to get their emotional reaction; rarely are their explanations or analysis of the situation aired on the news. The job of explaining the truth of the situation is generally reserved for higher class people.

Sexism, racism, and ethnocentrism all act similarly to class bias. Our society is structured around inequalities of race, class, and gender and those inequalities have an enormous effect on how we interpret the world. They frequently lead to perspective problems in encounters between members of different sexes, races, and cultures. Like class bias, they have lead at times to perspective problems in anthropology.

DOUBLE VISION

Your position in the social structure can affect what you 'see.' The group with less power frequently has a 'double vision' that gives a broader knowledge than is generally possessed by the more powerful group.

Double vision
The ability, resulting from one's subordinate position in an unequal social structure, to interpret events both from a subordinate point of view and to some extent from the perspective of the dominant group.

Note that in the fast food example, while neither group had a corner on the 'truth,' the workers had a fairly accurate understanding of the manager's situation, while the manager knew comparatively little about them. To some extent, the workers had *'double vision.'* They could see things from the manager's point of view as well as from their own.

Such double vision becomes more necessary for the less powerful group as inequality becomes more pronounced.

For instance, women in societies where gender inequality is severe, such as our own, frequently know more about the men they live with than the men know about them. This is particularly true for women who are dependent or abused. For such women, the ability to predict a husband's reactions may mean the difference between life and death, or may allow you to get what you need for yourself or your children. Enslaved Africans had a profound and necessary knowledge of their owners. Being able to predict an owner's reaction could help you at the least to avoid a whipping, and sometimes even allow you to manipulate your owner's decisions by carefully pushing the right buttons. The availability of whips, guns, lynching, castration, and the auction block meant that owners could generally get what they wanted from slaves without needing to respect them sufficiently or know them well enough to coax or persuade successfully. Secretaries generally know far more about their bosses, including about their private lives, than bosses know about their secretaries. This doesn't mean double vision gives you a corner on the truth. While an abused woman may know far more about her abuser than he knows about her, she may still have no idea why abuse is so common, and may even believe she deserves this treatment.

If you have never worked in fast food, then you will never know exactly how it feels to do that work and live that life. However, you can learn about things you have never experienced yourself. You can learn by truly listening to the voices of others, people with experience. And you can learn by reading, by making the mental effort to place yourself in someone else's shoes, as you learn about other peoples' lives and about the understandings of those lives that anthropologists present in ethnographies. You can do research into the ideologies, policies and laws that make it legal and generally morally acceptable to treat people this way, and you can find out whether it is true that most fast food workers are teenagers just wanting a little extra spending money. You may not develop double vision, but you can develop a perspective on the truth that takes account of the voices of a much wider range of people, including those with double vision.

Knowledge about the facts of people's lives is always created with some purpose, and serves some purpose.

Knowledge about people isn't 'pure.' 'Truth,' in other words, doesn't exist in anthropology in the clear way that, say, 2+2=4. Knowing the reason knowledge has been created (even if those collecting the information are unaware of it) helps you in evaluating that knowledge. Eventually you may find that you have to make some choices about whose side you are on in order to know whether a particular piece of interpretation of facts rates as 'truth' for the purposes you care about. In the fast food example, it is 'truth' to the manager that many workers are bad apples. Is that an analysis that you find useful for the purposes you care about? Will it help to get decent wages for the workers, or does it help to justify continued low wages? It may be a fact that some do call in sick a lot, but is describing them as something other than bad apples actually more useful? Would talking about this country's inadequate health care and child care system and the low wages that mean your car breaks down all the time get you further in understanding why they call in a lot? If those are the causes of most of the sick days, talking about bad apples won't do any good if you want to figure out ways to make life better for the workers. On the other hand, if you want to help make sure that the corporation makes as big a profit as possible, then the bad apples explanation is useful for the purposes you care about.

There actually are facts out there that you can't ignore and expect to come anywhere near a reasonable understanding of why people act as they do. You can't ignore the fact, for instance, that many people working full-time, year-round, as well as part-time fast food workers, earn so little they need food stamps if they have families to feed. How you interpret those facts, however, is most likely influenced by your own values and position in the social structure. Learning about new facts and about new perspectives does sometimes cause people's interpretations to change.

On top of all this, there is 'knowledge' that is actually false. That Saddam Hussein was connected with the attacks of 9/11 is a classic example of false knowledge; so is the belief held by many Americans that Islam makes people dangerous. When false knowledge is promoted by people with power, it is useful to ask what purpose is served by getting people to believe it. Anthropologists in this particular case are well aware that this knowledge is false and are working to bring out a more valid understanding of the societies involved. There are other cases of false knowledge that anthropologists did not realize were false. Sometimes this is simply due to incomplete knowledge; all the facts are not yet known. But incomplete knowledge can also be related to perspective problems.

For instance, Malinowski, one of the most famous of all early anthropologists, studied the Trobriand Islanders. He was unaware of the roles played by women in the socio-economic structure. As a result, his description of even what the men were doing was incorrect, as Annette Weiner discovered much later. Part of the reason he was unaware of what the women were doing was that his unconscious sexism, built into the culture he was part of, prompted him to ignore or discount what women did.

Inaccurate interpretation led Europeans in colonial Papua New Guinea to see 'cargo cults' as proof that 'the natives' were irrational, magically trying to get manufactured goods—cargo. Seeing only the religious/magical rituals of these 'cults' and not the rational resistance and self-help aspects justified 'teaching' them to work for Europeans for their own good, by force when necessary. Or the belief in cannibalism: some societies have funeral rituals in which small amounts of ashes or flesh are eaten as an expression of love or respect or honor—hardly a cannibal feast. Unconscious racism and ethnocentrism made it easy to believe in the 'savageness' of the people Europeans had conquered, and if you can believe they are irrational, or that they eat each other for dinner, then forcing them to become 'civilized' by taking their land and working them on plantations or in mines looks like a good idea—and is highly profitable.

THE PERSPECTIVE OF THIS BOOK

Anthropologists who come from the tradition of 'decolonizing' and 'engaged' anthropology are primarily concerned with using anthropology as a tool to help end oppression and exploitation. We think that to be valid, anthropologists can't just be impartial observers evaluating the behavior of 'other' people and explaining it for outsiders. Neither can we assume that other societies need to be changed, while our own is pretty much okay as it is. Nor can we assume that the exploitation of people in other societies has nothing to do with our own lives. We believe that greater equality around the world will benefit most people in our own societies as well as people in other societies.

Most importantly for this book, however, we believe that an engaged and decolonized anthropology will let us show you, the readers of our work, aspects of our world of which most of you are completely unaware. In fact, you could say that most of us are taught not to know this information—a form of learned ignorance.

Many of you reading this book will not approve of much of what is happening to the people you will learn about in the U.S. and in the rest of the world. Ideally you will read articles and ethnographies along with this book, and watch documentary films. As you read and watch, you may find yourself being shocked at the role *learned ignorance* has played in your own understanding of the world and the government policies you have supported. You may also find that in the long run you and your communities are being hurt by the very same policies that oppress other people in other parts of the world. You may even find that the ideas you have been taught about *'other'* people actually contribute to these oppressive policies, both here and in the rest of the world.

DECOLONIZED ANTHROPOLOGY

We called this approach 'decolonizing' anthropology because we are trying to create an anthropology that reverses some of the effects of anthropology's past. Historically anthropology developed as part of the attempts by the elites of the world's most powerful nations to take over the land and resources and people outside their own countries. The elite are the people in an unequal society who have power and directly benefit from controlling other people. The most powerful nations, the ones that did the

• **Want more?** Try Cultural Anthropology Hotspots http://www.culanth.org/conversations/4-hot-spots Or try Cultural Anthropology Fieldnotes http://www.culanth.org/conversations/9-field-notes

Learned ignorance
A lack of knowledge which is fostered to protect the distribution of power in a society.

'Other'
People defined as being irrevocably different from you and your group. *

conquering, were the ones that happened at the time to have the most effective weapons and the most efficient system for amassing wealth. What we now know as anthropology developed as European and then U.S. colonialism vastly increased the possibilities for creating wealth. Colonialism shifted the value of the work done by lots of other people in conquered areas into the pockets of just a few people, the elite, in the conquering country. These elites were helped and protected by the military, which did the conquering for them and put down revolts.

But more than a military was needed to make this all work.

Anthropological knowledge was needed to help colonial administrators conquer, control and extract slave labor or extremely cheap labor from their colonial subjects.

The societies of conquered peoples had to be reorganized so that profits would flow into the coffers of a few of the conquerors—the elites of the conquering country. Since this generally meant that most of the conquered people suffered to create these profits, they usually resisted, often fiercely. Anthropological knowledge gave administrators clues about the conquered people they studied, often making it easier to beat down resistance.

The soldiers, missionaries, and administrators of the conquering country risked their lives to benefit the elite, so they and their relatives in the middle and working classes of the conquering country all needed to be convinced that colonization was a good thing.

This process of convincing people is, of course, still necessary whenever people are being asked to risk their lives, and it often requires a great deal of work and propaganda to be effective.

During the colonial period it was often anthropologists who, frequently unwittingly, provided much of the grist for the propaganda mills of the elite. This was particularly important since most working people in the country doing the conquering didn't benefit from this process, although a middle class of bureaucrats, administrators, and managers did grow larger and was better off. They were well paid for their work in managing and controlling both people and profits for the elite.

But the English workers in textile mills of the conquering country weren't better off because the cotton they worked with was very cheaply produced by enslaved Africans in the American colonies. After all, their whole families, including little kids, worked twelve hours a day, six days a week, in the textile mills for literally barely enough to keep body and soul together. Nor did they benefit from the fact that the cloth they produced was sold at an excellent price in India because British administrators there had destroyed the local handloom industry. And it did textile workers no good that the cloth they made was valuable in Africa,

• **Want more?**
For pictures, try searching "textile mill workers, images, England." Also try searching "images, cotton and slavery." (Note that some images depict cotton picking after slavery ended)

where it was used to buy more enslaved people to grow more cotton more cheaply. Even the fact that they could buy cloth for themselves for less was pretty meaningless in the face of those twelve hour days and starvation wages. Nor did they benefit from the fact that the tea they drank as a stimulant to keep themselves going was grown and picked in India by people who had been displaced from the handloom industry and now were paid even less by the British tea planters than were the textile workers. And then there was the sugar in their tea, a quick energy booster—again produced very cheaply, by enslaved Africans and Native AmericansNative American in the Americas. Nobody benefited from this except the British elites and some of the upper classes in the Americas, in India, and in Africa, who reaped a tidy profit on cotton, cloth, tea, slaves, and sugar.

> *Ideas about 'race' and civilization and culture and progress all became very important in keeping the working people in the conquering countries from identifying with the people they helped to conquer.*

Since most didn't benefit, they needed other reasons to think colonialism was a good idea. This is where anthropological knowledge played a role. The 'natives' were described as being very different from themselves—so different, in fact, that they benefited from being conquered. Conquest was thus benevolent, although the people in England, for instance, would never think it was benevolent if they themselves were conquered.

Without such divisive ideas about 'other' people and 'races,' and about their 'immoral' cultures, parents might not have been so willing to send their children off, perhaps to die, to enrich the elite. Had many people in the conquering countries begun to focus on the damage colonization was doing to their own standard of living, as the elites became increasingly powerful and therefore able to push wages lower and lower in the conquering country, they might have been even less willing to support colonization.

Instead, however, fascinating anthropological images of cannibalism, of widows burning on their husbands' funeral pyres, of husbands making slaves of their wives, of women who had to be shrouded in black from head to toe, of 'strange' sexual practices, of hungry children and 'Oriental' splendor, and of unending tribal warfare—all these images served as a smoke-screen. Anthropological concepts such as the evolutionary progression from 'primitive' bands and tribes to 'civilized' states contributed to justifying conquest in the name of evolutionary development toward a better way of life. Even the terms 'bands' and 'tribes,' for types of egalitarian societies, as well 'chiefdoms' to describe ranked, more stratified societies, were created and used by administrators and by many anthropologists to claim that such societies have lower positions on the ladder of human progress.

European states were seen as the pinnacle of human intellectual and social development, at the top of that ladder. Most anthropologists no longer believe this. They see those ideas as a part of the racist ideology that helped to 'Other' colonized and exploited societies. This issue will be addressed in Chapter Three.

Most people of the conquering country couldn't see through the smoke created by these ideological beliefs about other people. They could not recognize the ways in which their lives were similar to those of the 'natives,' and they couldn't pull their attention away from the supposed benefits of 'civilizing' such 'outrageous' or 'backward' people long enough to look at the effects of colonization on their own country. And they had no way of examining the accuracy of these images. These ideas, in other words, became *hegemonic*—they became the unquestioned framework through which most people viewed the world. British elite control of the British empire, their own position of inequality in England, and the necessity of conquest all appeared natural, inevitable, and somehow 'right'.

Many anthropologists believed their work would benefit the people they studied. They generally had no intention of misleading their compatriots, nor of aiding in the conquest and increasing misery of the people they studied. Intentional or not, however, their work often played this role. Some, as they realized this, worked hard to oppose the policies of their own governments, trying to protect people they had come to care about and whose cultures they had come to value, from the devastating effects of colonialism and development. We will return to the issue of colonialism in Chapter Two.

> *But anthropology is also able to counter those images. Anthropology can be used to provide more accurate information and alternative perspectives. Anthropology can be used to help eliminate our learned ignorance. It can be used for decolonizing, rather than colonizing, for helping to convey rights, not deny them.*

ENGAGED ANTHROPOLOGY

Anthropologists now frequently talk about 'engaged' anthropology," and see it as the next step beyond decolonizing anthropology. Those involved in engaged anthropology believe that their role is not simply to learn about and write about the situations and people they encounter. They believe they need to pay attention to how their books and articles might be used. Are they written in such a way that they will provide fuel for propaganda, for anthropological images that will make it easier to exploit people? Or will they combat the learned ignorance of people who wouldn't approve of exploitation if they knew it was happening?

Hegemony
The dominance of a set of ideas or of a power structure that is so powerful and so entrenched that it goes unchallenged and is rarely questioned.*

• **Want more?**
Try *Why Anthropology Still Matters* http://www.huffingtonpost.com/gina-athena-ulysse/anthropology-still-matters-faye-v-harrison_b_4259423.html

Climate change
A process of change in overall regional or worldwide climate patterns, particularly referring to change resulting from global warming produced by the use of fossil fuels; this change includes for more rain and far more frequent and violent storms in some areas and droughts in others.

• **Want more?**
For a video about a community trying to cope, try *Community Climate Change Adaptation in Manus Province* https://climateadaptationcafe.wordpress.com/2013/06/13/community-climate-change-adaptation-in-manus-province-papua-new-guinea/

Studying up
In studying up, the anthropologist consciously decides to focus on the people who hold power in an exploitative situation, with the hope that the knowledge they gain will give clues about how to change the situation.

Social inequality
A system whereby certain individuals can gain more power, prestige, influence, or wealth than others. Social inequality becomes stratified when people who gain wealth, power, or prestige through their own efforts gain control of the means of production and can then pass their advantages on to their children.*

> *But in addition, doing engaged anthropology means involving yourself in people's problems and in their efforts to understand and fight the underlying causes of those problems. This means participation as a colleague, not as an expert.*

It means assuming you have much to contribute to grass-roots struggles, but so also do other people. People in a homeless shelter, for instance, know a great deal about homelessness and about their individual problems. They may know less about the underlying processes that cause the inequality and exploitation that makes some people homeless. They may be unaware that fifty years ago homelessness was rare in the U.S.; homelessness isn't inevitable. This is knowledge that an anthropologist can provide. Both types of knowledge are needed if anything is going to be done to eliminate homelessness. More recently engaged anthropologists have been working with people whose way of life is threatened by melting ice or rising sea levels, helping them to develop strategies and promote policies that could push back against the effects of *climate change*, and acting as expert witnesses in legal proceedings and lobbying efforts. Their ideas about the scientific causes of global warming can compliment local explanations, educating both the anthropologists and the local people.

A strategy some anthropologists use to gain knowledge that can be helpful is *studying up*. In studying up, the anthropologist consciously decides to focus on the people who hold power in an exploitative situation, with the hope that the knowledge they gain will give clues about how to change the situation. Choosing to study the CEO and upper level management of the fast food corporation, rather than the workers, would be an example. Studying the effects of the policies of the International Monetary Fund and World Bank would be another, as would studying Federal and State housing policies and bank loan policies to see how they created the dense concentration of poor people in the sections of New Orleans that were most vulnerable to flooding. Some engaged anthropologists point to the ways oil companies have worked hard to keep people confused about climate change—as tobacco companies did about the relationship between cancer and tobacco—by promoting the 3% of scientists who deny that climate change is real or caused largely by an economy that is dependent on fossil fuels, an idea that is then picked up and promoted by some politicians and news media.

Understanding *social inequality* in its various forms is critical to understanding how exploitation and oppression are possible. In some societies everyone equally can get and use the resources they need. In other societies certain categories of people don't have that right. Understanding how a society conveys rights or denies rights to its members plays a primary role in explaining the social conditions under which people live. It is also critical to understanding the ideologies (such as various kinds of learned ignorance) used to keep people from noticing, resisting, or helping others to resist exploitation. Because a decolonized and engaged anthropology has to look at the world in ways that take seriously the experience and the knowledge of people being exploited, an understanding of social inequality is basic to this perspective. I hope that you will be reading articles and ethnographies describing a variety of societies, and that you will apply the ideas outlined in this book to them. I believe you will find that this perspective is the most straight-forward way to clarify the largest number of issues in people's lives all around the world, including in our own.

This book will have been successful if, as you watch the news, you find yourself saying, "But wait a minute…" You will then be questioning what you are being told about members of different race, class, gender, and ethnic categories in the United States and in other countries, and wondering what role those images play in damaging or benefiting them or yourself.

TALKING OF RIGHTS

The perspective I have been describing takes inequality as its organizing principle. Rights are conveyed to people in some kinds of societies; in others most people are denied a wide range of rights, creating inequality. Rights, as I am using the term, does not refer simply to legal permission to access a resource or opportunity—as in the right to vote or to own property. I am using the term much more broadly, reclaiming it from the limited and limiting sense it has been given by those who take an individualistic approach to understanding how people become rich or poor, powerful or oppressed. In that perspective, once an individual has been given the right to own property, for instance, it is then up to the individual. The fact that an individual may have no money and therefore is far less likely to actually be able to exercise that right than is someone born into wealth or given a good education is considered to be irrelevant. Both have equal rights, so those who wish may disregard the inequality that actually exists between the two people.

Although this legalistic conception is included in my use of the word, I am actually using it to denote the structures and their accompanying ideologies that encode a peoples' beliefs about what is proper and moral for members of their society to be able to do, to have, to use—what should come to them as humans with needs, desires, longings and loved ones. Some societies— those that create inequality—claim that what should come 'by right' to some is very different from what should come to others, and the accompanying social structures in those societies ensure that, in fact, some do have far more than others. These claims that inequality is right and moral, or at least inevitable, are commonly based on race, caste, class, birthright, and gender in varying combinations and in varying ways. We will factor each of these in as we go through the book, looking at various ways of creating inequality. Claiming and fighting for rights in the legalistic sense can be, and sometimes is, an important step toward gaining rights in a broader sense—the sense which says having the right to eat is not the same as actually having food, and that all should have food.

And it is also true that the language of rights is not the only way people make claims on food or anything else. Children get fed by parents and kin, not because it is their 'right' but because the adults experience love, obligation, and duty. We give gifts at a wedding shower, not because the bride has claimed a right to a gift, but because of friendship, obligation, or fear of appearing stingy or impoverished. This is true around the world, and different types of societies provide people with different methods of laying obligations on each other. But at the same time, all these different methods do convey (or deny) to individuals and groups access to the resources that they need to use as humans with needs, desires, longings, and loved ones. This is what I am trying to capture with my use of the word 'rights.'

A WORD OF WARNING

As you read this book, you will be trying to understand your own and other people's culture—their way of life, including their social organization, economy, values, norms. In other words, you will be trying to understand why people act as they do. We all grow up and live as adults as members of particular 'race,' ethnic, class, and gender categories. We are often taught that members of other categories are silly, backward, inferior, irrational, or immoral, or just don't know any better. We are taught to be blind to the good reasons 'other' people have for their actions—another example of learned ignorance. This is particularly true if you come from a category that has political or economic control of another group of people, or if your beliefs are shaped by the people in political or economic control of other categories of people. The elites who profit from cheap labor still need to convince us that the people they exploit and oppress 'deserve' or benefit from this treatment, just as they did during colonization.

If we believe that other people are in some way inferior, then it is easier to get us to blame them for their problems, rather than seeing the ways in which their problems are caused by the elite who are exploiting them.

The European elite of the conquering countries did this when they promoted ideas about 'natives' who needed to be 'civilized,' so that working class sons and daughters of the conquering country would be willing to risk their lives to help control the 'natives' and turn them into a profitable source of cheap or slave labor, or take away their land. English elites promoted this idea by referring to England as the 'mother country,' implying a nurturing relationship with the people they exploited. A similar process is at work if we believe that most of the people who are poor are poor because they are lazy or don't care or made poor choices, rather than because jobs are scarce, and often are poorly paid and part-time. This belief works to prevent us from questioning the elite policies that make wages low and jobs part-time. And if we don't question, then there is nothing to prevent the elite from continuing to increase their profits at the expense of the people who are doing the work.

These ideological beliefs are often related to ethnocentrism. Most of the time, most people feel most comfortable living in their own culture, since that is the one in which they grew up. People in exploited groups sometimes use defense or revival of their culture as a potent form of resistance, emphasizing that their culture has great value and beauty. This can provide people who are otherwise being devalued with a sense of worth and a means for standing up against oppression. This is not what anthropologists mean by ethnocentrism.

Ethnocentrism
Judging the members of another culture or subculture by the standards of one's own culture, with the assumption that one's own culture is best and that it is the way all rational people would naturally choose to live.

Ethnocentrism means taking that feeling of comfort in your own culture a step further, and consciously or unconsciously deciding your culture is also better than all other cultures. People who are being ethnocentric don't see, or they deny, the values and beauties of other cultures, and don't see, or deny, the problems within their own. We tend as Americans to assume that other people 'naturally' want to live as we do. We also assume that the way we live is right, or the best, so other people are ignorant or silly or unfortunate if they live in other ways or have different beliefs. This attitude that your culture is best, not just more comfortable for you, is called ethnocentrism. Americans have no corner on ethnocentrism; it is a common attitude all over the world. However, when people in a group or society with political or economic power over other people act on their ethnocentrism the consequences for the less powerful people can be devastating. Ethnocentrism directed at you without power backing it up can make you pretty angry, or unhappy, or uncomfortable, but it can't destroy your group or the values you care about.

To develop an anthropological perspective you must try not to be ethnocentric, because ethnocentrism prevents understanding your own culture and other cultures, and can contribute to policies that hurt both you and other people.

You need to realize that other people's lives and values are just as reasonable and just as important to them as yours are to you. Every culture has a long history that has shaped it just as much as our history has shaped ours. We may think of ourselves as independent individuals who make our own choices. But our behavior and our choices are deeply influenced by our culture, just like people everywhere in the world.

You may eventually conclude that you believe that particular features of a culture are cruel. But don't allow that to make you ethnocentric: for every problem you see in another culture, be clear that our own culture has features that are every bit as bad. And remember that people in other cultures see our culture as riddled with cruelty and irrational behavior. Warehousing the elderly in nursing homes until they finally die is just one example. And don't forget, we lock up a woman who goes out without clothes above the waist. Think how irrational and oppressive that could look to women who can go naked above the waist if they wish—and aren't expected to wear the harness we call a bra! But in fact most of us don't think being forced to wear clothes above the waist is oppressive; many Muslim women who cover themselves up outside their home don't find it oppressive either.

CONSOLING ADVICE

Don't be upset if these first pages aren't totally clear to you. In fact, it would be surprising if they were, since anthropology, particularly decolonized and engaged anthropology, is introducing you to a very different pair of glasses for looking at the world, one that may contradict much of what you grew up believing. What you have just read will ferment in the back of your mind as you immerse yourself in the ethnographies and articles chosen to accompany this book. In about three weeks, come back and reread these pages. Wait a bit and do this again, several more times. Each time you do this you will understand more. At some point you will wonder why this wasn't all obvious the first time you read it.

Anthropologists often talk and write in 'anthropologese,' a habit that makes reading anthropology difficult until you learn the language. This book uses plain English as much as possible; however, there are words you will need to learn as you go along. Some of these words have different meanings in plain English, some you will never hear of outside of anthropology, and some will allow you to talk about things you may have known were happening but had no convenient words for. These last, in particular, may become handy tools for analyzing your own and other people's experiences. For instance, if you are the fast food worker described earlier in the chapter, you might find that the anthropological analysis summed up in the word 'exploitation' fits your situation exactly and allows you to talk about what is happening more easily. Words in anthropologese are printed in bold italics the first time they are used in a technical sense in this book, where it is important to know the definition, and are defined in the margin. They are also defined in the glossary. But in many cases the full definition, and the explanation that would be helpful to you, is too long to include in the margin. If the definition in the margin is a shortened version it will be marked by an asterisk. In that case it will be much to your advantage to look in the glossary, but the short definition will at least get you through reading the sentence.

I have tried to make the glossary 'user-friendly' and informative, and I suggest that you use it heavily as you read.

Also, at the end of each chapter you will find a list of books written by anthropologists, and others, who have described examples or theorized about the kinds of situations and perspectives I have synthesized in this book. If you are curious about where the ideas and information in this book came from, that is where to look. It is also where to look if you want to do further reading on a particular topic.

THE REST OF THE BOOK

The rest of this book will look at how societies have organized equality or inequality. Inequality and the denial of rights can be based on a number of different factors, alone or in combination, and as we go through the book each chapter will introduce more of these factors. These factors tend to pile up, one on top of another, so that the inequality in a severely unequal society is based on a combination of many factors. The focus will be on understanding inequality, but, so that you can see that there truly are other ways of organizing societies, that inequality isn't part of human nature, we will also talk about societies that are comparatively egalitarian, where the unequal consequences of Hurricane Katrina would make no sense, and where the wealthy owner of a fast food chain would be expected to give away his or her wealth or be laughed out of town.

You will quickly see that equality or the lack of it affects every aspect of a society, and every aspect of the lives of the people who make up that society. Everything from marriage to religion to the kind of work you do—the question of equality comes into it all. Other issues are also involved, of course, but this one is probably the most basic to setting the framework within which people live.

Please note that as this book describes societies with different degrees of inequality, it simply describes typical characteristics. Each society combines the factors of inequality in its own way. As you read various ethnographies, you will find that most, but not all, of what you read here will fit the particular society you are reading about. Be aware of these differences.

REFERENCES/SUGGESTED READING

On decolonized and engaged anthropology:

Harrison, Faye V., ed. 1991 Decolonizing Anthropology. Washington, D.C.: American Anthropological Association.

Hyatt, Susan and Vin Lyon-Callo, Special Issue eds. 2003 Anthropology and Political Engagement. Urban Anthropology and Studies of Cultural Systems and World Economic Development 32(2):133-251.

Lyon-Callo, Vincent 2004 Inequality, Poverty, and Neoliberal Governance: Activist Ethnography in the Homeless Sheltering Industry. Peterborough, Ont.: Broadview Press.

Smith, Linda T. 1999 Decolonizing Methodologies: Research and Indigenous Peoples. New York: Zed Books.

On collaborative and 'Third World Anthropology'

Connell, Raewyn 2007 Southern Theory: Social Science and the Global Dynamics of Knowledge. Cambridge: Polity.

Kingsolver, Ann, and Sasikumar Balasundaram with Vijayakumar Sugumaran, Jennifer Engel, Timothy Gerber, Craig Spurrieli, Colin Townsend, and Kristen Wolf. 2010. Collaborative Research On Food Security In The U.S. And Sri Lanka. Practicing Anthropology 32(4):24-28.

Ntarangwi, Mwenda. 2010 Reversed Gaze: An African Ethnography of American Anthropology. Urbana: University of Illinois Press.

On the involvement of anthropology with oppression

American Anthropological Association 2007 Executive Board Statement on the Human Terrain System Project.

Baker, Lee 1998 From Savage to Negro: Anthropology and the Construction of Race, 1896-1954. Berkeley: University of California Press.

Stocking, George 1991. Victorian Anthropology. New York: Free Press.

On the ideological role of anthropological and other images

Berkhofer, Robert 1979 The White Man's Indian: Images of the American Indian from Columbus to the Present. New York: Vintage Books.

Mantsios, Gregory 2007 Media Magic: Making Class Invisible. In Race, Class, and Gender in the United States: An Integrated Study. Paula Rothenberg, ed. Pp. 636-644. New York: Worth Publishers.

Miner, Horace 1956 Body Ritual among the Nacirema. The American Anthropologist 58:503-507.

Said, Edward 2003[1979] Orientalism. New York: Penguin Classics.

On the working poor and welfare reform

AFL-CIO 2008 Executive Paywatch. Electronic website, http://www.afl-cio.org/corporatewatch/paywatch.

Ehrenreich, Barbara 2002 Nickel and Dimed: On (Not) Getting By in America. New York: Henry Holt Paperbacks.

Fuentes, Annette 2003 [1997] Guiliani's Workfare: Slaves of New York. Baltimore Chronicle. Electonic document, http://www.baltimore-chronicle.com/workfare.html, accessed June 10, 2008.

Skurnik, Jonathan and Kathy Leichter 2002 A Day's Work, A Day's Pay. 57 min. Harriman, NY: New Day Films. Spent. An online game. http://playspent.org/

On the relationship between the working classes in England, India, and North American slavery

Baptist, Edward. 2014. The Half Has Never Been Told: Slavery and the Making of American Capitalism. New York: Basic Books.

Beckert, Sven. 2014 Empire of Cotton: A Global History. New York: Knopf.

Lappe, Frances Moore, and Joseph Collins 1977 Why People Can't Feed Themselves. *In* Food First: Beyond the Myth of Scarcity, Frances Moore Lappe and Joseph Collins. Pp. 99-111. New York: Random House.

Mintz, Sidney 1986 Sweetness and Power: The Place of Sugar in Modern History. New York: Penguin Books.

Williams, Eric. 1973. British Industry and the Triangular Trade. IN The Slave Economies Vol. I. Eugene Genovese, ed. Pp 185-194. New York: John Wiley and Sons.

On Human Rights

Harrison, Faye V. 2005 Introduction: Global Perspectives on Human Rights and Interlocking Inequalities of Race, Gender, and Related Dimensions of Power. *In* Resisting Racism and Xenophobia: Global Perspectives on Race, Gender, and Human Rights. Faye V. Harrison, ed. Pp.1-31. Walnut Creek, CA: AltaMira Press.

Speed, Sharron 2008 Rights in Rebellion: Indigenous Struggle and Human Rights in Chiapas. Stanford CA: Stanford University Press.

On climate change

American Anthropological Association Statement on Humanity and Climate Change. 2015. http://s3.amazonaws.com/rdcms-aaa/files/production/public/FileDownloads/pdfs/issues/press/upload/AAA-Statement-on-Humanity-and-Climate-Change-2.pdf

Baer, Hans and Merrill Singer. 2014 The Anthropology of Climate Change: An Integrated Critical Perspective. New York: Routledge.

Crate, Susan and Mark Nuttall, eds. 2009 Anthropology and Climate Change: From Encounters to Actions. Walnut Creek, CA: Left Coast Press.

(see also references for Chapter Four)

Miscellaneous—Topic Identified by Title

Buck, Pem Davidson 1991 Colonized Anthropology: Cargo-Cult Discourse. IN Decolonizing Anthropology. Faye V. Harrison, ed. Pp. 24-41. Washington, D.C.: American Anthropological Association.

Jordan, Brigitte 1992 Birth in Four Cultures: A Cross-cultural Investigation of Childbirth in Yucatan, Holland, Sweden, and the United States. Prospect Heights, IL: Waveland Press.

Miller, Jean Baker 2007[1976] Domination and Subordination. *In* Race, Class, and Gender in the United States: An Integrated Study. Pp.108-114. Paula Rothenberg, ed. New York: Worth Publishers.

Nader, Laura 1972 Up the Anthropologist-Perspectives Gained from Studying Up. In Reinventing Anthropology. Dell Hymes (ed). Pp 284-311. New York: Pantheon Books.

Pardes, J. Anthony, guest ed. 2006 In Focus: The Impact of the Hurricanes of 2005 on New Orleans and the Gulf Coast of the United States. American Anthropologist 108(December): 637-813.

Ryan, William 2007[1971] Blaming the Victim. *In* Race, Class, and Gender in the United States: An Integrated Study. Paula Rothenberg, ed. Pp.688-697. New York: Worth Publishers.

Weiner, Annette 1988 The Trobrianders of Papua New Guinea. Belmont CA: Wadsworth.

CHAPTER 2
IMPERIALISM, COLONIALISM, AND NEOCOLONIALISM

As anthropologists look around the world, go off to do fieldwork, or look at the way our own communities operate, we see everywhere the effects of policies that have shaped people's lives. These policies have created varying degrees of equality or—most commonly—inequality. They are largely the result of decisions made by people with power, working to enhance their own power by making wealth for themselves. Ordinary people, people without the power to enforce policies on other people, have sometimes collaborated with those policies, sometimes have killed each other in the name of those policies or to get a bigger piece of the economic pie for themselves, and sometimes have cooperated with each other to resist policies that hurt all of them. In any case ordinary people have had to cope, one way or another, with the consequences of policies over which they have little control. Those coping mechanisms sometimes involve a creative engagement with each other or with outsiders and with influences being imposed on them. The way of life a community follows is influenced by the interaction between policies designed to exploit and the processes of accommodation, resistance, and creative ideas about new ways to be.

In this chapter we will talk about the various systems elites have developed to expand their power—and thus their ability to exploit—to an ever-larger number of people. States, as we will discuss, are actually formed by this process. Empires, likewise, are made this way. Extending power over other people is based on conquest, but conquest comes in many forms. It can take the easily recognizable form of violence exerted by a military. But violence comes also in less obvious forms. We will talk about both forms in discussing imperialism. We will begin a discussion of *'globalization,'* and will return to that discussion in Chapter Seven, where we examine how it both resembles and differs from that of the multitude of empires that have grown and disappeared in the past on every continent except Australia.

It is important to understand that the desperate conditions people deal with on a daily basis in many of the ethnographies you will be reading or films you will be seeing are not accidental, nor are they a result of the shortcomings of the people themselves. Without a clear understanding of these policies it will be hard for you to make sense of the reasons for changes in people's way of life. Nor will the causes of the conditions you read about and of people's strategies to deal with them make sense—be they based

Globalization
The process by which the economies of the world are becoming increasingly interconnected, so that powerful (core) nations and transnational corporations control the economies of the rest of the world without necessarily directly controlling the governments of the world.*

on a cooperative effort to achieve social justice, or on divisive efforts to gain more for their own group, or on individualistic efforts to 'better themselves.'

The processes of colonialism, neocolonialism, and imperialism are based on policies meant to organize exploitation—to make wealth from around the world end up in the hands of a very few people. The elites—the people who organize and benefit from this process—are in a never-ending competition with each other for power. They use their wealth to increase their power relative to other elites. But to do this they need resources, both human and material. They need control of the means of production and they need labor, and they use state power to gain that control and to expand their reach to new resources.

Elites who are contending with each other on a national level, who are all members of the same *state*, generally first use resources from within their state. This is different, as you will see in the next sections of the chapter, from what happens later, and from what happens when elites from different states are in direct competition and expand their control to resources and people outside the state. Nevertheless, the expansion process itself is similar in both cases, and although expansion within the state is not generally called 'imperialism,' the subject of this chapter, looking at expansion within the state can clarify expansion outside the state.

EXPROPRIATION OF VALUE FROM OTHER PLACES AND 'OTHER' PEOPLE WITHIN THE STATE

There are a number of policies elites can pursue in attempting to add additional people and places to exploit within their own state. All involve doing some reorganizing so that the value available from this new source can be taken away and fed into their own pockets, and all involve using (and if necessary, creating) one or more of the factors of inequality to excuse the resulting exploitation. Frequently a state pursues several of these policies of *expropriation* at once. The most common are expansionism, labor importation, internal colonialism, and creating labor reserve areas. Since labor reserves take their most obvious forms in adding exploitable people and places outside the state, they will be discussed in the next section.

EXPANSIONISM

A state pursuing an *expansionist* policy is trying to annex more territory to be included within the state. Nearly all the states that exist today were formed in this way. We tend to think of a state like the United States as a *nation-state*; that is, we think of the people in it as a *nation*, 'one people' who all share a common history, culture, basic values, language, and perhaps religion. In reality, however, there are very few true nation-states today. Many states, such as Spain, were created when one small group—often a

State
A political entity that exercises sovereign rights over a territory, has a monopoly on the use of force within that territory, and exercises power through centralized, hierarchical bureaucracies to enforce control of the means of production, collect revenue in taxes or tribute, and enforce laws and norms about members' duties and rights. States are stratified societies in which some groups monopolize wealth, power, and prestige.

Expropriation
The taking of profits or goods away from the people who produced them.*

Expansionism
A policy of trying to annex more territory, and the ideologies which get people to believe this is a good idea.

Nation-state
A state whose citizens are all members of the same nation.*

Nation
A group of people who consider themselves to be 'one people.'*

true nation, perhaps a small kingdom or chiefdom—conquered or made alliance with neighboring groups, who often spoke a different language or in other ways were a different culture. To some extent those cultural differences may still exist, but all are within the borders of what is now a single country and are administered by the same government. Others, like India, were created by the decision of an imperial power, in this case the British, to glue many small kingdoms into one big country called India. Iraq was formed in much the same way, in the post-World War I and II divisions of the world.

Conquest state
A state formed by the forcible annexation of territory and people outside its former borders; the state's borders are expanded to include the new territory.

> *These states, and most modern states, can be called conquest states. The United States is one of these.*

It was formed by the conquest of the territories of countless Indian nations as well as by wars in which the US took half of Mexico in 1848 in the Mexican War and in the Spanish American War in 1898 took the Philippines, Guam, and Puerto Rico from Spain, and also annexed Hawaii. Other sections were purchased—the Louisiana Purchase from France in 1803 and Alaska from Russia in 1867.

Citizenship
A legal status conveying the rights and obligations of membership in a particular country.

Civil rights
The rights that belong to all full citizens of a state; for instance in the United States the right to vote and the right to trial by jury.

In most **conquest states** those who were forcibly brought into the state are seen as culturally and/or racially inferior. They are seen by the dominant group as 'other,' as 'those people,' as different from 'us.' They may not be given full **citizenship** and denied the **civil rights** that belong automatically to any citizen. For instance, they may be denied the right to vote or to own property. In some cases, if they no longer form an important source of cheap labor and no longer have any claim to the resources that led elites to want to conquer them in the first place, they may be granted full citizenship if it had previously been denied. They may, with the passage of several generations, be eventually largely assimilated into the dominant culture—if they are willing to abandon their own culture. Some may be more willing than others to do this, and may become part of the middle collaborator class. Even with full civil rights, however, if they continue to be used as cheap labor, discrimination from the dominant group may make it nearly impossible to exercise those rights fully.

As former Mexican territory was incorporated into the U.S. its inhabitants technically became U.S. citizens. However, treaty rights to land were ignored, and most Mexican landowners lost their land. Anti-vagrancy laws, discriminatory enforcement of tax laws, and restrictions on voting similar to those used to eliminate Black and poor White votes in the southern states all made a mockery of civil rights for people of Mexican and Spanish descent. Mexican laborers, mainly Indians or of mixed ancestry, whose work formerly had gone to enrich wealthy Spanish landowners in the hacienda system, instead now worked as laborers to enrich Anglo (English-speaking people without Spanish ancestry) enterprises. Paid a pittance or caught in debt peonage, they built railroads, did housework, irrigated the desert, minded Anglo children, mined, and did nearly all of the physically exhausting and dangerous work of the Southwest. In the early 1900s their labor was supplemented by that of tens of thousands of people coming from Mexico, 'welcomed' by U.S. employers in search of very cheap labor for factories, domestic work, and agriculture. Particularly in agricultural work they were not truly free: debt and labor contracts, both enforced with legal and illegal violence, kept many men and women in a system close to slavery and similar to that enforced with vagrancy laws against Black workers in the South. Segregated schools, for those children who were able to spend time in school, were designed to provide such an inadequate and demeaning education that children would have no option but to take as adults the same sorts of jobs that their parents had.

Divide and rule
The strategy of getting people to be controlled to fight each other rather than to fight those who are controlling them.

• **Want more?** For deportation try http:// usatoday30.usatoday.com /news/nation/2006-04-04- 1930s-deportees- cover_x.htm

Many Anglos saw people of Mexican and Indian ancestry, regardless of their citizenship, as a threat, taking jobs at very low wages and thus lowering everyone's wages. Instead of directing their anger at employers, however, they went after workers like themselves: a classic case of divide and rule.

Citing racist reasoning and fear of racial impurity, they claimed that they, although often the descendants of recent immigrants themselves, had a right to the U.S. while descendants of Native Americans and Mexicans, who had been here for generations, or, in the case of people of Aztec or Mayan decedent for thousands of years, had no such right. They pushed for laws excluding these 'dangerous' people. Employers fought back, pushing for a system that would allow them to bring in labor when needed but force them to return to Mexico when not needed. In the process tens of thousands of U.S. citizens, as well as immigrants, were forcibly sent to Mexico, sometimes packed like cattle into railroad boxcars, in the 1920s. The Nazis used the same method of transportation not long afterward. During World War II Latinos bore more than their share of casualties, but, like Blacks, found on their return that the democracy they had fought for overseas did not apply to them at home. And civil rights violations continue. For instance, thousands of Latino/as (along with many other people of color) were effectively denied the vote in recent presidential elections. Or another example, in areas dependent on immigrant labor 'wage theft' has become common—the employer withholds wages or pays illegally low wages, frequently with the threat of deportation for those who are now organizing to enforce their rights. And while many of you are probably aware of sex trafficking, labor trafficking is actually far more common, giving employers nearly absolute control over workers in a situation close to slavery. Recent laws in several border states put citizens' civil rights in jeopardy in the name of border enforcement.

As their land was incorporated into the United States, Native AmericanNative Americans were defined as wards of the state—giving them the status of children unable to govern themselves or make decisions about their own resources. Legally even their reservation lands were held in trust for them by the U.S. government—thereby giving access to it for the elites who might want to use that land or the resources, such as oil or coal, lying under it. It wasn't until 1924, after almost 500 years of occupation by the British, French, Spanish, and then the U.S., that Native AmericanNative Americans became citizens by law. Nevertheless, some states denied them the right to vote until 1948.

Human rights
Those rights that are believed for moral reasons to belong to all human beings.*

> *However, being granted the right to vote and other civil rights does not give you the right to eat—a human right. The granting of civil rights is not the same thing as granting full human rights.*

Human rights are hard to define without being ethnocentric, but basically include access to resources that all societies define as necessary for human survival with dignity. In a conquest state it can be many generations, if ever, before people who have been forcibly annexed are seen as equally deserving of human rights. While human rights are hard to define, civil rights are not. Civil rights are those granted legally to citizens in good standing by the government, and usually by the constitution, of a country. States vary in what they define as the rights of a citizen. In the U.S. for instance, citizenship brings with it as civil rights the right to vote, the right to own property, the right to be free of search and seizure without due process of law, freedom of speech, and the right to confront your accusers. You should be aware, however, that those rights have been under siege since the destruction of the World Trade Towers on 9/11/2001.

> **Rights that have been granted can also be denied, and frequently are, first with the claim that the denial applies only to people defined as 'other' and that the denial is necessary for 'our' safety. Later those denials can be applied to everyone.**

IMPORTATION OF LABOR

Labor importation
Acquiring workers, legally or illegally, from outside the borders of a state to work within the state, usually at very low wages and usually without granting them rights within the state.

The denial of civil rights generally also accompanies policies of *labor importation*. Importing labor—bringing in additional people to work, usually at low wages—is another policy that allows for expanding the availability of people to exploit. The extreme version of labor importation is slavery. Slavery, at least as practiced in the U.S., involved a total denial of civil rights and of human rights. But slavery everywhere, even when not involving quite such an absolute denial of rights, is a system for forcibly bringing in people from outside the society and making them available as an unpaid labor force. Labor trafficking and some forms of contract labor are close relatives of slavery.

• **Want more?** Try
*Transient Servitude: The
U.S. Guest Worker
Program*…http://
combatingglobalization.co
m/articles/
transient_servitude.html
Also **try** *Using Jailed
Migrants as a Pool of Cheap
Labor* http://
www.nytimes.com/2014/
05/25/us/using-jailed-
migrants-as-a-pool-of-
cheap-labor.html?_r=0

Other systems, usually not based directly on force, include contract labor, the granting of temporary work permits or guest worker programs, and the recruitment of people without legal permission to enter a country. Many countries in Europe, for instance, have a system of 'guest workers' that allows people to immigrate without granting civil rights. No matter how long they stay they cannot become citizens, creating a kind of caste system of citizens and permanent non-citizens. The U.S. 'bracero' program, from 1942 until 1964, was similar. This program was the compromise that resulted from racist objections from Whites to people of color getting jobs and employers' insistence on importing people who would work for less. People from Mexico, mainly young men, were recruited for agricultural work and sent back to Mexico at the end of the season with what was left of their pitifully small wages. No matter how long they participated in the program, and no matter that their work was the basis of much of U.S. agriculture, they could never live here year round and could never become citizens. Both human and civil rights were denied.

Some of the proposals concerning immigration being considered in the U.S. Congress come very close to reviving this program. In the U.S. at present the recruitment of people without legal permission to enter the country is a massive source of extremely cheap labor. Simply 'failing' to fund adequate inspection of work sites or to seriously prosecute and punish employers who are found in violation makes this source of labor available to the elite. Punishing or threatening the employee but generally imposing at most light penalties on the employer makes the employee vulnerable and therefore more exploitable. Without civil rights the worker can't protest illegally or inhumanly low wages, fight for higher legal wages, or expose employers for unsafe working conditions. Ongoing discrimination makes it possible to deny not only civil rights, but human rights as well. All of this is a bonanza for the elite. Strawberry growers in the South, for instance, protested mightily when state anti-immigrant laws were tightened, cutting off their labor supply during harvest.

INTERNAL COLONIALISM

Internal colonialism
Treating one section of a
country or one group of
people as if they were a
part of a colony, so that
what they produce goes to
benefit outsiders.

Internal colonialism is a system for reorganizing an area within a state so that it produces greater profits for the elite. It means corporate and governmental policies that make it possible to treat one section of a country or one group of people as if they were a part of a colony, so that what they produce goes to benefit outsiders. Generally this involves an area that is not totally dependent on working for wages but has resources that are needed to expand major enterprises within the capitalist economy. The object of internal colonialism is to tie the area more tightly into the capitalist economy. This is done by getting control of the resources of the area—such as coal, silver, oil, or copper—by buying, stealing, tricking, or passing laws.

Since this usually means that lots of people loose their rights to the means of production, it also accomplishes a second goal: getting the people who live there dependent, or more dependent, on wages, so that they will provide a low wage labor force to be used in extracting the resource.

In other words, poverty has to be created, so that people will be 'willing' to work for very little. Poverty is not natural, any more than wealth is natural. Both are made to happen.

Resource-extraction industries tend to be dangerous, with high death and disablement rates. So people are working for very low wages in jobs that are likely to leave them unable to work at all within just a few years. They were being treated as what some anthropologists call **disposable labor**. Ideological justification is needed for treating people this way, so that people in the rest of the country as well as the middle collaborator class managing the workers and others in the internal colony all believe the extraction industry is doing a good thing for 'those people.' This is often accomplished by claiming that the people in the internal colony are inferior, usually by defining them as a different race or by using other race-like designations, as well as by claiming that their culture is inferior. The claim that the men are lazy or vicious and mistreat women is common. All of this is used to claim that the people benefit by being forced to change their ways, and that the extraction industry is therefore doing a good thing.

A classic U.S. example of an internal colony is the coal-producing region of Appalachia. Anthropologists would say that most people there were not poor before the coal companies came in, according to the anthropological definition of **poverty**. It is true that many had relatively little money.

Disposable labor
A term that implies that people are being treated like disposable paper plates: health and safety of workers is being ignored, and when workers are 'used up'—ill or disabled or dead—and therefore are no longer useful, they can be tossed aside and replaced.

Poverty
The inability, due to lack of resources, to participate in a society as people in that society say people should.

But most anthropologists don't use money to define poverty. Anthropologists define poverty as the inability to participate in your society as people in that society say people should.

If money were the criterion for judging poverty, then you would have to say that all those people living perfectly okay lives in hunting and gathering or small scale farming societies are desperately poor. But if you live in a society where money is needed, then the lack of it is a real problem. So anthropologists look instead at people's lives, rather than at their money. For example, if where you live a car is necessary in order to do things your society expects, then lack of a car, or of a car that is dependable, is a sign of poverty. But if you live in a big city near public transportation and the store is around the corner and you take a subway to work, then lack of a car is not a sign of poverty. If you are supposed to give gifts at a wedding, and can't afford to, you are not participating as your society expects. Poverty isn't a state of mind. It is a real lack of resources that has real consequences in terms of health and many other aspects of well-being.

You may have a loving family and a happy outlook on life, but you are nevertheless living in poverty, and your attitude doesn't change that.

So, returning to the situation in Appalachia: lives there were not totally dependent on the working for wages or selling goods or crops. Many people were farmers, raising almost everything they needed and selling the excess. Some had small crafts businesses, but also had big gardens and raised a hog each year. The fact that they had very low incomes did not make these people poor. They had access to the means of production. They were able to participate in their society as people said was right. There were some people who truly were poor, who didn't have access to the means of production and were tenants or sharecroppers, or worked for very low wages without a place to raise a big garden. But overall, the poverty rate was not particularly high. That changed when Appalachia was made into an internal colony.

The coal companies used trickery to convince people to sign away their right to their land or to the minerals under it for extremely low prices. Many couldn't read, or couldn't read the legalese of the contract they signed, and to people who saw very little money each year, the amount offered was tempting. Eventually land loss made people dependent on wages, and advertising campaigns convinced others that they really needed the consumer goods that a steady wage or the sale of land or mineral rights could bring them. A study in the late 1970s showed that 72% of the land in Appalachia was owned by absentee owners, and that a mere one percent of the owners, most of them huge corporations, owned 53% of the land. But almost the only work available was in the mines, since the coal companies kept other businesses out. And mining was so dangerous that once a man or boy started working underground, his working life expectancy was short. In parts of Kentucky you were safer going to war than going into the mines. If a man became disabled or died his family would be thrown out of their home in the company town, unless other family members went to work in the mine. He wasn't even paid in money, but in scrip—an IOU that could only be spent at the company store.

The company, in other words, simply recycled the miners' wages. Prices were high at the company store, and wages were low, so most families lived on credit from the company store. Anthropologically speaking, they were now living in poverty, despite having a bigger income than their parents had had. *Debt peonage* laws kept them in bondage to the company. Mining families revolted until finally in the 1930s there was actual war between the coal company owners and the miners. It took many deaths to establish unions that were gradually able to force the owners and government to convey back to the workers some of the rights that had been denied to them. By the late 1960s and the 1970s owners had to pay higher wages—in actual money—and had to bear the costs of making mining a bit safer. By the 1980s the

• **Want more?** Explore *Kentuckians for the Commonwealth* www.kftc.org or view *I Was There—The First 30 Years of KFTC* https://vimeo.com/30448462

Debt peonage
A system of involuntary servitude that allows employers to force people who owe them money to work for the employer until the debt is paid off. Charging exorbitant rates for room and board and paying low wages often allows the employer to keep the worker in debt indefinitely; no longer legal in the U.S.

power of the unions was being undermined, and eventually even compensation and health care for people with black lung was under siege.

To justify all this, Appalachian culture and people were portrayed, starting toward the end of the 1800s, as deeply flawed. Terms such as feuding barbarian, hillbilly, and white trash were used to factor in race-like designations to claim that Appalachian people weren't 'true' White people, and that they, especially the men, were so dangerous and lazy that putting them to work in the mines was good for them and for the women in their families. Missionaries were sent to 'civilize' them, to give them charity to compensate for their abysmal wages, and to tell them that God wanted them working hard and obediently in the mines. Contributing to those missions made outsiders feel virtuous; accepting needed help made some Appalachian families feel inferior and persuaded them to blame themselves, rather than the coal companies, for their problems. Nevertheless, miners revolted over and over, even crossing race lines established to keep the miners from cooperating with each other, and were able to reclaim at least some of their civil rights and their human rights. But those race-like designations are still alive and well, and are still used to justify the continuing poverty of Appalachian people. The term hillbilly, with the addition of redneck and trailer trash, now has expanded to justify the poverty of many other poor White people who are part of the **reserve labor force** or are living somehow on **dying wages**. Whole mountain tops have disappeared to the coal industry despite local and national protest; pollution from the coal industry is so severe that water is literally undrinkable. Emotional pain and depression are common as the landscape people loved and identified with is irrevocably destroyed, leaving people feeling powerless and betrayed.

Combined with the effects of poverty, both emotional and physical, and with the prevalence of pain resulting from disabilities from mining and other dangerous work, and corrupt or inadequate medical care, Appalachia now is in the grips of an epidemic of overuse of pain medication. Instead of looking at the root causes of problems in Appalachia, many use those stereotypes to blame the victim, while for the most part industry behavior is seen as 'normal' or 'inevitable.' The consequences of such conditions is seen also in the unexpected rise in death rates among poorly educated Whites, whose income has dropped precipitately in recent years.

Very similar processes have been at work in many societies around the world, as you will probably see in films and in the books you are reading. As you will see, similar processes have also made it possible to exploit people and places that are external to the state, and have had comparable intense effects on the lives of people all over the world.

• **Want more?** Try searching for video *Harlan County USA*

Reserve labor force
Those people in a capitalist society who do not have a job but would take one if it were available, or who work part-time but would work full time if a job were available.

Dying wages
Another term for super-exploitation, used only when super-exploitation is occurring in a capitalist economy where people are selling their labor, but for extremely low wages.*

• **Want more?** For rising white death rate try http://prospect.org/article/shocking-rise-white-death-rates-midlife-and-what-it-says-about-american-society

EXPROPRIATION OF VALUE FROM OTHER SOCIETIES AND 'OTHER' PEOPLE OUTSIDE THE STATE

Imperialism
The policy and practice of conquering areas outside the state, keeping them to some degree separate from the conquering state, and expropriating value from the conquered area for the benefit of the elite in the conquering state.

Empire
Areas that are under the formal control of another state, but are not incorporated into the controlling state itself, although the empire is governed and exploited by the controlling state.

> *Imperialism in its various forms provides exploitable places outside the boundaries of the state. When the state's control of external exploitable places is tight and formal, we speak of empire.*

Imperialism is nothing new; nor has it disappeared with the breakup of the British Empire and the Soviet Union. In fact, you live in a state that was formed by processes little different from those that form *empires*. The line between conquest states and empires can be fuzzy. What distinguishes an empire from a conquest state is that in the state the conquered groups are brought into the state and live under the same government. The borders of the state are simply expanded to include them. In an empire, the conquering country remains at least to some extent distinct from the countries it has conquered. This accomplishes two things. First, the conquered people can be ruled by their traditional system, so long as the local rulers acknowledge and obey their conquerors. In this system ordinary people may not notice much difference in the conduct of their daily lives and may continue to see their rulers as legitimate. This means the local elite, who are likely to feel a significant loss of prestige and power as a result of conquest, may have a lot of trouble rousing ordinary people to follow them in a revolt. Secondly, keeping the conquered country separate removes any obligation to treat the people and land in the conquered area in ways that are compatible with membership or citizenship in the conquering country. Separate laws can govern conquered areas, and the economy of the conquered area can be carefully organized to produce profits for the conquering elites. If labor is needed within the conquering country, or for enterprises in other conquered countries, people can be pressured, tempted, or forced into migrating or signing labor contracts, or they can be enslaved if slavery is legal.

EMPIRES BASED ON TRIBUTE

• **Want more?**
For pictures of Aztec tribute, search 'Aztec tribute images.'

Some of the early empires, created by kings conquering other territories, such as the Aztec Empire or the early days of Roman imperial expansion, made minimal changes in the social structures of many of the areas they conquered. If elites already existed among the conquered people, little was needed except to require that those elites collect and hand over tribute. Others, such as the Inca Empire, conducted major realignments of the societies they conquered. The Inca followed policies that included moving people from one conquered area to another, creating a number of enclaves within a newly conquered area, each of which spoke different languages and did different jobs. One enclave might consist of farmers, another of soldiers, unable to communicate with each other and unable to communicate with the local population—a classic example of the principles of divide and rule. Tribute was collected and used locally to support these enclaves, to support the Inca administration and religious establishment, to build and maintain fortifications and roads, and to maintain storehouses of basic supplies such as grain for use by people working for the state and for use in times of shortages. In some cases, such as the Spanish empire, a system very much like the European feudal system was replicated in conquered areas. The encomienda system in Mexico is an example.

CAPITALIST EMPIRES

Capitalism

An economic/social/ political system in which the means of production and distribution are privately owned by individuals (or by corporations legally acting as individuals) and operated for personal profit; land and labor are commodities that can be bought and sold.

Aristocrats

In a ranking system, those people who are members of families or of lineages that receive privileges by birth, have inherited rights to positions of power, and usually have control of the means of production.

Colonialism

The establishment of a relationship between two countries in which one country goes to another and reorganizes its culture, economy, and resource use so that the colonizing country can extract cheap labor and cheap resources from the colonized country.

With the development of market economies and of *capitalism*, the character of empires began to change. As elites competed with each other to create wealth and the power that accompanies it, they began to want direct access to resources and labor. Tribute could not be expanded indefinitely, at least not without killing off the work force from starvation or causing massive revolts. And tribute usually could not be productively invested in order to make more wealth. And the competition was no longer restricted to *aristocrats* by birth. A rising merchant class in many parts of the world had entered the competition. They did not have rights by aristocratic birth to tribute, but they were beginning to have capital. They needed to invest it. Colonies provided the means to do so.

Colonialism

Colonialism has influenced and reorganized, to greater or lesser degree, the cultures of most of the world's people, and thus most of the people traditionally studied by anthropologists, including even foraging people who might appear totally isolated from such influences. Colonialism means the establishment of a relationship between two countries in which one country goes to another and reorganizes its culture, economy, and resource use, so that the colonizing country can extract cheap labor and cheap resources from the colonized country. In order to do this, conquest was generally necessary. The conquering country 'owned' the colony and sent administrators to govern it. Ideological justification was needed, as usual, to get people in the conquering country to agree that sending their sons and daughters off to risk their lives, or at least their health, to increase elite wealth was a good idea. This is where the idea of 'the White man's burden' came from—the belief that White people were racially and culturally the most advanced people on earth and therefore had to accept the 'burden' of 'civilizing' and governing the rest of the world in the early 1900s. Many people in Japan had similar ideas about their superiority over Koreans as they colonized that country. In another ideological move, in the British Empire England was referred to as the 'mother' country, implying that conquest brought nurturing governance and gave birth to a better society. One of my students once suggested that 'vampire' would actually be a more accurate term.

Settler Colonies

There are different ways of organizing a colony. The first, and the one you are probably most familiar with, is the settler colony. In a settler colony, invaders come to settle permanently. They want to use the land themselves and often expect to provide at least some of their own labor, for instance on family farms. Thus their most immediate goal is to drive out the original inhabitants. The original inhabitants are killed or removed, especially in areas where family farming predominates. U.S. history is full of examples of this process. An obvious one is the Trail of Tears, when Cherokees and other southern Native AmericanNative Americans were forced at gunpoint by the U.S. army from their homes and farms in Appalachia and made to walk to Oklahoma in Indian Territory, outside what was then the United States. Thousands died on that walk. Australia, South Africa, and New France (Quebec) are other examples of settler colonies.

Generally settler colonies are established in areas where no big profits are expected by the government of the conquering country. Establishing taxable farms and business and taxing imports appears to be the most effective way of shifting value from the colony to the elite of the conquering country. The conquering country retains control of the sale of produce from the settler colony and taxes the colony's production. Whether small family farms or plantations are established depends on the ecology of the area, on the probability of large profits, and on the availability of a source of cheap labor. Plantations are most likely in relatively tropical areas where the kinds of plants suitable for growing on a large scale for export are extremely labor intensive, and where it is possible to establish a system of slavery or very cheap labor. Less labor-intensive crops, like corn, are far more likely to be grown on family farms.

True settler colonies often serve as a 'safety valve' for the discontented in the conquering country; they can emigrate rather than revolt. Or unwanted (by the elite) people can be forced to emigrate, as were many who were shipped from England as indentured servants. Forced emigration is more likely to occur when the colony needs a huge labor supply, as was the case in the Southern colonies in North America, where labor intensive crops were being grown.

Company Colonies

Company colonies are the other likely form colonialism takes. However, many colonies were intermediate between the settler form and the company form; others started as company colonies and eventually shifted away from that model.

• **Want more?**
For pictures try searching 'soldiers trail of tears image.' Also try *The Cherokee Trail of Tears* http://www.dailykos.com/story/2010/05/06/864063/-Indians-101-The-Cherokee-Trail-of-Tears

Company colonies are formed by corporations as profit-making enterprises. The entire colony can be under the direct control of the corporation (for instance the British East India Company in India or Jamestown under the Virginia Company), or there may be a number of smaller corporations formed to operate within the colony, which remains under the direct control of the conquering country (for instance Del Monte in the Philippines and Dole in Hawaii). The corporation can be privately owned, or it can be a government entity. Many of the British colonies in North America were initially started by corporations bringing in settlers, expecting to profit from the colony. The southern colonies retained some characteristics of company colonies, while the Northern ones rapidly shifted into settler colonies.

In company colonies individual colonizers come temporarily to the colony as representatives of foreign governments and companies or of wealthy absentee landlords; they do not make their permanent home in the colony. The foreign government or its representatives maintain permanent control of the colony. This form is most likely to be preferred by the elites of the conquering country in areas where tropical agriculture or mining is profitable and is adapted to production that uses much labor and comparatively little money. Unlike in a settler colony, the original population is not driven out; they are needed as a labor supply.

A common policy was establishing apartheid and the creation of labor reserve areas. A *labor reserve area* is organized to provide people who receive very low wages and go away from home to work, voluntarily or involuntarily, often on plantations or in mines. Their families are left behind in the labor reserve. The colonial administrators leave the social structure and economy of the labor reserve more or less alone, except for the absence of a significant number of people. A labor reserve area has the additional advantage that in economic downturns, when fewer workers are needed, the unemployed can be reabsorbed back into the families and kin groups they had left behind. When they are needed again in the capitalist sector of the economy they can be brought back out again. In Papua New Guinea, for instance, colonial administrators allowed labor recruiters to take only a stated percentage of men from a village and required them to be returned at the end of their contract period. The object of these laws was to make sure that there were enough men left to do their part of farming so that the original economy was able to continue functioning. So long as the kin groups were able to continue producing food for the families of those who were gone working on plantations or in mines, the employers could pay extremely low wages because those wages were not needed to feed families. This means that the capitalist portion of the economy (the plantations and mines designed to produce export goods to provide a profit) was receiving a subsidy from the village kin groups. That subsidy came from the families, and particularly from the women, in the labor reserve who made it possible for families to survive without

Labor reserve area
A section of a colonized country where the traditional subsistence economy and related aspects of a culture are kept relatively unchanged so that the traditional economy can supplement low wages.*

• **Want more?**
For pictures about Papua New Guineans taken to Australian plantations try searching 'Blackbiding in Australia images.'

wages. Capitalist profits, in other words, were built on exploiting the village economy.

> *You might want to argue that the companies were on welfare from the people in the labor reserve—just like the fast food owners, and many other low-wage corporations are on welfare from the state. In essence, by providing food stamps and other subsidies to people paid too little to live on, the state—and taxpayers—pays part of the wages that the fast food place ought to be paying.*

Creating a Cheap Labor Force

> *Strategies backed by force are needed to create a low-wage labor force in egaltarian societies where people have access to the means of production and therefore no need to work for wages. Once people were absorbed into the cash economy and depended on money for many necessities, physical force was no longer needed. People were now 'willing' to work for very low wages because poverty had been created.*

Creating a cheap labor force required elites to pursue some very definite policies. Taking away land and turning it into private property owned by the conquerors and protected by police or the military eliminates access to the means of production and is part of the process. Instituting taxes forced people to get money to pay the tax and was very important in transforming a society to provide cheap, *docile labor.*

Docile labor
People working for a company who cannot afford, either economically, politically, or socially to object to the policies of the company, or to the laws regulating company policies.

Conquerors, whether a neighboring kingdom, such as the Aztec or Inca invading a tribal group on the edge of their territory, or the more recent European colonizers, often had a hard time making the tribes they conquered into a productive source of labor or tribute. Tribes had no central authority to conquer; there was no chief or king with the right and the power to speak for the entire group and direct their behavior. Instead individual clans or villages had to be conquered one by one, and most had well-trained fighters and a tradition of frequent skirmishes that often resembled what we now call guerilla warfare. Women, particularly in matrilineal societies, often had considerable say in questions of land redistribution and land use, and frequently objected strongly as colonizers took over. So there was no guarantee that a tribe would stay conquered. People in tribes are used to shifting allegiance from one Big Man (an informal leader) to another; they did not have to be loyal either to a Big Man whose policies toward the conquerors displeased them, or to conquerors whose rule they had officially accepted. Moreover, they had no expectation of working for the material benefit of others. Their economy was based on gifts, not working for wages. They *exchanged* valuables;

they *gave* gifts. They believed giving gave you the right to expect a return, and hoped for a good return on those exchanges. Becoming poor and working harder to benefit an elite who gave very little in return made no sense at all. Tribal societies, even after decades of intervention by outsiders who were trying to reorganize them for profitability, often were able to maintain their own agendas within the new context, at least so long as they retained control of their land. And some are still fighting to retain control of their land and their lives.

When European colonizers took over an area and tried to turn egalitarian people into a plantation or mining workforce, they had real problems with egalitarian 'laziness.' People used to working three to four hours a day on their own schedule, and on work that directly benefited them and their group, found the European demands excessive.

The colonizers who dealt with societies that were fairly egalitarian generally thought they were a pain in the neck—lazy, undependable, vicious—and had to invent elaborate techniques to turn them into a profitable labor force. This often meant coming up with ways to put someone in charge of a tribe—making someone into a 'chief' or headman and using the military to enforce his power over 'his people.' It often meant reducing women's influence in matrilineal societies by putting land legally under men's control, and it often meant figuring out ways to convince tribal people that the conquerors actually were giving them something in return. This could be done, for instance, by fomenting wars between tribes and then providing military assistance or protection to those tribes that 'behaved.' Missionaries often played a critical role in European conquest, claiming that they brought God's blessing to those who converted and accepted Church authority. In areas where tribal people had become hungry as a result of being driven off their land, missionaries also provided food and housing in return for labor. Instituting a 'head tax' that had to be paid in money or labor was another effective means for creating a labor force, especially when backed by prison terms at hard labor for those who failed to pay. This was all seen as part of the European 'duty' to 'civilize' 'savages.'

Conquerors often found it far easier to siphon off profit from ranked societies where chiefs or kings had some degree of power over 'their' people and could demand tribute or tax, than from more egalitarian societies. Chiefdoms could usually mount a fierce war of resistance, but if the colonizers won, they automatically gained control of the entire territory of the chiefdom. Furthermore, the people they conquered already had some expectation of authority from people above them, and were already used to the idea of giving tribute or labor. They were already adjusted to the necessity to produce some surplus. The conquerors simply had to put themselves above the chief or paramount chief, forcing him or her to turn over most of the tribute to them. The chief or paramount chief could continue as chief, exercising traditional authority. The right to rule came by inherited position and so was seen as legitimate by most commoners and aristocrats. If the chief was cooperative, this meant an easy job of ruling for the conquerors. Backing from the conquering army often meant that the chief gained far more power over both commoners and other aristocrats than he had had before, sometimes to the point of becoming a puppet king—so long as he stayed in the good graces of the conquerors.

The colonizers dealing with chiefdoms often had a lot of respect for the chiefs and thought the ordinary people made good servants and trustworthy laborers. They worked hard at maintaining political alliances with high level chiefs, or at replacing chiefs who wouldn't cooperate. By controlling chiefs, they had a chance at controlling the entire society, although they had to be on the lookout for chiefs who served as a focus for rebellion.

> *At the time when British elites were creating a cheap colonial work force, the European working class was fighting to get down to a ten to twelve hour workday. European elites had hoped to get more work from their colonial subjects at even lower wages.*

Since egalitarian people have the right to join relatives elsewhere, they tended to leave, and Europeans tended to complain, "These people need to be taught to work." Missionaries tried to convert them to Christianity and the belief that God wanted them to live by the sweat of their brows. Generally speaking, hunting and gathering peoples in particular were unimpressed and refused to become the workforce colonizers envisioned until so much land had been taken that there was nowhere left to go. In some cases Europeans took to hunting such people as if they were predatory wolves who had to be cleared out so the land would be available for farming and ranching. Many Europeans defined them as less than human to legitimize their actions.

IMPERIALISM WITHOUT EMPIRE: NEOCOLONIALISM

> *Neocolonialism (or dependent development) is organized to ensure that capitalist enterprises in the conquering countries continue to receive their subsidy from people around the world, but without the political control colonialism provides.*

Colonies around the world fought for independence, sometimes politically, sometimes with guns, sometimes taking advantage of the opportunity presented by wars fomented between competing elites of the conquering nations. Some gained their independence; others were assigned as 'mandates' or 'trust territories' to the conquering Allied nations in the post World War I and World War II divisions of the world. The U.N. charter mandated eventual independence, and by the early 1970s most were granted independence.

Hawaii and Alaska voted to become states of the United States, thereby providing U.S. elites with permanent outposts, largely for Cold War control of the Pacific, far outside of the former boundaries of the U.S. A few colonies, such as Puerto Rico, which is designated a Commonwealth of the United States, remain in an ambiguous status under the control of one of the conquering powers. However, political independence for most former colonies, with the exception of a few such as India, definitely did not bring autonomy. Those new nations that provided important natural resources or grew profitable cash crops were particularly subject to a revised system of control called **neocolonialism** (or sometimes **dependent development**). Generally these colonies were not granted political independence until their economy was thoroughly dominated by the corporations owned by elites of the conquering country or other more powerful nation.

The economic ties that were put in place during the colonial period are still in existence, so that the original conquering country (or other more powerful nation) still has enormous influence over political and economic processes in the country being dependently developed. Those ties are used to guide the neocolony's development in such a way that they can continue the expropriation of labor and resources, much as corporations did during the period of colonial control. As we shall see in Chapter 7, however, there are examples of development that is based on local community needs and values, rather than on the needs of corporations. Development could, if elites can be resisted, enhance, rather than diminish, the well-being of ordinary people.

> *Neocolonialism ensures dependent development. What development is allowed is dependent on the needs of the corporations operating there. Dependent development does not mean that the country is dependent for its survival on the controlling country or its corporations. In reality, it is the elites of the controlling country who are dependent on the former colony for labor and resources.*

When people in the U.S. think about countries with high rates of poverty (variously called 'Third World,' *'peripheral,'* 'underdeveloped,' 'non-Western,' 'least industrialized,' and most recently 'the *Global South*,' all terms that have problems, leaving us without a good generic term) we tend to think that they are poor because they have few resources, or because they lack education, or because they haven't developed their infrastructure, or because they have too many droughts or wars, or because they have too many children, or because they just don't know any better, or because they don't care about human life, or because they

Neocolonialism (dependent development)
Development in a country which is politically independent, but whose economy is dependent on other more powerful countries who guide the dependent country's development in such a way that they can continue the expropriation of labor and resources.*

Peripheral nation
World system theory analyzes the relationships between nations by dividing them between core nations and peripheral nations—those exploited nations which supply labor and raw materials to the core nations.*

Global South
A term which is used in place of terms such as underdeveloped or third world, both of which have negative implications, to refer to those parts of the world which have been and continue to be exploited by more powerful nations referred to as the Global North.

have corrupt leaders. In reality none of these explanations work. Some, such as lots of children, are results of poverty, not causes. Others are simply wrong, such as they don't know better, or don't care about human life. Others have a grain of truth in them, but don't explain anything, such as the corruption of leaders. Many countries, including our own, have had corrupt leaders; they aren't all poverty-stricken nations. Nevertheless, corruption does increase stratification, as it has done in the U.S. with tax breaks for the wealthy and the destruction of the social safety net for the poor, the granting of huge war materials contracts to buddies, and the manipulation of accounting, resulting in loss of jobs and of lifetime savings. Basically what these explanations do is blame the victim. That is why everyone learns them in school. They are a part of the learned ignorance necessary in maintaining a stratified society. This learned ignorance keeps us from questioning the policies that create wealth for elites, don't benefit most of us, and create massive poverty in much of the rest of the world. If we don't know what is happening, we have no reason to do anything about it.

In reality, just as labor reserve areas and internal colonies are the result of specific policies carried out by the elite or by governments in the interests of the elite, so also poverty and 'underdevelopment' are the results of similar policies, with similar purposes: to maintain exploitable areas and exploitable people, in a system that is sometimes referred to as Global Apartheid. Poverty is a result of policies carried out to benefit elites. It is carefully developed. The January 2010 earthquake in Haiti has put the consequences of such policies into stark relief.

Neocolonialism: Developing dependent development

Dependent development depends on having collaborators in the former colony as it gains independence, generally local elites, who will run the new national government for the benefit of the corporations operating there—as well as for their own benefit. This works best if the local elites have been well indoctrinated with the ideologies that make *global apartheid* appear reasonable and inevitable. Most in major decision-making positions have received an education in one of the dominant nations, and have come to believe the 'trickle-down' theory of economics. This theory says that by making things really good for people at the top of the stratification system, so that they can make big profits, you actually benefit the whole society because those at the top will invest in expanding their operations, thus creating more jobs. And people with jobs will spend more, thereby creating more opportunities for other smaller businesses to open up, again creating more jobs. The wealth at the top, in other words, will 'trickle down' to everyone. Those ideas are then repeated in speeches, newspapers, and television and become widely accepted among the wealthy

Global apartheid
A term used by some anthropologists to describe the relationship of powerful countries to less powerful countries as similar to that which existed under apartheid in South Africa.*

and among those with middle class social control jobs. This is the same argument used by many in Congress to argue against raising taxes on the wealthy and instead to cut programs that benefit primarily the poor, women, and the elderly in order to balance the national budget.

It is usually a fairly easy task to convince many people in the upper part of an unequal system that dependent development is a good thing, since they are likely to benefit from it. Convincing those in the middle is sometimes harder, since although they may benefit in some ways, with jobs in the corporations or as professionals or in other social control positions, many will have wages that are fairly low, and many will be in direct contact with people who are clearly suffering from the policies being followed by the elite. Racist, classist, and sexist ideologies are generally needed to provide them with enough learned ignorance to get them to buy into the system.

Instruments of Outside Control

Transnational corporation
A term now used for multinational corporations that have become so powerful that they transcend the power of most nations.

Multinational corporation
A company with headquarters in one country (usually an industrialized one) and branches in many different countries around the world. See also transnational corporation.

Dependent development is carried out under the joint control of multinational or *transnational corporations*, international financial institutions, the government of the dominant country, and the national government of the country being dependently developed. Export industry and agriculture are at the basis of dependent development. Production in these industries is not even partially aimed at meeting the needs of local people, most of whom can't afford to buy the products they help produce. Development of export crops and industries is done by permitting or encouraging *multinational corporations* to establish factories or plantations. Multinational corporations have their headquarters in one country, usually one of the powerful industrialized countries, and have branches in many countries around the world. Their big stockholders and CEOs are generally citizens of the country where the headquarters are located. (These huge corporations are now slightly different and are called transnational corporations as will be discussed in Chapter Seven,) Land is sold or leased to the corporation, tax holidays and other incentives are provided, and the local police or military squash union activity and outright rebellions and kill or jail their leaders. As a result, production is extremely profitable. But that profit goes to the owners of the multinational, while most of the people who work for the corporation get only very low wages, so that poverty is wide-spread. Although those wages mean there is more money in the local economy as a result of dependent development, most of it is in the hands of the local elites and the well-paid portion of the collaborator class.

Even though ordinary people may have higher cash incomes, their standard of living generally drops because they are now dependent on wages, and those wages are so low that they can't buy what people used to provide for themselves in the old economy. For many, this means truly desperate conditions—serious malnutrition, contaminated drinking water, no medical care, little protection from the elements— and no way out.

This may sound familiar, though more extreme, to those of you who live in areas in the United States that have been treated as internal colonies or as something like labor reserve areas. Dependent development happens in the United States, too, although it can't take quite such drastic forms here as it does outside the dominant countries. Crossing the border into Mexico will make the difference immediately clear to you: we have laws that prevent corporations from being quite as exploitative as they can be in Mexico. That, of course, is why corporations chose to go to Mexico. Multinational corporations are free to go wherever they can get the cheapest labor and resources. This means that one effect of dependent development is that the working classes of countries all around the world are in competition with each other for jobs. Dropping real wages and job loss in the U.S. are among the results of this competition, since in effect the corporation has not just the U.S. reserve labor force to draw on, but instead has an enormous world-wide reserve labor force. And it means that dependent development outside our borders hurts many people in the U.S., not just in other countries. In fact, this helps explain why the owners of the fast food joint in Chapter One can pay employees so much less than they need to live on.

Dependent development involves both industry and agriculture. We will look at agriculture first. Instead of growing food to be eaten locally, agricultural products are chosen for their salability in the dominant countries, where more people can afford to pay high prices for them. In many tropical countries plantation agriculture is common, mainly providing industrial centers with products such as sugar, bananas, rubber, and coffee. All products of a plantation are exported; typically food for workers and machinery is imported—which means profits for corporations in the dominant country. Plantations may be broken up when labor becomes more expensive. Local people are then encouraged to grow the export crops on their own, but the distribution and processing remains in the hands of the former owners. In this case debt and taxes, or sometimes laws, keep the small farmers continuing to grow export crops for needed cash, and therefore unable to grow adequate food for themselves. Often they are tenants or sharecroppers.

Most of the good farmland in the country is devoted to export crops. Huge local landowners own some of it, and some is

• **Want more?** Try *Mexico's Maquiladora Labor System Keeps People in Poverty* http://www.mcclatchydc.com/news/nation-world/world/article24730981.html

owned or leased by multinationals. This means that there is nowhere near enough farmable land left for ordinary people and for growing food for ordinary people. Plenty of cheap agricultural labor is available, since local people have been driven off their land, either during the colonial period or during dependent development, and can no longer feed themselves. Many of you are probably acquainted with the saying, "Give a man a fish, you feed him for a day; teach him how to fish, and he can feed himself forever." This statement completely misrepresents why people can't feed themselves.

> *It isn't lack of knowledge—of farming or of fishing— that keeps people hungry. It is the denial of the right to fish in the lake, the denial of rights to the means of production, and, of course, the refusal to pay decent wages.*

But the fish statement is one of those powerful ideological statements that help keep us from understanding what is happening, and therefore from doing anything about it that would actually help. And just as there was plenty of food in Ireland during the Irish potato famine, but people's wages were so low they couldn't afford to buy it, so also there is plenty of food produced in most countries with high rates of hunger, but growers won't sell it at prices people can afford, and instead sell it overseas for bigger profits.

Agriculture generally comes nowhere near providing enough jobs for all the people who no longer have access to the means of production. This is partly because some of the agriculture is mechanized, but it is also because landowners and multinationals own many times more land than they use, but refuse to allow ordinary people to farm on the unused land. The result is a lot of very desperate people who will work on the plantations for almost nothing, and those without jobs make an enormous reserve labor force for incoming industries. They go to the cities, where some are able to get jobs, most of which pay miniscule wages, although some get somewhat better jobs, especially if they have had some education. With so many trying to live on dying wages, or turning to begging or prostitution or crime, it is no wonder that there is an extremely high infant and maternal mortality rate, and that life expectancy can be 20 or more years shorter than in the dominant countries and than the elite of their own countries. And it is no wonder that industries in search of low wages and high profits chose to establish factories in dependently developed countries.

Making all this happen requires the cooperation of the local government, but it also requires the cooperation of the government of the dominant country. Both foreign and domestic policy of the dominant country need to be geared toward the needs of the multinational corporations. For instance, laws in the dominant country will have to provide tax structures favoring multinational corporations' ability to move around the globe. Laws will have to curtail the power of unions to insist that corporations have real responsibilities to the people who have made their profits, and to their communities—that in fact in some sense the corporation belongs to the community and can't simply leave because it could make bigger profits elsewhere. And the effects of dependent development policies on people in the dominant country will have to be disguised or downplayed. The destruction of the rain forest caused by the massive export of lumber from the Amazon, for instance, is a major contributor to the global warming that leads to climate change. What if that were clearly understood in the US, and if it were clearly understood that climate change is even now causing devastation here—Hurricane Katrina being perhaps the first clear example of far more powerful and frequent storms—and if unchecked will continue to raise sea levels to the point where coastal sections of the US simply disappear? What if we wondered where the displaced population of New York City would go when they became climate change refugees? Might we be inclined to insist on changes so that corporations couldn't place profit ahead of the welfare of the Amazon rain forest?

Foreign policy toward particular countries (peripheral nations, or nations of the Global South) will likewise have to favor the interests of the multinational corporations operating there. Political leaders in neocolonies who favor the presence of multinational corporations have often been backed or installed in power by the CIA and similar branches of other internationally powerful nations (*core nations*, or nations of the *Global North*). The influence over government policy in the dominant country is maintained by the presence of the multinational corporation 'representatives' in the government itself, usually in appointed positions, such as secretary of state, and sometimes in elected positions, such as vice president. These are government officials who maintain close ties with particular multinational corporations, revolving back and forth between government positions and management positions in the corporations as well as through ownership, stockholding, and board membership. This is particularly noticeable in the United States in relation to the oil industry. With their enormous wealth corporations are also able to lobby extremely extensively—they represent by far the most powerful 'special interest' in the United States—and can provide funding for political campaigns of people who will favor their interests.

Finally, the World Bank and the International Monetary Fund provide funds on the condition that receiving nations develop production for export. Loans from dominant nations fre-

• **Want more?** Try video *Amazon: Lungs of the Planet* http://www.bbc.com/future/story/20130226-amazon-lungs-of-the-planet

Core nation
According to world system theory, core nations are those that control the financial and investment centers of the world and often the final and most profitable aspects of manufacturing. They absorb raw materials and labor from the peripheral nations.*

Global North
A term which is used in place of terms such as First World or developed, which have positive implications, to refer to those parts of the world which exploit the rest of the world.

quently require that the money be spent on products manufactured by corporations in the loaning country. So for instance an agricultural loan can require that fertilizer be bought from U.S. companies, rather than from local companies. This means that the fertilizer is far more expensive, and that local companies don't get the business. As the only major market for export products, the dominant nations have an additional source of control.

Structural adjustment is frequently required when indebted nations try to get help. The local government is required to adjust the structure of society to cut back on its expenses as a condition of the loan. An example is the 2012 crisis in Greece, with massive unemployment resulting from government spending cuts mandated by the more powerful European Union nations as a condition for receiving loans. Some anthropologists would also argue that a similar structural adjustment is happening in the US in order to pay for the wars in Iraq and Afghanistan. Such austerity measures specifically target social welfare programs, thereby both forcing people to work for even less as well as cutting government expenditures. So if the government used to provide free hospitals, or subsidized the cost of food, for instance, or provided school lunches, they have to cut back or even stop. The result is greater suffering, more intense **structural violence**, the brunt of it borne by women and by children, since they are the ones most frequently benefited by social welfare programs. Human rights are denied, and multinational corporations have an even cheaper labor supply.

RESISTING IMPERIALISM

At this point I doubt that I have convinced you. You may be saying, "Okay, then it is the fault of the people in the country that they are poor—if they wanted to change it, they should elect better people and pass better laws." So let's see what happens when they do exactly that, when they resist exploitation.

Resistance includes attempts by the exploited group to create more favorable conditions for themselves. It involves attempts to take some power away from the exploiting group, such as strikes or economic self-help movements. These efforts are often interpreted as irrational or destructive or out of touch with economic reality by the exploiting group, who use this interpretation to justify using legal or even military means if necessary to stop them. We have seen such reactions frequently in U.S. history, for instance as Appalachian mining families went on strike or as Blacks refused to sit in the back of the bus, or as women insisted on the right to vote, and now as Latino/a people resist being defined as criminals for taking a job in the U.S. Such movements have been common all over the world as people try to take back the rights that have been denied to them.

Structural adjustment
The imposition of austerity measures to cut government spending, mainly on social welfare and social justice programs, thus adjusting the structure of a society so that poorer people have fewer options and will work for less or will be more docile.*

Structural violence
Violence that is not a result of individuals or the state taking direct action to harm others. Structural violence generally results from inequality built into the social structure and results in deaths, maimings, malnutrition among those most seriously exploited. A death resulting from a society's refusal to commit adequate tax money to care for the poor is an example of structural violence. A death caused by murder is not.

Resistance
The refusal to accommodate (see accommodation) the exploitative demands of those with more power; the refusal to do something against one's will.*

Socialism
A socio-economic system
in a state society in which,
unlike capitalism, all or
some of the means of
production are owned by
the state as representative
of the members of the
society. *

• **Want more?**
For democratic socialism
try exploring this site:
Committees of
Correspondence for
Democracy and Socialism
http://www.cc-ds.org/

Socialism is one approach to creating a more egalitarian social structure. Actually, socialists were involved in all the resistance movements I listed in the previous paragraph, and have played an important role in shaping the U.S. Since socialism involves various ways of lessening the difference between haves and have-nots, and since it conveys greater human rights to ordinary people and denies to the elite some of their rights to exploit, it also is not as efficient a system for conveying wealth to the elite. Those who believe that they and their society benefit by denying rights generally object to a socialist government. Since they hold power, their objections may prevent a shift to socialism or may derail a socialist government. They frequently turn to force, especially if they continue to control the military. If they need help in putting down rebellions or stifling unions or socialist parties, they often can get it from other capitalist countries, particularly ones whose elites use resources or labor from the socialist country. With their leaders killed and their jobs threatened, with jail looming, with news media and mainstream religious establishments describing socialism as an invention of evil and its adherents as lazy immoral whiners wanting a handout, and even perhaps with the army marching in or bombs falling, attempts at more egalitarian government often fail.

Despite all the strategies for imperial control, revolts are fairly common, both among peasants and industrial and plantation workers. And they do sometimes succeed, but only if a broad coalition of the working class is formed, ignoring divides such as race and gender, thus creating power for themselves through sheer force of numbers.

Colonies and former colonies have frequently attempted to establish socialism. In order to alleviate the dire poverty present in such countries one of the first steps of a socialist government upon gaining power, whether by revolution or election, is likely to be land redistribution—returning to ordinary people their rights to the means of production. So the major landowners and the multinationals operating in a country are likely to lose at least their unused land. Some of the major resource extraction industries may be nationalized, on the principle that resources such as coal belong to the nation as a whole, to everyone in the country, not just to a few wealthy people or multinational corporations. These efforts to improve the lives of ordinary people mean that the reserve labor force will decrease. Wages will go up, and profits will go down. When this happens many of the local elite will be furious. They are likely to join with the multinationals in attempting to overthrow the socialist government. If this appears to be difficult because the majority of the population supports the socialist government and, being spread over the countryside, can engage in quite effective guerilla warfare, the elite and their multinational allies turn to the government of the dominant

• **Want more?** Try *September 11, 1973: A CIA Backed Military Coup* http://www.democracynow.org/2003/9/11/sept_11_1973_a_cia_backed

country for military help, weapons, and money. So, for instance, the U.S. military was deeply involved in overthrowing duly elected socialist democracies such as Allende's Chile, Ortega's Nicaragua, and Arbenz's Guatemala.

Chile, for instance, had its own 9/11 when, on that date in 1973 planes in a U.S. backed coup bombed the capital, killing well over 3,000 people, with another 20,000 murdered shortly thereafter, 60,000 tortured, and one million going into exile. After the coup, during which thousands of ordinary people often died, puppet governments favorable to the interests of U.S. multinationals were installed.

Other socialist countries, often the ones with particularly strong socialist aspects, have been dictatorships, such as Cuba, China, and the former USSR. The hold of the elite in these countries under the previous regime, before the socialist dictatorship, was so pervasive—for instance Russia was a particularly exploitative feudal monarchy—that armed revolution was needed to dislodge them from power. Their elites were largely killed or expelled, as was the middle class bureaucracy that supported them. This bloodbath (generally smaller than many that have been carried out by governments supported by the U.S. government) was justified with the understanding that the elite had been conducting a quiet bloodbath of their own for generations. For large numbers of ordinary people, these socialist dictatorships provided decent jobs and the hope that most of their children would live for the first time in memory. Compared to other former colonies, and even compared to poor people in the U.S., their standard of living was relatively high. It is also true that they were not free to pursue great wealth or to purchase many commodities, and they did not have the civil rights U.S. citizens have.

Resistance to inequality and imperialism appears to be on the rise again, in the U.S. and around the world, much of it, as resistance often is, lead by young people. For instance, since approximately 2010, there has been the Arab Spring—the widespread revolt against dictatorships in many Middle Eastern countries, many of which have since been undermined by war and the effects of climate change. There is the Occupy Movement, which started with the occupation of Wall Street, spread around the U.S., and then abroad, protesting the growing wealth of the rich and the environmentally and financially devastating policies that have greatly increased the divide between haves and have-nots. Protesting another U.S. divide is BlackLivesMatter, a movement initially responding to police killings of unarmed young Black men under conditions where young White men almost never die, but now pushing hard for racial justice and equality in all areas, not just in the criminal justice system. Riots and resistance have greeted the imposition of greater and greater austerity measures on indebted European Union countries such as Greece and Spain. Wisconsin's teacher-led resistance to union-busting, spreading to members of the state legislature and then to other states, Iceland's

• **Want more?** Try Black Lives Matter http://blacklivesmatter.com/ Search for 'Occupy Movement images' **Or explore** #OccupyWallStreet https://owsanalysis.wordpress.com/

Chapter 2 Imperialism, Colonialism, and Neocolonialism 55

refusal to give in to the demands that tax-payers bail out banks, indigenous Bolivians rising against development of a road through the rainforest, the widespread protests for women's rights sparked by the garment factory fire in a Bangladesh Walmart supplier and by the shooting of Malala Yousafzai, a student activist for women's education in Pakistan, resistance to fracking and to the construction of the Keystone XL Pipeline which rouses concerns about climate change by enabling the exploitation of the tar sands... the list could go on and on. Most of these examples of resistance are directly or indirectly responses to the Neoliberal policies we will be studying in Chapter 7.

People who are being exploited do not simply sit back and passively accept the way they are being treated. Revolts are frequent, but even when they fail, people continue pushing back trying to find ways to beat the system. People engage in a complex combination of accommodation and resistance.

ACCOMMODATING IMPERIALISM

Accommodation
The process of adjusting oneself to difficult circumstances you are powerless to change. In particular, the term applies to situations of inequality, where the person with less power must somehow learn to live with the demands of more powerful people.*

Accommodation comes in a variety of forms. As used by anthropologists the term generally refers to ways individuals and groups adjust themselves to inequality, ways in which people with less power learn to live somehow with the demands of more powerful people. So a wife may accommodate herself to having to do all the housework, an employee accommodates an employer's unexpected demand for overtime work. People who are poor and have little power may accommodate themselves to their lack of resources, believing for instance, that God will somehow take care of them. However, accommodation isn't really an individual matter; a group or an entire society develops cultural patterns that guide people's likely individual responses. So, for instance, if the society says housework is women's work, the wife may find it easier to cope with if she knows her friends and relatives are all doing the same thing and believes that this is just the way things are and that her husband is not doing anything immoral by refusing to help.

Imperialism frequently means that the old system of accommodation no longer works. New patterns are needed. Those changes come about partially as a direct result of imperial policies, and partly because people actively figure out how to deal with new economic and social realities. This is often done by reinterpreting elements of the traditional culture so that people can fit into the new socio-economic situation without feeling as if they have lost all their previous values and culture.

RELIGION

Religion plays an important role in maintaining inequality and in helping people deal with it (see Chapters Three and Six). Consequentially people often turn to it as part of accommodation. This can be a two-edged sword. Some of those accommodations represent efforts on the part of people who were formerly relatively privileged to regain that privilege at the expense of others, usually people defined as inferior by race or gender. This does, in a sense, also involve an element of 'resistance:' resisting changes that convey rights to a wider range of people. The recent rise of Christian, Hindu, and Islamic fundamentalisms is an example, with their emphasis on patriarchy, traditional forms of authority, and obedience to those in power. Others are more inclusively egalitarian and tend to have a complex mix of elements of both accommodation and resistance.

Liberation theology, for instance, focuses on using religious arguments to convince the group in power that their exploitative behavior is immoral and assures the oppressed that it is not their fault that they are poor. This movement has been particularly important in Latin America. Liberation Theology maintains that to do God's will, you must work to end the inequality and social injustice that is the root cause of poverty. Giving charity is not enough. Liberation theology is often a religious basis for resistance. While the recently selected Pope Francis rejects some aspects of Liberation Theology, nevertheless his position has much in common with that tradition. He says that the present socio-economic system is unjust. And because it kills people, it is contrary to the commandment "Thou shalt not kill" and therefore contrary to God's will. Profits cannot be put ahead of people or ahead of the welfare of the earth. He points out that the earth produces enough food for all, and greater equality would end hunger. Inequality, he says, is at the root of all evil, and until we reject the rule of the market and of financial speculation we will not be able to solve any of the world's problems—from climate change to homelessness to war.

Revitalization movements are another response. They play parts in both accommodation and resistance, and are most likely to arise early in a society's experience of imperialism, for instance when colonial authorities first institute far-reaching economic changes and insist that the society's previous way of life was immoral. Revitalization movements are religious movements that attempt to revive a society that has been conquered or otherwise damaged. They try to build a new society, using some aspects of the traditional religion, as well as new aspects. Cargo cults in Papua New Guinea were revitalization movements that were to some extent accommodation but were at the same time resistance movements and self-help movements. The colonial authorities used police and the legal system to squash them with the excuse of claiming that people in these cults had lost it and

Liberation theology
A religious doctrine and movement, primarily within Catholicism, but spreading beyond, that emphasizes justice and social activism on behalf of the oppressed.*

• **Want more?** Try video *Pope Francis' Speech to Congress*: https://www.washingtonpost.com/local/social-issues/transcript-pope-franciss-speech-to-congress/2015/09/24/6d7d7ac8-62bf-11e5-8e9e-dce8a2a2a679_story.html

Revitalization movement
A social movement, frequently religious or with strong religious aspects, that attempts either to bring new life to a society which has been conquered or otherwise damaged, or to bring to life a new society in its place.*

become irrational when they came in contact with all the material goods that Europeans had.

FAMILY, HOUSEHOLD, AND GENDER ROLES

The use of families to subsidize capitalist enterprise often means changing the family structure to allow some family members to be away for long periods or to spend all of their time working at the capitalist enterprise. Others in the family continue to help support the family with 'traditional" economic work outside the capitalist system, for instance raising food, making clothes, exchanging labor with neighbors and kin. Similarly, the U.S. family structure has had to change to allow many more women to work outside the home for generally low wages. The prevalence of fast food is one such change along with the disappearance of the obligatory daily family meal. Gender roles are changing to some extent also, with more men taking on some responsibility for childcare and housework. It is no longer unusual for a man to cook, at least in middle class homes; interestingly, that is also the most creative and most thanked aspect of housework.   Middle class women have had to learn to manage both home and job, as poorer women have been doing all along.

Typical family structure may also change. Extended family households may break up as individual wage earners follow jobs and, when those jobs pay enough, sever their economic ties with the extended family in order to 'better themselves' by unloading some of their financial responsibilities toward less well-off members of the family.

Nuclear families may get bigger, particularly in societies where a long postpartum sex taboo or other restrictions on intercourse previously limited pregnancies. A changing way of life or religious changes may mean more frequent pregnancies, and in societies where vaccinations and clean water are effectively introduced, more of the children may live. The higher birth rate may be to some extent offset by a rising death rate due to lack of immunity to new diseases, genocide, or the consequences of poverty among people who previously were not poor by the anthropological definition of poverty. These consequences include prenatal and postnatal malnutrition, inadequate health care, and the spread of disease with urban crowding. However, among well-to-do families the birth rate and family size may drop considerably as people come to believe that their children will live and that their security comes best from investing in the education of just a few children. Middle class parents in India, who themselves had five or six siblings, now often have only one child, especially if the first child is a boy. If the first child is a girl, they often try a second time.

The relatively carefree childhood found in most egalitarian societies often disappears as those societies become severely unequal as a result of imperial policies. Children may have to become wage earners at an extremely early age. Child labor is an important source of profits for many sweat shop owners, and sometimes also for the bigger corporations. To some extent this pattern is seen in the United States also, as more middle class families believe their children benefit more from flipping hamburgers than from doing homework.

GENDER INEQUALITY

• **Want more?**
For pictures try searching 'Child labor images'

> *The position of women frequently becomes worse as patriarchal and patrilineal definitions are imposed by colonial authorities or by lending institutions in dependent development.*

Wage labor
Selling your labor to someone who owns the means of production.

When land held by whole kin groups is reassigned as private property by colonial authorities, it is generally men who are given title to the land. Women thus become dependent on husbands, fathers, brothers, or sons for access to the means of production. Even in societies where women were the principal farmers, but were farming on land held by their husband's kin group, they generally had control of the crops they produced. This source of power disappears when men instead are defined as the farmers and are the only ones crop buyers for corporations and representatives of lending institutions will deal with. As more and more people are driven into dependency on *wage labor*, and most of the jobs that pay slightly better wages are available only to men, women again become increasingly dependent on men. Men may also be inclined to spend a significant portion of their wages on themselves. The availability of wage work also makes it more possible for men to abandon their families, or to leave for long periods in the hope of finding work and sending wages home. If war is added into the mix, as it frequently is, the situation for women becomes even worse.

As a result, women and their dependents frequently suffer the worst effects of inequality in terms of malnutrition and lack of necessities. It may be their rights that are most effectively denied. Their labor may be organized as the cheapest available, and corporations may refuse to hire many men. Women are thus forced to work for very low wages to feed their families, as well as continue doing housework and childcare. Their labor both enriches the elite and makes men of their own class a bit more comfortable. Previous sources of income, such as selling farm produce, crafts, or cooked food, may disappear as locally made products are replaced by industrial products.

However, there may be contradictory effects at work for women in elite families and in families in the well-paid and professional classes. For instance, there are more women in the legislative bodies of some former colonies—including Iraq and Afghanistan—than in the U.S. and other former colonial powers.

Many have had female heads of state; the U.S. has never even had a woman run for president as the candidate of one of the major parties, much less win.

RACE AND ETHNICITY

Many societies in areas being colonized did not have rigid boundaries between groups. People from different small-scale farming societies, for instance, often married each other, and your membership in your kin group and your relationship with your spouse's kin group mattered far more on a day-to-day basis than which tribe you identified with. Animosity between these groups did exist, but who was a member of which group was fairly fluid, and animosities themselves shifted frequently. Colonial administrators wanted clearly defined groups for administrative purposes—such as tribes in some areas or castes in India. They also needed groups that could be severely exploited and other groups to act as collaborators in managing exploitation. Definitions of inferiority, sometimes already existing within the conquered society, and sometimes more or less manufactured, were needed to justify exploitation and to gain consent of the collaborators. So tribal, *ethnic*, and *racial* categories were rigidified or invented or elaborated upon to reflect the system of inequality in which the colonized, dependently developed, or internally colonized are kept in exploited positions at the bottom. These differences were used as needed within the conquered society for purposes of divide and rule.

Ethnic group
A group of people within a larger society who are thought to share the same national or cultural heritage, which is different from that of other groups in the society; generally created in the context of conquest or migration.

Race
An artificial grouping of people invented to fill ideological needs in situations of massive inequality.*

In addition, differences between the conquered group as a whole and the conquerors were needed. And in the 1800s and the first half of the 1900s anthropologists and other social scientists put enormous effort into trying (and ultimately failing) to define racial, biological characteristics that would clearly show the source of inferiority in the conquered group. Inferiority was supposedly proven, for instance, by head shape that differed from that of the supposedly typical head shape of the conquerors.

The conquered or exploited group is defined as a racial or ethnic group, and the physical or cultural differences from the more powerful group are defined as important. These differences are used to define the group as 'other,' not like 'us,' and inferior or backward.

Once these definitions have been made and at least to some extent accepted, the social construction of reality takes over. Despite being based on lies, such definitions can have real consequences. Alleged inferiority justifies discrimination, and discrimination ensures that most of those defined as inferior will remain in subordinate positions, making it appear to be true that the inferior group actually lacks talent and initiative. And thus it appears natural that the conquerors are in power and natural that the conquered group needs guidance and should be grateful for the opportunity to learn by working for the conquerors. Since their culture has been defined as inferior, they should also be grateful for the civilizing influence of the conquerors. An entire ideology, in other words, is now available to free those in the conquering group from guilt and to help collaborators see their role as benevolent.

Within a conquest state these same processes are at work, defining the group brought in by conquest or other forms of expansion as unworthy of the rights of full citizens. Just as in expansion outside the state, the groups being *super-exploited* are usually defined as a separate race. Groups that are less exploited are likely to be defined as ethnic groups, differing from the dominant group only in culture, rather than in the supposed biological differences of race. The Irish, for instance, used to be called a race when they were being super-exploited in the U.S.; now they are seen as just another ethnic group—and that seems to matter only on St. Patrick's Day. Ethnic groups can also arise when two different groups share power in a country they both invaded. Ethnicity can be used in the fight for power between the two groups. However, if the groups have or gain approximately equal power, ethnicity may serve simply as a form of personal identity with little prejudice and discrimination involved, as is the case now for the Irish.

Boundary markers are used to distinguish the groups. These markers can be seen as relatively minor, such as food preferences, accent, or a slightly different religion. Or those differences can be defined as major, such as language or religious differences that are said to be very important. In the U.S., the differences between Protestantism and Catholicism were said to be critically important when some of the groups being super-exploited were Catholic, coming from Ireland and later from Southern and Eastern Europe. Many Protestant Americans in the 1920s believed that Catholics couldn't be 100% Americans because they were supposedly unable to think for themselves and obeyed the Pope, who was not an American. Few Protestants feel this way any longer. Strong and very marked boundaries are one indication that ethnicity is being used to place people very unequally in the stratification system. The country's myths, jokes, and its teaching of history also reflect a group's placement. Subordinate groups are often excluded, or their role is downplayed, or they are included in the myths and history in ways that appear to justify their subordination.

INDIGENOUS PEOPLES EMBEDDED IN STATES

Today most *egalitarian* societies, bands and tribes where all people have access to the resources they need, no longer exist as relatively independent societies, although until very recently a few were still to be found in areas unsuited for agriculture or for other means of producing a surplus. But bear in mind that even these

---

Super-exploitation
People are left with so little of what they produce, or are paid so little for the work they do and the value that they produce, that they cannot pay for the cost of raising the next generation, or of maintaining themselves as workers.*

Boundary markers
Characteristics which are said to demonstrate or indicate membership in a particular group, often an ethnic group.*

Egalitarian
A system of relationships in which everyone equally has access to needed resources. In the most egalitarian societies, no one can be denied access to the means of production. Leaders have no real power, their position is not passed on to their descendants, and they have no more material possessions or food than anyone else.

societies, like all the societies studied by anthropologists, have been affected by colonialism, imperialism, and globalization. The arrival of the anthropologist marks the point at which a group has become 'study-able.' Transportation has become available, or they have more or less given up fighting the colonial police or military, or treaties have been signed, or ranchers are encroaching on their land. What may appear to be a 'traditional' way of life has already changed. And it has changed many times in the past, when new people move in, for instance, bringing with them new subsistence strategies or new forms of organization, and perhaps conquest.

Contrary to what most Americans assume, egalitarian groups as independent societies have not died out due to inefficiency, starvation, backwardness, or a 'natural' desire to become part of more stratified societies.

Some egalitarian societies have disappeared due to their own internal changes, with gradual increases in the ability of one group to take away and use for its own benefit the surplus produced by members of other groups, perhaps becoming powerful kingdoms.

However, this shift toward stratification is not a one-way trip. Societies sometimes shift back toward equality, sometimes as socialist societies have done, but historically more often as the Maya in Central America did around 1400 CE (AD), before the arrival of the Spaniards. They quit building huge palaces and temples; royalty lost control of their kingdoms and could no longer muster armies or collect tribute and taxes from their subjects. Local farming families organized themselves into more or less self-governing villages in which everyone had the right to use the land surrounding the village. Groups of family elders made or had a lot of say in decisions that affected the whole village.

While in some cases states such as kingdoms have existed side by side with more egalitarian societies, states, being organized for war and for profit, tend to conquer or develop neighboring societies and in the process make it much harder for them to maintain egalitarian values.

The equalitarian societies that survived the recent rounds of colonization and dependent development did so because they were in areas such as deserts or tropical forests that did not have the abundance of resources that allowed for the development of inequality. And for the same reason other, more powerful, people didn't want it. Social inequality did exist among those foraging societies that lived in an environment that was so rich that it was possible to produce a surplus easily, and could support a *sedentary* population—people living in one place year round. However the same resources that underwrote their inequality made them attractive to colonizers or to more powerful neighbors, or to transnational corporations.

Sedentary
A way of life built around staying in one place year-round, for many years at a time. The opposite of nomadic.

The elites of powerful societies can become more wealthy and powerful from using the land or the labor of a neighboring egalitarian group, and they have authority over their own people and can tell them to go out to fight and conquer other people. So decision-makers in such societies are likely to see conquest as an attractive option. Egalitarian societies, particularly foraging ones, are not organized around the needs of war and defense and are vulnerable to conquest. After being conquered they are in one way or another put to work producing a surplus, which gets turned over to the conquering elites. They are no longer an egalitarian society; they have lost their ability to convey rights to all. Those rights have been appropriated by the conquering group, who deny them to most people. Denying those rights forces the conquered group to go to work for their conquerors in return for food and shelter.

Indigenous peoples
The descendants of the people who inhabited an area before conquest and now exist as minorities within the borders, or straddling the borders, of countries that are highly stratified.

• **Want more?** Try exploring
The Republic of Lakotah
http://www.republicoflakotah.com/

Nevertheless, although indigenous independent societies practicing an equalitarian way of life have largely disappeared, the descendents of people who lived in such societies are still here.

While some have been absorbed into the dominant culture of the stratified society in which they live, many continue to identify with the society of their parents or grandparents, adopting new ways but adapting those ways to their own needs and values. Such people are often described as 'indigenous,'—the descendants of the people who inhabited an area before conquest and now exist as minorities within the borders, or straddling the borders, of countries that are highly stratified. An example might be the Lakota Nation which in 2007 declared independence from the United States, or the highland Indian people of Chiapas, Mexico, who have been the backbone of the Zapatista movement for human rights.

Indigenous people, embedded in states, live lives that are shaped by the interplay of their own local situation and the global economy in which they participate. Many non-indigenous people find images of a tribal leader carrying a bow or with a lip ornament speaking on a cell phone both incongruous and symbolic of globalization, but such images actually disguise the reality of indigenous life today. Most indigenous people around the world have been dispossessed of their local land base and disenfranchised through the processes of colonialism, neocolonialism, and imperialism. Poverty in indigenous communities is rampant, due largely to these same processes of dispossession and disenfranchisement. Having lost access to the means of production, the old system of kin group landholding no longer works. Some farm individual plots of land, but in an economy where money is a necessity and without the security offered by membership in a larger group. Many others try to find jobs locally, where they can sell their labor. Globalization is far more likely to mean working in a sewing factory paid pennies an hour making blue jeans for people of the Global North than it is to mean chatting on a cell phone with friends and family half a world away. Some do have access to technology such as cell phones and computers; the vast majority does not.

Participating in a global economy may indeed mean having friends and family half a world away, or in a neighboring country: people often deal with local poverty by emigrating, or by crossing back and forth over national borders, in order to find jobs. Frequently those who leave send money back to their families, who remain involved in the local economy where they spend the money sent back. Some local economies are heavily dependent on such remittances. Those who do well may be using their cell phones and the internet to maintain contact with families, but many more remain poor. Jobs for immigrants frequently pay very little, and remittances to the family at home may absorb what little extra there is. Nevertheless, immigrants do travel back and forth and do maintain contact with family, and they also develop indigenous communities in the new country. In a sense, the indigenous culture has become *deterritorialized*. A culture that was once connected to a particular territory, a particular area of the world, is now to be found in various forms in numerous parts of the world, and even to some extent in cyberspace.

Globalization for many has meant exploitation on a very basic, biological level. The blood of indigenous people has been taken for genetic research and their knowledge of medical plants is mined for cures for those Western peoples who can afford the best of medical care, while many indigenous people live under conditions that cause illness, created by the poverty that accompanies neocolonialism or imperialism. The plant varieties they have developed over many generations are taken and patented by major agricultural corporations, in some cases making it illegal to save and plant the seed they have used for generations. Indigenous children have been taken—adopted—to provide children to well-to-do people in the Global North. For some communities in the U.S. so many children have been taken by Social Services that Native American activists talk of cultural genocide.

Deterritorialized
A culture, or significant aspect of that culture, is no longer associated only with the territory or geographical area in which it originated.

• **Want more?** Try *How the Blood Came Back to the Yanomami* http://center-yanomami.publicanthropology.org/

All of these conditions together have led to massive resistance on the part of indigenous people around the world.

While egalitarian societies no longer can govern themselves independently, and are enmeshed in the consequences of being forcibly absorbed into stratified societies, many of their descendants fight to maintain their integrity as a people, their control of their land, and the values of their ancestors.

Austerity program
A program pursued by a national government to reduce spending, usually by cutting programs and subsidies that benefit the poorer segment of a society; often instigated by international financial institution as a condition for loans to the national government.

Ethnotourism
Tourism based on organizing tourist attractions by exhibiting the 'traditional' way of life of indigenous groups.

NGO
Non-Governmental Organization; private or non-profit organizations frequently associated with development in failed states and in countries with a history of colonialism and neocolonialism. Often funded by organizations of the Global North.

• **Want more?** Try *Protecting the Amazon Includes Defending Indigenous Rights* http://therealnews.com/t2/index.php?option=com_content&task=view&id=31&Itemid=74&jumival=12281

In the process the very meaning of their identity as a people is often manipulated, both by indigenous communities and by outsiders. Outsiders bent on dispossession may question whether people who have adopted and adapted new technologies, new ways of making a living, or new ways of dressing, are 'authentic' indigenous people. They are no longer living as the outsiders imagine indigenous traditions require, and if they are not authentic indigenous people then their right to protections granted by treaty, law, or international conventions can be challenged. States, particularly those subject to *austerity programs* imposed by international financial institutions, may turn to *ethnotourism* as a source of income. Indigenous people are hired by tourist agencies and resorts to dress up, demonstrate crafts, and dance like 'real' tribal men and women, thus being commodified in return for usually extremely low wages. Namibian farmers, however, are taking over the control of wildlife tourism, managing wildlife conservancies to regulate animals, tourists, hunting, and other Namibians to provide profit for themselves and even a surplus to support benefits such as HIV/AIDS care.

Indigenous groups within a state who previously had no particular reason to define themselves as 'a people' may, in the face of oppression, work to build the numbers and strength needed for resistance by creating a pan-indigenous identity. Doing so may also help them meet *NGO* definitions that make them eligible for financial support for organizing efforts or for humanitarian aid. Some are cooperating across state borders. Indigenous peoples around the world who have access, perhaps through their own middle class status or through local indigenous organizations or NGOs, to the communication and transportation technologies of the global economy, are coordinating their efforts. They are organizing indigenous congresses and conferences, forging a world-wide indigenous alliance or even a world-wide pan-indigenous identity.

Indigenous people have been at the forefront of many environmental initiatives. For instance, they are leaders in efforts to save genetic material and to resist genetic alteration of crops and animals. They have joined with other indigenous people and other allies around the world to save the environment in which they live, and thus their way of life. They have worked to stop pollution, toxic dumping, over-fishing, and destruction of animal habitat. Stopping global warming and the ensuing climate change would help save environments all around the world for all indigenous peoples, but actually for everyone else too. Indigenous people are among those most likely to be already feeling the direct effects of climate change, since the places where they are most likely to still have communities tend to be land nobody wanted badly enough to drive them out—mountains, deserts, islands, low-lying coastal areas. Rising sea-levels that flood fields with salt water or submerge land, homes, and whole communities, higher temperatures, longer droughts, melting glaciers, changed animal migration routes—these are all issues indigenous people, as well as others, are experiencing today. A history of colonialism and dependent development has left many indigenous communities with few resources and little money with which to fight against climate change or to accommodate it or rebuild lives and livelihoods elsewhere.

Other descendants of indigenous people, as a result of a long history of rape, intermarriage, slavery and other forms of unfree labor, education (often forced), adoption (often forced), and relocation (also often forced), no longer identify or are identified as indigenous people. If you are in a typical U.S. classroom, for instance, a number of the people in the room who identify themselves as White, African American, or Latino/a undoubtedly have Native American ancestors. Some may be aware of that fact; others may not. Some may be trying to reclaim that ancestry.

> *Indigenous people have not disappeared; they are still here despite the efforts of hegemonic forces to eliminate them, assimilate them, or at least make them invisible in the public eye.*

RECAP

What you have seen in this chapter are the policies that have made it possible for an enormous proportion of the world's wealth to accumulate in the pockets of a very small number of people. Many of you will see films or read books or articles that document the conditions that have resulted, with some people benefitting from the process but far more suffering from structural violence and others from genocide and war. Much of the rest of the book talks about how this kind of behavior is disguised, so that much of the time people are not even aware that rights are being denied.

REFERENCES/SUGGESTED READINGS

Empire and resistance outside the U.S.

Buck, Pem Davidson 1991 Colonized Anthropology: Cargo-Cult Discourse. *In* Decolonizing Anthropology. Faye V. Harrison, ed. Pp. 24-41. Washington, D.C.: American Anthropological Association.

Enloe, Cynthia 1989 Bananas, Beaches, and Bases: Making Feminist Sense of International Politics. Berkeley: University of California Press.

Gunewardena, Nandini and Ann Kingsolver, eds. 2008 The Gender of Globalization: Women Navigating Cultural and Economic Marginalities. Santa Fe, NM: School for Advanced Research.

Kingsolver, Ann 2001 NAFTA Stories: Fears and Hopes in Mexico and the United States. Boulder, CO: Lynne Rienner Publishers, Inc.

Moksnes, Heidi 2004 Militarized Democracies: The Neoliberal Mexican State and the Chiapas Uprising. *In* State, Sovereignty, War: Civil Violence in Emerging Global Realities. Bruce Kapferer, ed. Pp. 89-106. New York: Berghahn Books.

Richter, Robert 1984 The Business of Hunger. 28 min. Maryknoll,NY: Maryknoll World Films.

Rothenberg, Paula, ed. 2006 Beyond Borders: Thinking Critically About Global Issues. New York: Worth Publishers.

On Indigenous Peoples

Brower, Barbara and Barbara Johnston 2007 Disappearing Peoples? Indigenous Groups and Ethnic Minorities in South and Central Asia. Walnut Creek, CA: Left Coast Press.

Escobar, Arturo 2008 Territories of Difference: Place, Movements, Life, Redes. Durham: Duke University Press.

Joyce, Christopher 2011 To Save Wildlife, Namibia's Farmers Take Control. National Pubic Radio October 10. http://www.npr.org/2011/10/10/140445502/to-save-wildlife-naminias-farmers-take-control

Muehlmann, Shaylin 2009 How Do Real Indians Fish? Neoliberal Multiculturalism and Contested Indigeneities in the Colorado Delta. American Anthropologist 111(4): 468-479.

Maybury-Lewis, David 1997 Indigenous Peoples, Ethnic Groups, and the State. Boston: Allyn and Bacon.

Smith, Linda T. 1999 Decolonizing Methodologies: Research and Indigenous Peoples. New York: Zed Books.

Sylvain, Renée 2008 Disorderly Development: Globalization and the Idea of "Culture" in the Kalahari. In The Anthropology of Globalization: A Reader, 2nd Edition. Jonathan Xavier Inda and Renato Rosaldo, eds. Pp. 403-432. Malden MA: Blackwell Publishing.

The effects of imperialism on the U.S.

Buck, Pem Davidson 2008 Keeping the Collaborators on Board as the Ship Sinks: Toward a Theory of Fascism and the U.S. 'Middle Class.' Rethinking Marxism 20(1):68-90.

Dawson, Ashley and Malini Johar Schueller, eds. 2007 Exceptional State: Contemporary U.S. Culture and the New Imperialism. Durham: Duke University Press.

Enloe, Cynthia 2007 Globalization and Militarism: Feminists Make the Link. Lanham MD: Rowman and Littlefield.

Harrison, Faye V. 2008 Outsider Within: Reworking Anthropology in the Global Age. Urbana: University of Illinois Press.

Lutz, Catherine 2002 Homefront: A Military City and the American Twentieth Century. Boston: Beacon Press.

Starr, Paul. 2015. A Shocking Rise in White Death Rates in Midlife—and What It Says about American Society. The American Prospect, November 2. http://prospect.org/article/shocking-rise-white-death-rates-midlife-and-what-it-says-about-american-society. Accessed Nov. 15 2015.

Vogel, Richard 2007 Transient Servitude: The U.S. Guest Worker Program for Exploiting Mexican and Central American Workers. Monthly Review, January. Electronic document, http://monthlyreview.org/0107vogel.htm, accessed June 12, 2008.

On internal colonialism, ethnicity, and racial inequality

Appalachian Land Ownership Task Force 1983 Who Owns Appalachia? Landownership and Its Impact. Lexington: University Press of Kentucky.

Buck, Pem Davidson 2008 Rural White Stereotyping. *In* Encyclopedia of Race and Racism. 3 vols. John Hartwell Moore, ed. Pp 507-511. Detroit: Macmillan Reference USA.

Gaventa, John 1982 Power and Powerlessness: Quiescence and Rebellion in an Appalachian Valley. Urbana: University of Illinois Press.

Greenberg, Stanley 1980 Race and State in Capitalist Development: Comparative Perspectives. New Haven: Yale University Press.

Handler, Richard 1994 Is 'Identity' a Useful Cross-Cultural Concept? *In* Commemorations: The Politics of National Identity. John Gillis, ed. Pp. 27-40. Princeton: Princeton University Press.

Hill, Jonathan 1996 Introduction: Ethnogenesis in the Americas. *In* History, Power, and Identity: Ethnogenesis in the Americas, 1492-1992. Jonathan Hill, ed. Pp.1-19. Iowa City: University of Iowa Press.

On Latino/as and the conquest of the Southwest

Alamaguer, Tomás 1994 Racial Fault Lines: The Historical Origins of White Supremacy in California. Berkeley: University of California Press.

Brennan, Denise. 2014 Life Interrupted: Trafficking into Forced Labor in the United States. Durham: Duke University Press.

Brooks, James 2002 Captives and Cousins: Slavery, Kinship, and Community in the Southwest Borderlands. Chapel Hill: University of North Carolina Press.

Krisberg, Kim 2012 On the Border of Change: A portrait of the Workers' Rights Movement in El Paso. July 27. http://scienceblogs.com/thepumphandle/2012/07/27/on-the-border-of-change-a-portrait-of-the-workers-right-movement-in-el-paso.

Takaki, Ronald 1993 A Different Mirror: A History of Multicultural America. Boston: Little, Brown and Co.

Talavera, Victor, Guillermina Nunez-Mchiri, and Josiah Heyman 2010 Deportation in the US-Mexico Borderlands: Anticipation, Experience, and Memory. In The Deportation Regime: Sovereignty, Space, and the Freedom of Movement. Nicolas de Genova and Nathalie Peutz, eds. Pp. 166-195. Durham: Duke University Press.

On empires

Berdan, Francis 1982 The Aztecs of Central Mexico: An Imperial Society. Belmont CA: Wadsworth

Burbank, Jane and Frederick Cooper. 2011 Empires in World History: Power and the Politics of Difference. Princeton: Princeton University Press.

Doyle, Michael 1986 Empires. Ithaca: Cornell University Press.

On non- and postcapitalist economies

Escobar, Arturo 2008 Territories of Difference: Place, Movements, Life, Redes. Durham: Duke University Press.

Gibson-Graham, J.K. 2006 A Postcapitalist Politics. Minneapolis: University of Minnesota Press.

On Haiti

Farmer, Paul 2004 Pathologies of Power: Health, Human Rights, and the New War on the Poor. Berkeley: University of California Press.

Ulysse, Gina. 2015 Why Haiti Needs New Narratives: A Post-Quake Chronicle. Middletown CT Wesleyan Press

On climate change

See references for Chapter Four

Pope Francis and Liberation Theology

Cox, Harvey. 2013 Is Pope Francis the New Champion of Liberation Theology? The Nation. Dec 13. http://www.thenation.com/article/pope-francis-new-champion-liberation-theology/

Pope Francis. 2013 Joy of the Gospel. Apostolic Exhortation http://w2.vatican.va/content/francesco/en/apost_exhortations/documents/papa-francesco_esortazione-ap_20131124_evangelii-gaudium.html

Thistlethwaite, Susan. 2013 Is Pope Francis a Liberation Theologian? The Huffington Post. http://www.huffingtonpost.com/rev-dr-susan-brooks-thistlethwaite/pope-francis-liberation-theology_b_4373538.html.

CHAPTER 3
PRINCIPLES UNDERLYING EQUALITY: THE COMMUNAL MODE OF PRODUCTION

> *Although we now live in a world of severe inequality, it is important to know that the world has not always been this way.*

Wealth
Items which can be owned and have money value or and exchange value (see also ceremonial valuable).

The world as we know it is a place where some die of malnutrition and inadequate access to medical care, where some suffer the horrors of wars which leave them homeless, mourning their dead, and struggling to care for the living—for damaged bodies and minds—with utterly inadequate resources, while others live in unimaginable luxury on *wealth* coming from the work of people paid pennies an hour. Even in the U.S. inequality is so extreme that the average life expectancy of poor people is years shorter than that of the well-to-do, and many people have to make weekly or daily choices between food, electricity, and heat. This is a world that has been created partially through the processes of colonialism, imperialism, and neocolonialism—the processes by which powerful countries have extracted land, resources, and labor from people around the globe to create immense wealth for the few, opportunities for middle class comfort for some others, and untold misery for hundreds of millions who do the labor that supports the rest.

But wealth extraction by powerful countries is only part of the process that has created misery. Around the world for the last several thousand years there have been societies called states. These are societies that have been organized to provide an elite with the power to exploit people in their own societies. They are based ultimately in the fact that states control the use of force within their territory. Elites in a state can enforce the process of extracting resources and labor; states work hard to maintain the *stratification* that determines who is likely to be an extractor and who will have to submit to extraction. It is by building off the power created for elites within their own societies, employing the processes of expropriating value from within the state described in Chapter Two, that some societies have been able to dominate others through colonialism, imperialism, and neocolonialism. In other words, some societies developed massive inequality for themselves, while others have had it imposed from outside.

Stratification
A system which enables one group to maintain control of the means of production and use the labor of those who don't; a stratification system shifts surplus into the hands of those who control the means of production.*

• **Want more?** Try
*Mondragon: Spain's Giant
Cooperative Where Times Are
Hard But Few Go Bust*
http://
www.theguardian.com/
world/2013/mar/07/
mondragon-spains-giant-
cooperative

Surplus
Production beyond the
subsistence needs of the
producers (see also
accumulation of a surplus).

But this unequal world is not the world that has always existed. We tend to think that poverty is inevitable, that it is natural that some have more than others, even much more than others, that all through history 'it has always been this way.' It *hasn't* always been this way, and if we don't know this, it is much harder to imagine a future world where human rights are taken seriously. And if we don't know this it is much harder to recognize the value of societies today that are attempting to prioritize human needs before profits, both as some indigenous societies and as socialist societies are doing, or even as some organizations are attempting with community economies, such as the Mondragon network in Spain. This would be a world where people, regardless of who they are, have a right to the basic resources they need, where the well-being of people, and of future generations, counts for more than the profits a coal company reaps while making local water supplies poisonous. The well-being of the world would count for more than people's desire to drive cars that burn huge amounts of gasoline and contribute to the global warming and climate change that is predicted to have disastrous effects on all of us.

So before we go on to examine the anthropology of stratified societies and states, where inequality and the resulting structural violence is rampant, we need to look at other ways of organizing human societies and see how they differ from stratified societies. That is what this chapter will do. But first a word of caution. As you read about egalitarian societies, bear in mind what Chapter One had to say about the role of anthropology in the colonial project. Egalitarian societies don't produce a **surplus** that can be accumulated as wealth, don't have a system for exploiting people, and were not good at all in furthering the extraction of wealth. So colonial or imperial states needed to change them, and those changes were made to seem 'good' by claiming they represented progress.

In Chapter One I've talked about ethnocentrism, and I've talked about how propaganda about conquered and colonized people was used to make taking their land, enslaving them, or organizing them to produce cheap labor seem to the colonizers as a good thing to do. I've even stated that ideas about bands, tribes, and chiefdoms were used to make it appear that the people being conquered were inferior beings who had not evolved, and maybe never would evolve without 'help,' into 'civilized' societies. These images of 'primitive' bands, savage 'tribal' societies, and tyrannical, bloodthirsty chiefs were all ways of making states—the sociopolitical structure of countries like England, and more recently the U.S., Canada, Australia, South Africa, Germany and the other 'Western' nations—appear to be the pinnacle of human development. This was a blatantly ethnocentric view of the world.

In fact, the whole process of coming up with the categories called bands, tribes, chiefdoms, and states was a part of the colonial ideological project. Colonizing administrators needed ways to categorize the people they governed and exploited in order to discuss them, to strategize about how to control them, and to pass that information along to their governments and to new incoming administrators. As used by the administrators, and by several generations of anthropologists, these terms were seen as ways of talking about a society's 'level' of development—their place on the ladder of social, economic, and political evolution. Stratified societies were seen as the result of greater intellectual or social development, the inevitable outcome of human history and human nature. Thus forcing egalitarian societies along the road to wealth production could appear to be a kind and wise project for colonizing powers. But stratified societies don't represent progress for the majority of people in them in terms of human well-being. They are much better, however, at creating wealth for the few.

Most anthropologists no longer think that societies can be ranked in this way; they do not think that one way of life is more 'evolved' than another. Some have rejected these terms altogether, seeing them as hopelessly enmeshed in colonialism. Some even say that it is fruitless to try to categorize human societies at all. Each society must be taken on its own terms.

My problem is that although I say I am working in the tradition of decolonized anthropology, I do use the terms—band, tribe, chiefdom, state—which have often been used in ways that are racist and exploitative. Ideally, I would abandon such colonialist terms. But I am focusing this book on the ways in which societies are constructed to convey or deny rights, based on various factors of inequality. It is the socio-political structure of societies which primarily organizes conveying and denying rights; without those structures there would be neither equality or inequality, and at present we have no other words to indicate the different ways of organizing societies to do this. So I do use those words, but, as I will reiterate from time to time throughout the book, I do not use these terms in the evolutionary sense. States are definitely a different way of organizing humans from the way people organize themselves in bands or tribes, but they are in no sense a better or more evolved way of life. They do not indicate a higher level of intellectual development or more complex thought processes, just somewhat different ones.

During most of the last few thousand years, since the time of the first stratified societies, most parts of the world have had a wide range of societies in existence at the same time, ranging from very egalitarian to quite stratified. Societies around the world influenced each other, changed from within, shifted from one way of living to another, and back again, became more egalitarian, less egalitarian, bigger, smaller—the human history of change stretches back for many thousands of years. Human societies have never gone on for untold generations doing exactly the same thing—contrary to what we are often told about so-called "primitive" societies, as egalitarian societies are often called.

WHAT IT MEANS TO BE EGALITARIAN

• **Want more?** Try http://river-films.com/ BAKA_People_of_the_Rai nforest.html Or do a search for 'Baka: People of the Rainforest' for video

During almost all of human history people have lived in various kinds of egalitarian societies. Egalitarian societies are designed to convey rights to all members, rather than to reserve special rights for a privileged few, so there are no haves and have nots, as there are in stratified societies. A surplus, produced by the work of a lot of people, but handed over to just a few, is the basis of inequality. Egalitarian societies don't let this happen.

In other words, the power to exploit people by denying them access to the means of production or to benefit from their labor is a fairly recent phenomenon. But people do not 'naturally' form societies based on equality, any more than they 'naturally' form societies based on inequality. Maintaining equality or inequality both require finely tuned and carefully maintained forms of social organization. So, how do equalitarian societies do this?

Maintaining equality is based on the following underlying principles:

- *Everyone has equal rights to the means of production—the resources belong to everyone and all have a right to use them.*

- *Nobody has power over other people—so someone can't force you to do something against your will.*

- *No surplus is produced—people produce only as much as is actually needed; or, if there is a small surplus it is in some way shared by everyone.*

- *There is no system for benefiting yourself by using other people's labor or taking away their surplus—you can't increase your own prestige or wealth by getting other people to work for you or hand over to you things they made or grew.*

Prestige
Higher standing, importance, deference, and respect given to someone than is given to the rest of the people in the group.

COMMUNAL MODE OF PRODUCTION

Communal mode of production
All members of a specific group jointly control resources, to which all have rights.*

Mode of production
The social and physical organization that is associated with producing food and other necessities in a particular society.*

Kin-ordered mode of production
One form of the communal mode of production, where production work is organized by kinship.*

Band
A small kin-ordered egalitarian group that follows a foraging subsistence strategy.*

Lineage
A group of matrilineal or patrilineal relatives all descended from a single known common ancestor, who act as a unit.*

Clan
A descent group formed by all those who believe they are descended from a common ancestor.*

Subsistence strategy
The methods used by a group of people to get food and other resources, such as foraging or horticulture.*

Foraging
A subsistence strategy that is built around primary dependence on wild plants and animals.*

Nomadic
A way of life based on moving from place to place as resources become available.*

> *In the communal mode of production everyone has an equal right to food and to the other necessities of life. Everyone has that right because everyone in the entire society is a member of a group that jointly uses resources.*

Historically, most egalitarian societies have been organized around the *communal mode of production*. A *mode of production* is the system by which people organize the work of getting everything produced that is needed by their particular society—how you organize producing food, making tools, building houses, making jewelry and everything else that is needed.

In the communal mode of production everything is organized so that the food and other necessities are produced either by everyone in the group working together or by individual families within the group all using the group's resources to produce their own food and other items. The communal mode of production has usually been organized through kinship. This form of the communal mode is sometimes called the *kin-ordered mode of production*. In this version of the communal mode it is kinship that gives you membership in a particular group such as a *band*, *lineage*, or *clan*, and your right to use resources is organized through these groups.

Bands are quite small, often like a large extended family. Band social structure gives no one power over others; people who know what they are doing form the core of a band, but they can't boss others. People pay more attention to what the core members suggest, but make their own decisions. No one owns or controls the band's resources, which all have the right to use. Bands are connected to other similar bands, which are all politically and economically independent of each other, although speaking the same language, sharing the same culture, and being interconnected through marriages and kinship. There is no overall political structure joining the bands into one larger unit.

A band's *subsistence strategy*—how they make their living—is *foraging*. Bands are generally at least somewhat *nomadic* within their territory, moving before they deplete the resources in that one area, so that plants and animals can reproduce and be plentiful when they return next year. Being nomadic helps to make their way of life sustainable. Since the resources belong to all, everyone in the band shares in the wild meat, vegetables, and fruit brought in by various group members. Everyone equally has the right to build whatever shelter is appropriate using materials from the band's territory.

Fictive kinship
Building kinship rights and obligations by claiming an actually non-existent kinship relationship.*

Bilateral
Tracing descent from both parents. *

Patrilocal
Residence of a married couple with the husband's kin.

Carrying capacity
The sustainable number of people that can be supported on a particular area of land.*

Tribe
A pastoral or horticultural group organized through kinship and led by people who gain their position by ability, rather than by birth.*

Chiefdom
A society with hereditary ranking but minimal stratification involving a much larger number of people than does a band or tribe.*

Horticulture
A subsistence strategy that involves primary dependence on farming that involves cultivating plants without the use of non-human energy.*

Pastoralism
A subsistence strategy based on primary dependence on raising large herds of animals.*

Descent group
A kin group whose membership is based on a rule of descent, either matrilineal or patrilineal.*

You can be part of a band because you were born into it, or you can be married into one, or you might be kin to someone who is already a member. You might even be *fictive kin* to people in the group—many egalitarian societies have a system of making you into kin and treating you as kin even if there is no biological kinship. Bands are usually **bilateral**, meaning that you are considered to be equally related to both the mother's and father's sides of the family. As a result, it is not at all unusual for bands to include people who are related to each other through their mother's side of the family, as well as other people who are related through their father's side. However, a slight tendency toward **patrilocal** organization is typical of bands. Thus it is slightly more common for a married couple to live with the husband's group than with the wife's. As a result, related men and their families tend to live together. Since you are equally related on both sides of the family, however, and can typically forage wherever you can establish kinship, people have the possibility of joining many different bands. This flexible social organization makes it much easier for families and bands to move around, congregate, and disperse depending on the availability of resources, so that they don't exceed the **carrying capacity** of their territory. It also makes it easier to organize groups with sufficient able-bodied adult members of both sexes to keep everyone in the group fed, including dependent children, the elderly, and the sick or incapacitated, the incompetent and the unlucky.

Lineages and clans are a different, much less flexible, method for assigning group membership and organizing the communal mode of production, and for controlling the means of production. They exist in fairly large societies, sometimes called **tribes** or **chiefdoms**. These are mostly societies whose subsistence strategy is raising food, as **horticultural** farmers or as **pastoral** herders, rather than depending primarily on fishing, hunting, and gathering wild food, as do bands. These societies include a number of unrelated extended families. These families may be organized into larger kin groupings, **descent groups** called lineages. In more complex societies the lineages may be grouped into clans of related lineages, and sometimes into even larger groupings of related clans.

Corporate group
A group of people who form a single legal entity in relation to outsiders and jointly control resources.*

Each lineage, or sometimes each clan, acts as a *corporate group* within its larger society. This means that each lineage or clan has its own land or other resources as their means of production within the territory held by their society. This makes these societies quite different from bands, which don't have internal divisions making separate groups with their own resources. If you are a member of the corporate group or married to someone in it, then you have the right to use that group's resources. You don't have rights to the resources of other corporate groups. So within the area held by your corporate group, where you have your rights, you might be assigned a place to garden by the elders of your group, or you might graze your cattle along with everyone else's, or you might hunt and gather wild food on your group's territory. But nobody *owns* these resources: they are held by the corporate group as a whole. The corporate group as a whole acts as a unit in relation to other groups, and is jointly responsible for the behavior of everyone in the group.

You are a member of only one of the lineages and clans in your society, so you can't be considered to be related in the same way to your mother's as to your father's side, as you are in bilateral societies, which don't have lineages. Generally descent groups are either patrilineal or matrilineal, although some societies have different systems. Patrilineal societies have been particularly common in Europe and Asia; matrilineal societies, although not as common, are more likely to be found in the Americas and sub-Saharan Africa.

Matrilineage
A lineage based on descent through the mother—a matrilineal lineage.

Patrilineage
A lineage based on descent through the father—a patrilineal lineage.

Exogamy
A pattern, preference, or requirement to marry a person who is not a member of one's own social group or category.

In a matrilineal society you are a member of your mother's lineage, called a *matrilineage*; in a patrilineal society you are a member of your father's lineage, a *patrilineage.* In both cases you maintain ties with the lineage of the other parent, but your rights are conveyed to you from your own lineage. Most societies require lineage *exogamy*. Exogamy means you must marry outside of your own group, so lineage exogamy means you must marry someone from a different lineage. Clan exogamy may be expected as well. But you do not change lineage when you marry, even if you go to live with your spouse's lineage. This is a very important part of maintaining rights: you never loose your rights in your own lineage. You can always go home. A death or divorce may leave you miserably unhappy, but not homeless and hungry; a miserable marriage can be ended without worrying about how to feed your kids. And you continue to have rights and obligations to your own lineage during your marriage. You can call on the support of your lineage in providing both help and the valuable goods needed for weddings, funerals, and other events, and they can call on you.

Matrilocal
Residence of a married
couple with the wife's kin.

Household
A group of people who
live together in one house
and are economically
interdependent.*

Kinship
A way of defining a group
of people with whom you
have mutual rights and
obligations due to shared
ancestry; they are people
defined as being 'related'
to you by blood or
marriage.

If a society is both matrilineal and *matrilocal* (a married couple lives with or very close to the wife's family or lineage) then land and houses generally belong to the matrilineage. A group of **households**, or even an entire little village, may be based on groups of related and cooperating women living together, along with their husbands and children. In a patrilineal, patrilocal system the group would be a patrilineage formed around a group of related men, along with their wives and children.

In some matrilineal, matrilocal societies the husbands work together on the land of their wives' matrilineage. Frequently, however, husbands do at least as much work for their own matrilineage. Anthropologists argue about the control of lineage resources in such societies: is control held by the men of the matrilineage, even though they live elsewhere with their wives, or is control a joint operation of the older brother/sister pairs, or is control of lineage resources really held by the women of the matrilineage? At the very least there appears to be considerable variation, but matrilineal, matrilocal organization does mean that men and women are closer to equal than they generally are in patrilineal, patrilocal societies.

Any of these forms of organization means that you live with kin and you share resources with kin. The term kin-ordered mode of production is used to emphasize the fact that not only are your rights to the means of production organized through *kinship*, but so also are work and distribution of goods and decision-making. Who you work with, who you live with, who you make exchanges with, who you listen to, all is largely determined by how you are related to various people. You work because you have kinship obligations—much as we take an elderly mother-in-law to a doctor's appointment whether we like her or not, or take out the trash or do the laundry whether we like our spouse or not. We do this because we have kinship obligations to them, and they have reciprocal kinship obligations to us. We have different obligations to different kinds of kin. It may be your responsibility to take your mother-in-law but not your cousin to the doctor. In the kin-ordered mode of production *all* work is done through kinship—from making baskets to making arrows to clearing land for farming to gathering berries to making music. Just what your obligations are, and to what relatives you owe them, vary enormously from one kin-ordered society to another.

THE ECONOMIC SYSTEM: WHO WORKS, WHO GETS

In egalitarian societies all adults work—and all get. But they often aren't working terribly hard, since they don't have to produce lots more than they need, either to sell in order to have money to pay for food and shelter, or to provide huge amounts of surplus in order to support a non-producing elite. And in many egalitarian societies those who work harder don't get more to keep for themselves—although they may get more prestige.

Sexual division of labor
The assignment of a society's tasks according to sex. In some societies the division between the work that men do and the work that women do is very clear. In others there is considerable overlap.

Economic system
A society's organization for the production and distribution of goods and services.

Production
Taking raw materials from nature and making them into goods that are useful to humans (see also mode of production and means of production).

Distribution
The assignment of goods and services to members of a society.

Exchange
The process of distributing goods and services by transferring them from one individual to another.

Reciprocity
The exchange of gifts and/ or services between individuals, in which the goods and services given and received are expected to be approximately equal.

Generalized reciprocity
The exchange of gifts or services between people who are not keeping track of the exact amounts given or received.*

Egalitarian foragers and horticulturalists generally work only three to five hours a day to provide their food, and maybe a couple more hours processing food or making things they need. Most band societies have a fairly flexible *sexual division of labor*, and very little gender inequality. In farming societies the sexual division of labor is less flexible, and there is a tendency toward gender inequality, a subject we will address more thoroughly in Chapter Four. Since food is shared, and men and women have fairly equal work loads, and they have no need to collect a surplus, typically they can work far less than we do. A 30-40 hour work week takes care of everything; for us, if we are lucky, we have a 40 hour week followed by a second shift at home that is so long most of us rarely get enough time to sleep.

> *Our stress levels and lack of sleep would look rather peculiar from the perspective of egalitarian people.*

The organization of the *economic system* is thus clearly an important part of how egalitarian societies manage to stay that way. An economic system includes both *production* and *distribution.* This, of course, connects to the communal mode of production, which we have already discussed. But we haven't talked much about the various ways goods get distributed in egalitarian societies.

> *All societies have a system of distribution. These are the ways in which a society determines who will get what goods and services. In egalitarian societies people have approximately equal amounts of goods and services. The more unequal the society, the greater the difference between the 'haves' and 'have-nots.'*

People in bands and some horticultural societies distribute food and other goods through a system of *exchange* called *reciprocity.* Reciprocity exists in all societies, but is usually the major means of exchange in bands. The basic idea of *generalized reciprocity* is that individuals give gifts to each other without trying to measure their value or specifying when a return gift will be made. However, the recipient is obligated to make a return gift eventually. This system acts as a kind of social security system, giving you the right to receive later. The people involved are obligated to each other by kinship or friendship and are generally members of the same small group. In the United States close friends or kin often practice generalized reciprocity. I help you out today and can trust that when I need help you will be there. These "gifts" can range anywhere from a cup of sugar to help with a funeral to lending you the use of a car for months at a time. In reality, the exchanges may be quite lop-sided, but that fact is not acknowledged in generalized reciprocity.

People in bands use generalized reciprocity in sharing food routinely among all members of the group, so no family is without food, regardless of who actually gathered or hunted it. Since luck in foraging is unpredictable, and because people get sick or hurt or heavily pregnant and can't always forage for themselves, all members count on sharing in a system of generalized reciprocity. Since nobody *owns* the means of production, the animals and plants growing in an area don't belong to anyone. Everyone equally has a right to eat them. So a hunter doesn't own the meat he brings in. Nor does he have the right to use it exclusively for feeding his own nuclear family. He usually does have the right to give the meat away, and gets a certain amount of prestige for doing so. Plant and vegetable food is also shared, although it usually is not given away with as much display as meat is. You give today, tomorrow you will receive gifts and you will be eating food brought in by someone else. If you didn't go out hunting or gathering today, or had bad luck, you won't go hungry; like everyone else, you will be eating from the food brought in by everyone. Even those too old for hard physical work contribute to the well-being of the band, through child-care, story-telling, and shared knowledge.

This system means that you receive because you are human, because you are kin, because you are a member of the band. You receive for the same reason that in our society (and all other societies) everyone in a family gets supper (ideally, at least) even if some in the family did more work than others. And you work for the same reason; you can see that the work you do in making supper directly matters to the well-being of you and everyone you live with. Like humans everywhere, some in bands do more, or are more skilled, than others, and some don't hunt or gather as much as others. They eat anyway, but the rest of the band may not let them get away with being lazy for too long.

> In egalitarian societies people can push you around through various forms of **social control**, such as teasing, shaming you, or **shunning** you, to get you to act as you should, even though no one has the power to force you to do anything.

There is another form of reciprocity, called **balanced reciprocity.** When egalitarian foragers engage in balanced reciprocity, it is usually between people who aren't as close to each other. The people involved are often members of different groups, and the exchange can be part of forming and maintaining political alliances. In balanced reciprocity the exchanges can't get lop-sided: the gift and return gift should "balance" each other. The return gift is not made immediately; instead it is often made months or even years later.

Ownership
The right to use and benefit from a particular item or resource and to prevent other people from using or benefiting from it without your permission.*

Social control
Those processes, both formal and informal, in a society which lead most people most of the time to act according to the norms of their culture or subculture.

Shun
An informal type of social control, in which members of a group refuse to acknowledge the existence of an individual who has seriously offended the group's sense of appropriate behavior.

Balanced reciprocity
The exchange of gifts or services between individuals who are keeping track of how much is given or when a return gift is to be made.

In many small-scale farming societies, (often called tribes) as opposed to foraging bands, distribution is handled differently. Generalized reciprocity goes on among close family and friends, but in addition there is *egalitarian redistribution.* This is a system of gaining status by collecting and then giving away surplus—the small surplus that horticultural extensive farming can produce.

Egalitarian redistribution
A form of redistribution in which the person at the center of the redistribution collects gifts of surplus produced by other people but then gives away everything received and does not keep anything for personal use.*

• **Want more?** Try searching for the video *The Kawelka: Ongka's Big Moka*

Egalitarian redistribution is generally associated with societies that produce only a small surplus. In other words, either the environment or technology won't allow the production of a large surplus, or people have the political power to refuse to produce one. Consequently no one has access to the large surplus that could translate into enormous power if it were accumulated under the control of one person.

In egalitarian redistribution, when you are given something you are placed under an obligation to eventually give back the equivalent. But if you want to gain prestige, you actually need to give back more than you were given, thereby creating an obligation for the original gift-giver to give you an even bigger gift. It takes years of careful manipulation of such exchanges to get yourself to the point where so much is owed you that you can call in all your debts at once and then redistribute it all back out in an impressive feast and give-away. People give each other gifts in egalitarian redistribution on those occasions that call for it, much as we give gifts at weddings and showers. Since many exchanges are based on kinship obligations—gifts are given at weddings, births, deaths of relatives, and a groom must give *bridewealth* to the family of the bride—success in exchanging is built first on a solid basis of kinship. In some patrilineal societies, it is bridewealth that establishes that the husband and his lineage have rights to the wife's children.

Bridewealth
Objects important for their prestige value that are given by the husband's group to the bride's group in order to validate a marriage.

This process means that all men, and sometimes all women—usually in matrilineal societies—are to some extent engaged in collecting surplus, usually by giving gifts to kin to create a debt that can be collected later. To organize a big gift they may talk their relatives into helping to uphold the honor of the family or lineage by contributing their surplus to the feast. They also collect from their debtors. When all is assembled, they give away what they have received. Some is used for the feast, and some is given as a return gift to people you owe from previous exchanges.

Big Man
A leader in some tribal societies who has gained his position through competition with other men, primarily through giving away massive quantities of goods by becoming a center person in egalitarian redistribution.*

Ceremonial valuable (or valuable)
Sometimes called wealth item. Non-money items used in ceremonial exchanges.*

Redistribution
A method of exchanging goods in which the surplus produced by many people is given to a central person or institution who then redistributes it to group members and other people.*

In some societies this is done with great ostentation, trying to impress others with your display of generosity and your ability to give more than others—much as our politicians may make a great display of their ability to collect money allocated by Congress for projects in their own districts, or corporate donors try to impress the public with gifts to local charities or other projects. In other tribal societies this gift-giving is far less competitive, and is more like being extremely generous. Being that generous brings prestige. Such prestigious people are called *Big Men* or referred to as important women.

If you look back at the list of conditions that underlie equality (page 74), you will see that egalitarian redistribution, despite its name, doesn't maintain those conditions quite as well as reciprocity does. It pushes people to work harder to produce a surplus, and puts the surplus, very briefly, into the hands of someone who then gives it all away. This surplus can be food, or it can be *ceremonial valuables*—objects that are defined as important but are generally useless for practical purposes, although they carry great symbolic value and serve as a status marker, like a diamond ring or a Picasso for us.

> *Despite the fact that egalitarian redistribution creates prestige for some and not for others, it is called egalitarian because of a number of factors that make it quite different from the kind of redistribution in chiefdoms or in stratified societies.*

First of all, with egalitarian redistribution, everyone has access to the means of production, and generalized reciprocity is practiced between groups of close relatives. Nobody is dependent for their necessities on giving and receiving the gifts that are involved in egalitarian redistribution. In fact, most of the gifts are ceremonial valuables, not things you need to live on. Secondly, no one of the right sex is denied the right to participate in the competition for status, and all have rights to the resources needed for competition. Thirdly, although Big Men do get the surplus produced by other people, in the form of gifts, they can't keep it. They do the same work and live the same way as other people. When gifts are given back out, nobody's status means they get a better gift than others; who gets what is determined by kinship and by what is owed back to you in return for previous gifts. And finally, although successful manipulation of the system gives some people great prestige, it gives no one power. A Big Man can't order; he can only persuade. His status is built on his personal abilities, not on his inheritance or birthright. Attaining this status requires remarkable 'people skills,' great talent as a speaker, an incredible memory for people's genealogies and for many years' worth of economic transactions, skill as a war leader and negotiator, and a deep fund of wisdom and patience—and on top of all that, willingness to work harder than strictly necessary, and in the more competitive tribal societies, a driving ambition to outshine others.

Since reciprocity and egalitarian redistribution both mean you give back as well as receive, it can't be the major means of exchange for non-egalitarian societies where people are trying to get control of the surplus that other people produced—you would just have to give it all away again. Even in stratified societies, what reciprocity does exist is carried on between equals or within families.

THE POLITICAL SYSTEM: DECISION-MAKING AND RIGHTS

The word 'band' actually refers to the ***political system*** of egalitarian foragers, just as the word 'state' refers to our own political system. Both are political systems because they organize the distribution of power, and therefore ultimately the access to resources, among the people in the society. In a band there is no power to distribute, and the political system is organized to keep it that way. The system is based on kinship, as is band membership, which gives you rights in the band's resources. Leadership roles are heavily influenced by your position within the ***family*** and kinship structure. The older, core members of the group tend to have more influence than other people, and informal leadership roles are spread out among a number of people, with no one person being an authority on all matters, helping to avoid concentrating prestige, and perhaps ***power***, in one formal leader. ***Leaders*** lead by force of personality, persuasion, skilful ridicule, and shaming—but only if the rest of the group agrees. Since ownership is not an issue, there is no need for a higher authority to defend people's rights to keep good things to themselves. Nobody can say, as they can in our society, "This land, or money, or food is mine, and I don't care how hungry you are, you can't use it—and if you try we will put you in jail." Neither leaders nor anyone else has power or control over the group's resources. Nobody controls production and distribution.

Part of protecting the egalitarian lifestyle is the use of leveling devices such as gossip and teasing directed at people who get swelled heads or act like they think that being good at something makes them better than other people.

People do get prestige from being good at something, but not if they act like they know it. This is extremely important because in fact some people are better hunters or gatherers than others. One person may actually bring in most of the meat a band eats. Suppose that person were to say, "Look, without me you would all starve, so I am more important than you are, and I expect you all to be grateful to me for taking care of you. If you don't obey me, I will stop feeding you. And to show your gratitude you must all give me your best

---

Political system
A society's organization of the distribution of public power, and ultimately of access to resources.

Family
An intimate kin-based group, consisting, usually, of at least a woman and her children; forms the minimal social unit that cooperates economically and is responsible for the rearing of children.

Power
The ability to get other people to do as you want, even in the absence of their consent.

Leader
In egalitarian societies, refers to a person whose opinions and actions have significant influence on the behavior of the group and on decision making within the group, but who has no power or authority to direct people's behavior.

Leveling device
A means of minimizing differences in wealth, power, and prestige between people.*

• **Want more?** Try *Eating Christmas in the Kalahari* http://www.naturalhistorymag.com/htmlsite/editors_pick/1969_12_pick.html

baskets and jewelry and arrows." If this were to happen, it wouldn't be long before such people would claim that the means of production really belongs to them, and other people have to give tribute or pay rent to use it. So people who get swelled heads are given a very hard time; they are "leveled" and learn the hard way to downplay their skills and accomplishments—they are teased, ridiculed, ignored, laughed at, and generally made to feel miserable until they quit acting like they are important. An individual who can stand being ridiculed and ignored can't be forced to do anything. But the individual who can stand up long to this treatment is rare indeed!

In tribal farming societies the political system works somewhat differently, but it still prevents anyone from gaining power or control of the means of production. However, it does allow individuals to have enormous prestige and influence in a way that bands avoid. Egalitarian redistribution is both a political and an economic system. Each small scale farming society usually has several Big Men or important women. These are not formal titles or positions; you are not chosen, elected, or appointed. It is a term of respect and acknowledgement of a person's skill and generosity. It is a little like a town's "business leaders." They may own half the town and have an enormous effect on political and economic decisions, but it is not a formal position like the one held by the mayor of the town. Unlike the business leader, however, the Big Man cannot force anyone to do anything, and he is not wealthier than other people. A Big Man's prestige can evaporate if he becomes too demanding and people get angry and begin making their exchanges with other Big Men. Or if your exchanges don't work out, you can slide back down. Neither Big Man status nor your possessions nor your debts and obligations can be passed on to your heirs. It is a lot easier to get rid of the influence of an unwanted Big Man than that of an unwanted businessman.

Egalitarian societies are possible only if they are organized so that accumulating more of something does you no good.

Since egalitarian foragers don't produce a surplus (the economic system), there is no power available for leaders (the political system) through control of the economic system. If extra dead giraffes only rot because you can't eat that much, and can't be turned into money or power, then there is little incentive to try to control the labor of other people. You have no reason to want to boss them around and get them to kill extra giraffes for you. Nor do you have any reason to take away the giraffes that other people kill on their own. If the only way you can get prestige is by killing that giraffe yourself, dividing it up, and giving it away, you can't gain real power over other people, and you can't benefit from taking away what they produce. Egalitarian redistribution accomplishes a similar situation: accumulating and keeping for yourself does you no good. The only time having things does you any good is when you give them away.

THE ROLE OF RELIGION

Religion
The cultural assumption that there are supernatural forces or beings outside of human life and the physical world.*

In all societies, whether egalitarian or not, *religion* deals with the same set of issues. Religion everywhere is concerned with issues that relate to the subsistence strategy of the society (for instance rituals for rain in a farming society or praying for a job in ours); it deals with issues that are critically important but which the society can't control, giving a sense of hope or security despite the lack of actual control (for instance illness, good luck in hunting, survival during war); it acts as a tool of social control (giving religious backing to a society's norms, such as the belief that religion requires a certain form of marriage), it promotes social solidarity (often through group rituals that promote a sense of belonging and through shared beliefs); and religion reflects and justifies the distribution of power in a society. It is with this last that we are concerned here, since religion plays a critical role in making equality or inequality seem reasonable.

> *Religion all over the world justifies the distribution of power in a society. It makes the degree of equality or inequality seem right and natural.*

Since in egalitarian societies nobody has power over others, their religion reflects equality, reinforcing the idea that everyone has the same rights. For instance, everyone participates in rituals. Nobody is the "audience," everyone has an active part to play.

Shaman
Part-time religious practitioner who is believed to have the power to contact supernatural forces directly, on behalf of individuals or groups.*

There is no situation in which one person such as a priest is seen as having the authority to perform a ritual that others have no right—or the knowledge—to perform. Instead, *shamans* are common in egalitarian societies. They are part-time religious practitioners, seen as being particularly gifted in getting in touch with the supernatural. They are especially likely to act as religious healers, bringing religion and medical knowledge together to bear on an illness.

Self-fulfilling prophesy
A prediction that comes true because people believe the prediction and act in ways that make the prediction come true.*

Esoteric knowledge
Information or activities which are known about by only a few people, who are expected to keep the knowledge secret from all except those who have the right to know it.

Shamans, as part-time practitioners in egalitarian and fairly egalitarian societies, may be given a lot of respect, but they make their living in the same way other people do. They don't live off payments for their services. Their healing is frequently based on a thorough knowledge of herbal medicine (many of our pharmaceutical drugs were first used by shamans) and of skills such as bone-setting. In addition their use of religious trances and rituals can be extremely effective in convincing the patient and everyone else that healing is occurring, causing the *self-fulfilling prophesy* to actually help the patient get well. In egalitarian societies everybody learns at least something about shamanistic practices, although some may be better at it than others. This is not *esoteric knowledge*, kept secret from most people, as it is in stratified societies.

In egalitarian tribal farming societies no one has power, but there may be intense competition for status. Individuals are trying to outdo each other, and that competition is reflected in religious beliefs and practices. In their effort to outdo each other individuals may try to gain access to religious sources of power, such as spirits or the ancestors. This may be done through inducing an individual (rather than a group) *altered state of consciousness*, perhaps by fasting, meditation, inflicting pain, or use of narcotics.

The secret use of *magic* can also reflect competition for status. Magic gives a very specific kind of control by providing ways to coerce *supernatural* beings or forces into doing something you can't do for yourself. Using magic depends on knowing the laws that are believed to govern the behavior of the supernatural. So an individual may use magic to help a garden grow well. But even more important is that people *believe* an individual can use magic to destroy someone else's garden, or to make someone get sick or die, or in pastoral societies cause their cows to go dry or their sheep to have lots of dead lambs. Bad luck is often blamed on the jealousy of someone else, who used magic to cause your troubles. Such beliefs are self-reinforcing: when a cow dies that is seen as proof that somebody used magic, much as we believe that if someone gets measles that proves that they were in contact with someone who gave them measles—except we rarely believe the measles were passed along on purpose.

EGALITARIAN SOCIETIES AND THE MOTIVATION TO WORK

Americans, brought up to believe in individual hard work and individual responsibility, often have two contradictory reactions to the sharing and group responsibility of egalitarian foraging societies. One is, "Why in the world would anybody work at all if somebody else is going to take care of them anyway? They must be supporting a lot of lazy people. No wonder they're backward." The other common reaction is the romantic one of, "They're such wonderful people, everyone takes care of everyone else, it just shows you what is wrong with America today—nobody cares about anybody but themselves these days." In reference to tribal societies, where everyone by right has access to the resources they need, Americans tend to find it puzzling why anyone would want to work at gaining prestige if you don't get wealth or power out of all the work you put into the process of egalitarian redistribution.

The cure for these reactions is to realize that people in egalitarian societies are reacting to the pressures of their way of life and the social relationships it requires. Likewise, we are reacting to the pressures of life in a stratified, industrialized, capitalist society and the relationships that way of life requires. Neither way of life is 'natural;' both are socially constructed and take a great deal of work to maintain.

Norm
A formal or informal standard or guideline for appropriate behavior; specific norms vary from culture to culture.

Employing various types of social control, such as shunning and leveling devices, is an important part of that work. Among egalitarian people social control is exercised informally, but nevertheless it is very real and very powerful. In no society do people just do as they please—they are pushed and prodded into following the *norms* of their culture, experience unpleasant consequences in some way if they don't, and are rewarded with at least acceptance if they do. In bands, as is true in any society, some people are nice and some are not. The fact that they share and take group responsibility for children and the elderly isn't related to whether or not they are nice people. It has to do instead with the structure of their society: they are organized in such a way that they *have* to share, whether they want to or not, just as we are organized in such a way that it is very unlikely that we will share everything we have. This is not because we are particularly selfish; it is because if we give away everything we are very likely to go hungry. People in bands are likely to go hungry if they *don't* share. Likewise corporate groups provide resources for all their members and give gifts through egalitarian redistribution whether they are nice people or not.

And finally, bear in mind that in egalitarian societies it is perfectly obvious why various tasks need to be done, and it is perfectly obvious that you and everyone you care about will benefit from having those tasks done. Your work directly benefits you. And you are working with your friends, at least part of the time on fairly enjoyable or companionable tasks, and you are not working yourself to the bone. You can take a "vacation day" whenever you feel the need. How egalitarian people feel about work is probably quite different from how you may feel about work in our own society. Your work may well work you to the bone but leave you with barely enough to squeak by, while enriching someone else; your work in itself more directly benefits the owner of the means of production than it does you. And it may be work that is incredibly boring, day after day without change, and you may be exhausted. Your incentives to be lazy are far greater than those of egalitarian people.

RECAP: WHAT IT MEANS TO BE EGALITARIAN

Despite all the variation, the bottom line is that everyone in an egalitarian society has a right to the resources they need. The kin-ordered mode of production is one system for making sure this happens. Since everyone is part of a group that jointly has rights to resources, there are no classes in egalitarian societies: there is no such thing as a class that controls the resources and a class that has no resources and has to provide labor to those who do.

• **Want more?** Try
Review of *The Spriit Level:
Why Equality is Better for
Everyone* http://
www.theguardian.com/
books/2009/mar/13/the-
spirit-level

• **Want more?** Try
*What Americans Keep
Ignoring about Finland's
School Success* http://
www.theatlantic.com/
national/print/2011/
12/what-americans-
keep-ignoring-about-
finlands-school-
success/250564/

Institutionalized
Built into the social
organization and
institutions of a society.

If our own society were egalitarian, then if some mothers had the resources to let them stay home to take care of little kids, so would all mothers. If some fathers could spend lots of time with their kids, so could all fathers. Nor would you have some kids dying from asthma while others get the medication they need.

Generally people in egalitarian societies have been better fed, have had more leisure, have seen fewer of their children die, and have had more control over their own lives than have many people in stratified societies. This is less true, of course, for the elites and those closely connected to them in stratified societies—their lives are generally more secure. However, recent studies have compared the well-being of rich, middle and poor people in terms of health and many other factors in wealthy stratified societies. What they find is that everyone, even the middle and upper income people, are better off in the countries that are more egalitarian, where there is less of an income gap between those who are at the top and those who are at the bottom. For instance, rich people as well as poor people live longer in the more egalitarian Sweden or Japan as compared to the U.S. or England. And the Finnish educational system has no private schools, all children go to public schools that are equally funded, and the emphasis is on all children, rich or poor, having the same educational experience, rather than on competition. This egalitarian system produces far better educated children, including children of well-to-do parents, than does the U.S. with its extreme educational system inequality.

People in egalitarian societies all participate in the music, dancing, story-telling and other art forms of their societies. Their society doesn't create the highly *institutionalized* accoutrements of a stratified society—the arts, magnificent architecture, literature, etc. However, most people in stratified societies don't have access to those accoutrements either. When, for instance, was the last time you went to the opera, or ate in the leisured elegance of a restaurant where breakfast costs thirty dollars a plate and your orange juice appears in a goblet wrapped in a white linen napkin? How a world works where only some get those white linen napkins is the subject of the next chapter.

REFERENCES/SUGGESTED READINGS

On egalitarian Societies

Duffy, Kevin 1995 Children of the Forest: Africa's Mbuti Pygmies. Prospect Heights, IL: Waveland Press.

Flannery, Kurt and Joyce Marcus. 2014 The Creation of Inequality: How Our Prehistoric Ancestors Set the Stage for Monarchy, Slavery, and Empire. Cambridge: Harvard University Press.

Josephy, Alvin 1993 America in 1492: The World of the Indian Peoples before the Arrival of Columbus. New York: Vintage Press.

Keesing, Roger, ed. 1983 Elota's Story: The Life and Times of a Solomon Islands Big Man. New York: Holt, Rinehart, and Winston.

Kehoe, Alice 2002 America Before the European Invasions. London: Longman/Pearson Education.

Lee, Richard 2002 The Dobe Ju/'hoansi, 3rd ed. Belmont CA: Wadsworth.

Nairn, Charlie and Andrew Strathern 1976 The Kawelka: Ongka's Big Moka. 57 min. London: Granada Television International.

Partanen, Anu 2011 What Americans Keep Ignoring About Finland's School Success. The Atlantic. December. http://www.theatlantic.com/national/print/2011/12/what-americans-keep-ignoring-about-finlands-school-success/250564/

Turnbull, Colin 1987 [1961] The Forest People. New York: Touchstone.

Wilkinson, Richard and Kate Pickett 2009 The Spirit Level: Why Greater Equality Makes Societies Stronger. New York: Bloomsbury Press.

Wolf, Eric. 1982. Europe and the People Without History. Berkeley: University of California Press.

CHAPTER 4
PRINCIPLES UNDERLYING INEQUALITY: THE TRIBUTARY AND THE CAPITALIST MODE OF PRODUCTION

In this chapter we turn to societies that are stratified rather than egalitarian. They are organized to put the surplus produced by lots of people into the hands of just a few people. In other words, they are built around exploitation. But some of these societies have been far more exploitative than others, so we will be looking at a range, from chiefdoms to kingdom to modern states. Some of this will look very familiar to you; some will probably seem very strange, but all have exploitation as their bottom line.

Just as there are some basic principles underlying equality (see page 74), there are some very basic characteristics of any society that displays inequality.

All of the following underlying conditions must be met if a society is going to display true inequality:

- *The environmental and technological conditions permit a society to produce a surplus—more than the people in it need to provide for themselves.*

- *Social conditions push people to do surplus labor and work harder and produce a surplus—more than they need.*

- *Social structures and values allow the surplus produced by many people to accumulate in the hands of just a few people.*

Surplus labor
Work beyond what is needed to provide for yourself and family and therefore can be allocated to other uses, including non-necessities for yourself or to provide profit or other benefits for someone who has a claim on your labor, such as an employer or landlord or lord.

Stratified societies are set up so that a few people can accumulate a large surplus using other people's *surplus labor* and keep much of it for themselves, and all kinds of inequality, including gender inequality, are likely to be much more severe. However, the degree of inequality varies enormously. In truly stratified societies these conditions structure people into separate classes, with only a few owning the means of production, making a very efficient system for producing wealth and power for the elite. This is what makes stratified societies like ours so different from egalitarian societies.

Stratification conveys to a few people the right to take away the value produced by other people and use that value to enhance their own wealth, power, and prestige. They enforce this right by keeping control or ownership of the society's resources, including the means of production. This control allows them to deny rights to everyone else, so that the majority has little choice but to allow their work—their surplus labor— to benefit the elite. This denial of rights is the basic principle underlying stratification. Stratified societies create birthright, rank, race and/or class to add to gender as factors on which inequality and the denial of rights is based.

Severe stratification systems, ones that cause a large portion of the population to struggle for even bare necessities, are usually found in states. This is because it takes the exercise of power and the use of force to deny so many people the rights to the basic resources they need, while at the same time allowing a few to have control of the resources all need. Only states provide the kind of social structure that makes this possible and that gets most people most of the time to accept the use of force as natural and normal—and in fact often not even recognize that force is being used. A state has a monopoly on the legitimate use of force within its boundaries. That force is used to control the have-nots and to protect the right of the haves to keep control of the resources of a society.

SUMMARIZING EQUALITY AND INEQUALITY IN DIFFERENT TYPES OF SOCIETIES

There are many degrees of inequality, and there are many forms of inequality. So a society may have aspects of both equality and inequality. This is not an 'either/or' situation. Instead there is a continuum between equality and inequality, and societies range all along this continuum. A diagram of the differences between the various ways of organizing human societies may help you in making sense of all this—but bear in mind that this is vastly oversimplified; each society must be understood in its own right. Diagram 1 is meant to help you do this. As you read your ethnographies and watch films, try to place the societies being described on this diagram.

TYPES OF RANKED SOCIETIES: CHIEFDOMS AND KINGDOMS

Rank
A ranked society is one in which certain formal, prestigious offices belong to certain lineages, and must be held by someone who is a member of that lineage.*

Rank is one of the systems for organizing stratification, and is generally associated with the tributary mode of production.

Ranked societies are designed to deny rights of position and prestige to all but a few, based on birthright. These few control, but do not necessarily own, the means of production. They have the authority to exercise this control because they hold certain formal, prestigious titles that give them positions such as chief. They have the right to these positions because they were born into a high-ranking family or kinship group that passes a particular title on from one generation to the next. In ranked societies a privileged category of people is set above the rest of the society from birth. How much this matters for your daily life depends on whether you are in a chiefdom, a complex chiefdom, or a kingdom.

Diagram 1: Differences in types of human social organization

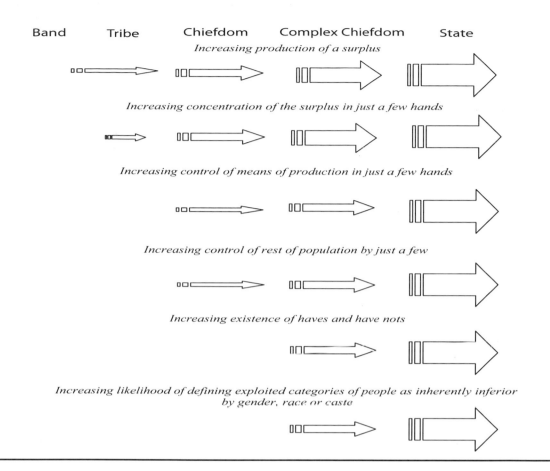

Band Tribe Chiefdom Complex Chiefdom State

Increasing production of a surplus

Increasing concentration of the surplus in just a few hands

Increasing control of means of production in just a few hands

Increasing control of rest of population by just a few

Increasing existence of haves and have nots

Increasing likelihood of defining exploited categories of people as inherently inferior by gender, race or caste

Ranked societies are not egalitarian. Instead, people are divided into two, and sometimes three, basic categories. One group consists of privileged lineages or of privileged families within lineages. These people are the aristocrats. By virtue of birth they are eligible for high status, formal positions giving them some degree of authority over other people. This is what it means to be a ranked society, much as England and other kingdoms once were. England, in fact, still has the remnants of that system. Queen Elizabeth is queen because she was born into the right family (and there were no sons). She has that formal position purely because of her birth, not because of any particular ability on her part. Her rank is above that of dukes and earls, who also got their positions because of birth into a family which had that title to pass on from one generation to the next. Everyone else is a commoner.

In a chiefdom, unless you are in the right family within a lineage you won't be given a particular aristocratic title or fancy ceremonial valuables, you won't marry people of high rank, and you probably won't have much say-so in political, economic, and social decisions. In return for acknowledging the authority and superiority of the aristocrats, and perhaps giving them ceremonial valuables as gifts or tribute, commoners have the right to use the means of production held by their lineage. But you don't need ceremonial valuables or titles to live well, in the same way that you don't need a Mercedes; you just need a dependable car of some kind.

The degree of inequality varies tremendously among ranked societies. Some are not too different from tribes. If a Big Man were able to pass his position on to his children, what you would have would be much like a chief in a fairly egalitarian chiefdom. In the more stratified chiefdoms, which usually were larger, there were a number of different subunits within their territory, each headed by a lower ranking sub-chief, whose territory may in turn be divided into village segments headed by village chiefs coming from even lower ranking, but still aristocratic, lineages. In addition, there are commoner lineages with no aristocrats at all in some very complex chiefdoms. In these more **complex chiefdoms** the privileged group can translate its prestige into real wealth, has control of the land held by all the lineages in the chiefdom, and has the authority to command other people to hand over their surplus in order to maintain their lineage's hereditary right to the means of production, and sometimes can use force to back up their position. This is the tributary mode of production which we talk about in a few pages.

This process of giving tribute is part of what some anthropologists call "**stratified redistribution**" to distinguish it from the gift-giving of egalitarian redistribution. People at the center of stratified redistribution in ranked societies do redistribute some of what they receive by providing for feasts at various ceremonies or to validate receiving a title. They support public works, and a large amount goes to other powerful members of the chief's or lord's own lineage and to the heads of other related lineages. This process increases the prestige of the titled people and helps to ensure the loyalty of other lineages. However, they do not give away all that they receive, and they and their lineage are better off than other people, since they are able to benefit from the labor of other people. They are able to use the redistribution system to create wealth for themselves, in addition to the prestige that egalitarian redistributors gain. In addition, they gain far more power than can egalitarian redistributors because the person in the political role of chief or lord is also the central person in redistribution.

• **Want more?**
For Kwakuitl chiefdom try exploring http://www.firstnations.eu/fisheries/kwakwakawakw-kwakiutl.htm

Complex chiefdom
A ranked society that grants far more wealth, power, and prestige to high-ranking people than do chiefdoms; divided into many administrative subunits.*

Stratified redistribution
A form of redistribution practiced in ranked and stratified societies in which people at the center of redistribution do not give away all that they receive, and they and their lineage are better off than other people, since they are able to benefit from the labor of other people.*

Stratified redistribution is a system that allows high-ranking people to collect surplus from commoners and use it to build their own political and economic strength. The people doing the work may get very little in return.

In chiefdoms and kingdoms the only people who participate in redistributing are members of the aristocratic category. Commoners do go to feasts and eat very well. But the gifts that are given out depend on your rank, with higher-ranking people getting gifts of ceremonial valuables that mark status and commoners receiving food and perhaps minor gifts.

In complex chiefdoms the *paramount chief* is probably not closely related to you, and may live in luxury in a far off town. Even your sub-chief may be at the head of a distant, aristocratic lineage, perhaps the head of your clan. This reduces their kinship obligations toward you; it also reduces your influence over who in the aristocratic lineage is actually given the right to a title. The demands for gifts made by chiefs in complex chiefdoms are likely to require far more work on your part; you are really paying tribute. The chiefs, in other words, are benefiting from the surplus labor you put into making those gifts.

In many chiefdoms there is a third class, below the aristocrats and the commoners, usually composed of war captives who have been enslaved, and their children. Or the third class may consist of people, particularly in societies dependent on horses or on herding, who, through bad luck or other reasons, have too few animals to support themselves adequately. Sometimes the resources held by some of the lineages are inadequate, leaving them dependent on the generosity of chiefs and obligated to provide labor or support to the chief. This third class is generally more evident in more stratified chiefdoms.

Most chiefdoms actually have many egalitarian aspects, despite the fact that some people are born into prestigious lineages where they may inherit titles, and despite the fact that handing over ceremonial valuables is a bit like paying tribute. Even in the more stratified chiefdoms there are limits on the power of chiefs and other aristocrats. Although theoretically the chief may even have the right to deny people access to their hereditary land or resources unless they provide tribute and loyalty, in reality most don't have enough power to get away with denying lineages their right to their resources. The chief's position is also limited by the fact that he is dependent on kinship for his position. Generally there are several people who are considered eligible to become chief, often the sons, brothers, and nephews of the previous chief. Lineage elders choose which of the eligible people should get the title. If a chief demands too much or makes poor decisions, people can withdraw their support and leave the chief with no way to exercise authority. In most chiefdoms the decisions made by even a paramount chief have to meet the approval of a council of elders or of other aristocrats.

The aristocrats' ability to accumulate wealth is also limited, since stratified redistribution requires that they make some return to commoners. They give feasts, but in addition, they are held responsible for the well-being of ordinary people. They are expected to communicate with the gods, ancestors, or spirits to keep them favorably disposed and ensure good crops and success in war. They are often expected to maintain large stores of food to be given out to commoners if there are food shortages. If they fail at these tasks, or if they demand more tribute than people think is

Paramount chief
The highest ranking chief in a hierarchy of chiefs of sub-units within a complex chiefdom.

• **Want more?**
Try exploring the website for the Powhatan Museum of Indigenous Arts and Culture http:// www.powhatanmuseum.c om/ Powhatan_Tribes.html

reasonable, or if they try to deny hereditary land rights, people are likely to revolt, probably by giving their support to an aspiring member of the chief's lineage or by claiming that the right to the office of chief actually belongs to another lineage. In some chiefdoms a titled person can actually be deposed—rather like impeaching a president.

> *Chiefdoms and complex chiefdoms, unlike kingdoms, prevent the privileged people from taking absolute control of the means of production. This means most people are going to be able to feed themselves and provide decently for their families and kin.*

Kingdom
A state that employs the tributary mode of production, is ranked, is stratified, giving absolute control of the means of production to an elite, gives the legal right to use force to the king, and acknowledges no kinship between elite lineages and ordinary people.

Tributary mode of production
An economic/political/social system in which low-ranking people activate their hereditary right to use the means of production by giving tribute in wealth, surplus, or labor to an individual of higher rank who has hereditary authority over the land or other resources that low ranking people use.*

Capitalism (capitalist mode of production)
An economic/social/political system in which the means of production and distribution are privately owned by individuals (or by corporations legally acting as individuals) and operated for personal profit; land and labor are commodities that can be bought and sold.

Theoretically there are two basic differences between complex chiefdoms and **kingdoms**. One is that in a kingdom the highest title carries with it absolute power. A king, unlike a paramount chief of a complex chiefdom, does not need the consent of other titled members of the aristocracy in order to exercise power. Second, the aristocracy that controls the means of production in a kingdom is totally unrelated to the people who work on their land. Their lineages are separate from commoners. The commoners who work the land are often in some form of bondage like that of feudal serfs, tied to an estate held by an aristocrat who may have nearly total power over them. This system allows for massive surpluses to accumulate in the hands of the elite. Kingdoms do use the tributary mode of production, as do complex chiefdoms, but without the kinship structures that characterize complex chiefdoms and put some brakes on the aristocrats' power and their demands for tribute. Demands in kingdoms can be so large that the commoners who work the land may be desperately poor. Kingdoms have a true system of haves and have-nots; complex chiefdoms do not.

MODES OF PRODUCTION: TRIBUTARY AND CAPITALIST

Stratified societies do not depend exclusively on the communal or kin-ordered mode of production. If they did they could not deny rights in order to create categories of people who have no access to the means of production, since the communal mode gives everyone the right to use resources and to share in what is produced using those resources. Instead, they employ some variation of the **tributary mode of production**, or of the **capitalist mode of production**.

The capitalist mode of production is used in most industrial states. The means of production is privately owned and used for personal or corporate profit. Unless you own the means of production—and most of us don't—you work for someone who owns the means of production to earn wages in order to buy what you need. This is the mode of production of most of the world today, including the U.S., and is discussed much more thoroughly in Chapter Six.

In the tributary mode you work to be able to pay tribute in return for being allowed to exercise your hereditary right to use land to produce what you need. In chiefdoms the tributary mode is combined with some use of the kin-ordered mode, but the more complex the chiefdom the greater the importance of the tributary mode. Kinship groups do work together using the kin-ordered mode of production to produce the tribute owed jointly by the lineage, as well as to feed themselves. They have rights together as a corporate group, but those rights are controlled and manipulated through the tributary mode, and a sizable proportion of what you produce on that land actually goes to the chiefs and other members of the aristocratic lineages. The chief who receives the tribute is likely to be a sub-chief, who in turn has to give tribute to the paramount chief to validate his own rights to control the land you and other commoners are working. So your work and your rights are organized by your tributary relationship. In kingdoms the tributary mode is completely dominant, and often takes a form of feudalism.

Feudalism

Kingdoms, until recently, depended on the tributary mode of production, although they often had groups of people, like merchants, who operated with some aspects of the capitalist mode. However, the tributary mode as practiced in kingdoms rather than in complex chiefdoms is far more exploitative and denies far more rights to far more people. The *feudal mode of production*, a variant of the tributary mode, was typical.

Kingdoms using some variation of the feudal mode of production have generally used a system that assigns people their positions in the stratification system at birth. *Birthright* and rank, along with gender, are the factors which are used to deny rights in the tributary mode of production in order to have a category of people available for exploitation. The rights to be conveyed to you, or denied to you, come automatically with your birthright position and your gender. Some kingdoms allowed more flexibility than others; as a commoner you might be able to move up a step or two as a reward for being a successful soldier, for instance. But in most kingdoms, the people at the very bottom of the stratification system, the people who did the hardest work and the agricultural work on feudal estates, were very tightly controlled and had no chance of changing their position.

In a feudal system all land is under the control of the king, although in weaker kingdoms, such as those of the Maya, he had trouble actually enforcing that control against the heads of other aristocratic lineages. In feudalism the king granted the right to the use of an estate (a fief) to an aristocrat. In return the fief-holder had to provide loyal support and tribute to the king. So long as this is done to the king's satisfaction, the fief would be passed by hereditary right from father to son. The very high-ranking aristo-

Feudalism/Feudal mode of production
A form of the tributary mode of production. It is a system of social and economic organization where estates in land are held by conferred right (in fief) by members of a privileged class, who can then command the labor of serfs who are attached to the estate.

Birthright
Rights that are conveyed to a person automatically at birth; such rights can include inherited position and privilege or rights of citizenship.

crats had enormous fiefs—whole districts. These fiefs were divided into numerous smaller fiefs held by lower ranking aristocrats. They in turn had to swear loyalty and give tribute to their own district lord, who held the overall fief from the king. Each fief-holder administered his (or very occasionally her) own estate.

With the estate came people who were tied to it, often referred to as serfs. They did not have the right to leave. But they were not slaves; they couldn't be bought and sold, and they couldn't be forced to leave. They had the hereditary right to work a piece of the lord's land for their own use but in return had to pay a form of tribute, either in labor or in produce. Regardless of the system, the tribute in time or crops usually left the serfs with barely enough to stay alive. However, their situation was slightly improved by certain rights. For instance many feudal societies specified that the lord had to allow serfs to gather firewood in his forest; some specified that the lord was to maintain a large store of food, usually grain, and in a bad year was expected to dole out enough to at least keep the serfs from actually starving to death. The lord was usually expected to provide enormous feasts on religious holidays, and there were many such holidays. In Europe, for instance, all the saint's days—and there were lots of them— were holidays. The lord's obligations were part of the system of stratified redistribution—returning a little of the tribute he received.

Between the fief-holders and the serfs was another category of people, many of whom were distant relatives of aristocratic families or were commoners but not serfs. These commoners generally lived in the cities or in the huge households of very high-ranking fief-holders. Some were retainers, acting as administrators and tribute collectors or as accountants or advisors or entertainers for the lords or king. Others were independent craftspeople, making goods for sale to aristocrats or to other city-dwellers. Others were merchants. The merchants and craftspeople in particular were edging into the capitalist mode of production. But even a wealthy commoner could not become an aristocrat and could not become a feudal lord. Some kingdoms also had slaves. As in complex chiefdoms their lives were often much like those of servants or apprentices and other retainers in the household, and they often performed equally skilled or demanding work. In many Asian and African societies slaves could gain positions of great prestige and power, for instance as administrators or soldiers, helping the king enforce the collection of tribute and control local lords or peasants who might revolt against the king's demands. There was usually some mechanism for regaining your freedom.

> *Both the tributary mode and the capitalist mode provide protection for the right to control or own property. Inequalities denying rights to certain categories of people, so that they don't have the means of production, could not last without some way to protect the property rights of those who own or control the means of production and claim wealth for themselves.*

• **Want more?**
For understanding how capitalism works, try the videos clips and short articles on http:// robertreich.org/

In both these modes someone has power over you. In both systems the elite lives off of the production done by ordinary people. Members of the elite may put in a lot of work, but it is likely to be political and religious work, or it may be supervisory, organizational work. In any case it is not productive work—it produces nothing that people can eat, use, exchange, or sell. Or members of the elite may use the wealth they collect from ordinary people to support retainers or pay wages, or buy slaves. This way they can get other people to do the administration and other kinds of non-productive work. And they can get other people to do the productive work they need done, such as making ceremonial robes, impressive architecture, statues, or jewelry, all important for marking their status as elite.

> *Both systems depend on being able to exploit labor—to take the value of the work they do away from the people who don't own or control the means of production. The difference is that some are able to demand a sizable compensation in return, while others can't.*

TYPES OF STATES: KINGDOMS AND RANK, REPUBLICS AND CLASS

Kingdoms are states and consequently are able to do a much more thorough job of denying rights than do chiefdoms, with complex chiefdoms in an intermediate position. Because this denial results in real suffering for large numbers of people, the elite in a kingdom, and sometimes in very complex chiefdoms, needs the right to use force to control ordinary people. They need a system for punishing disobedience and theft by hungry and angry people and a militia to provide bodyguards, property guards, and to put down revolts. Consequently, kingdoms are defined as states—they place the legitimate use of force under government control. In a kingdom this means that the only people who can legally use force are those who are authorized by the king or his appointees.

However, the line between complex chiefdoms and kingdoms is fuzzy. The more centralized authority is, and the more that authority is delegated to a bureaucracy, and the more stratified the society, with elite groups more able to monopolize wealth, power and prestige, the closer the society is to being a state. Whether a particular society gets called a complex chiefdom

• **Want more?**
Try exploring the website for Cahokia Mounds http:// cahokiamounds.org/

or a kingdom may well be a result of ethnocentrism among Western historians and anthropologists. Was King Arthur really a king, or was he a paramount chief? Why do we call him a king but call the highest-ranking person at the ancient mound site of Cahokia, near St. Louis, a paramount chief? Is it because Arthur really had more power, or because it is easier to define people we conquered as uncivilized if we think they never developed kingdoms, while ancestors of George Washington and Daniel Boone did?

> *In all states authority is held by a small group, whose members generally also control the means of production and the use of force. The state is organized to uphold the power of the elite to get control of the surplus produced by thousands of people, thereby ensuring them the wealth and resources that they use to keep themselves in power.*

This small group then delegates their authority to a bureaucracy that performs the actual work of governing—collecting taxes, running the legal system, maintaining roads, enforcing regulations and laws, controlling the police and military, and many other functions that vary from state to state, such as regulating education, controlling the religious establishment, building massive religious or governmental buildings, providing health services, or providing for the very poor. The bureaucracy forms an intermediate layer between the rulers and the commoners, controlling and supervising the commoners. All states do these things, but who is the head of the state and who makes decisions or is part of the bureaucracy varies enormously.

• **Want more?**
Try a search for documentary *300 Year Old Asante Kingdom*

In a kingdom it is birth into the right family that determines who is head of state. That birthright—having the right "blood"—means that the monarch is believed to generate all authority in the state, almost in the way that a power plant generates all electricity for a city. The monarch delegates this authority to the bureaucracy; with that authority comes the delegated right to use force if necessary. Ancestry also determines who controls the means of production, who is eligible for what positions in the intermediate bureaucracy, and who is a commoner providing labor. The commoners are often designated as inferior people who are believed by many to be *designed* for hard labor and exploitation. Kingdoms have typically been based on the tributary mode of production, often on a variant of feudalism. However, most kingdoms that remain today have shifted to the capitalist mode of production. In many of the remaining kingdoms, like England, the monarch is theoretically the source of authority, but in actual practice is a figurehead. Real power is exercised instead very much as it is in a republic.

> *Kingdoms are ranked states, but often develop a class system among commoners in addition to having a ranked aristocracy. Republics are states based on class, which is not automatically inherited. Republics don't have ranked, hereditary titles and positions.*

Republic
A state which is not a ranked society; positions of political and economic power are not directly assigned by ancestry or inheritance.

Capitalist
A person who owns the means of production in the capitalist mode of production.

In a *republic* ancestry does not directly determine who is head of state, who is a member of the elite controlling the means of production or a member of the bureaucracy, or who provides the labor that produces the surplus that is the foundation of the state. This is possible because republics are based on class as a major factor of inequality, and class does allow people to rise or fall in position. Capitalist republics use the capitalist mode of production, and *capitalists* are the people in the class that owns the means of production. Those who own huge portions of the means of production are the ruling elite, and they hold or control positions in the upper levels of the governing bureaucracy.

If the capitalist republic is democratic, then voting is used to determine who will hold these positions. In most cases the choice is between members of the ruling elite or, more often, between people who have been directly or indirectly designated as candidates by the ruling elite. A capitalist country can also be a dictatorship, where power has been seized from the elected government or from a monarch, as was Hitler's Germany and also some of the governments backed by the U.S. government, such as the Philippines under Marcos, Haiti under the Duvaliers, and Suharto's Indonesia, the Taliban in the 1990s in Afghanistan, Saddam Hussein in the 1980s in Iraq. A dictator, usually backed by the upper echelons of the military and by the most powerful capitalists, makes laws and governs without input from a representative body such as a Congress or Parliament.

SUBSISTENCE STRATEGY AND SYSTEM OF EXCHANGE IN STATES

In order to produce the large surpluses required to support an elite and their retainers in complex chiefdoms and the enormous surpluses required by states, most stratified societies depend on agriculture—intensive cultivation, not the extensive cultivation of horticulture. In addition there are many people not engaged in farming. They may be providing services to the elite, or they may be involved in manufacturing. Even in industrial societies agriculture remains critical, and is often responsible for a very significant proportion of the gross domestic product, as it is in the U.S.

Market exchange
A method of distribution
in which commodities are
bought and sold, generally
using some form of
money, without regard to
the relationship between
people, with the price set
by market forces such as
supply and demand.

Money
Objects that have been
assigned a standard value
and serve as a medium of
exchange in a wide variety
of transfers.*

Trading partners
A system of carrying out
(usually) balanced
reciprocity between
members of distant hostile
groups.*

Commodity
A product or service that
can be bought and sold
through market exchange.

• **Want more?**
Try *History of Money* http:/
/www.pbs.org/wgbh/
nova/ancient/history-
money.html

Stratified societies can't depend on reciprocity or egalitarian redistribution as their primary system of exchange. Reciprocity may well exist on the local level, among kin groups, family, friends, and neighbors, but stratified redistribution and/or *market exchange* are needed to allow surplus to accumulate in just a few hands. In a kingdom the monarch, along with the rest of the elite, controls production and distribution, often using a system similar to Europe's feudal system. The king, like the paramount chief, acts as the center for stratified redistribution, collecting the surplus produced by commoners, serfs, or slaves. The surplus is passed up through the hierarchy of the nobility to district rulers and on to the king. At each stage some of the surplus is kept by the person who received it; the rest is passed on up to the next level. Some of what the lords at each level receive is redistributed back out to the people by giving feasts, maintaining an army to protect people, and by giving charity. The elite, particularly at the higher levels, collect more and keep more for personal use than did chiefs or paramount chiefs, so that there is a much greater difference in wealth and power between elite and commoners in kingdoms than there is in chiefdoms.

In capitalist states, redistribution is carried out through taxation. Taxes are paid into the central bureaucracy. A portion is used to pay wages to the members of the bureaucracy; the rest is redistributed back out again in ways which are supposed to benefit the people of the state, including school systems, roads, welfare programs, and protection. There may be serious disagreement over what actually benefits people, as there is in the U.S.: should tax money go for health care for all, or should it go to pay for the military invasion of oil-rich countries, or should it be given back as a tax break for the wealthy?

Unlike most chiefdoms, states also rely heavily on market exchange. Market exchange involves the buying and selling of goods, usually using *money*, at prices set by supply and demand, not by kinship or by *trading partner* status, or by rights and obligations determined by your position in a society. In complex chiefdoms there is often some market exchange, but it frequently applies only to certain specified goods, not to everything. Other goods are exchanged through reciprocity or redistribution. In kingdoms generally most things can be bought and sold; that is, they can be exchanged as *commodities*. You can go to the market and buy food, cloth, weapons, cattle—almost everything people need. However, you can't buy land, and in many kingdoms you can't buy labor. You can't hire someone to work for you, pay them a wage, and that is the end of your transaction—their labor is not a commodity. But you may well be able to buy a slave: you are buying the person along with that person's ability to work. You aren't buying their work separately from the person. In some kingdoms it is possible to buy labor in some situations but not in others, but a great deal of work may be done by people who are tied to the land, as European serfs were. Kingdoms that have shifted to the capitalist mode buy and sell land and labor in the same way that capitalist republics do.

In capitalist republics such as ours, market exchange applies to the distribution of everything produced by the society. And we permit the buying and selling of the means of production. Land and labor are both commodities. That means that we have a *market economy*, not just a lot of market exchange as in kingdoms and some stratified chiefdoms. A market economy is an economic system in which almost all exchanges are made using market exchange including labor and the means of production. Those socialist nations that depend heavily on redistribution and exclude labor and the means of production from market exchange do not have a market economy, although they do have a lot of market exchange.

Market economy
An economic system in which everything, including land and labor, can be exchanged through market exchange. A society can have market exchange without having a market economy.*

THE JUSTIFICATION OF INEQUALITY IN RANKED SOCIETIES

> *Keeping a stratification system going is not easy. The vast majority of people are in the group being denied rights so that at least part of the value of the work they do can be taken away from them. Something has to convince them to let this happen.*

In chiefdoms comparatively little is taken away, so religious ideologies justifying the distribution of power and affirming the birthright of people of rank are usually adequate to get people to agree to hand over tribute or provide labor. The emotional strength of religion is harnessed to give the elite religious backing for their position of power.

In egalitarian societies people "do" much of their religion for themselves. In those egalitarian societies anyone has the right to become a shaman; your ability and inclination, not your parentage, determines whether you actually get the training needed to be a shaman. This is because in egalitarian societies it is common for all people to individually be able to gain access to the supernatural. An individual vision quest, for instance, lets anyone communicate directly with the supernatural. But in ranked societies it may be thought that ordinary people need help because they can't contact the supernatural themselves. Many of the rituals having to do with the well-being of the group as a whole, such as rituals for good harvests, solstice ceremonies, and other *calendric rituals,* must be performed for commoners by an aristocrat with the right birth, who has the right training and is authorized by chief or monarch. Aristocrats may also monopolize the performance of *crisis rituals* such as marriage, funerals, and initiation. Knowledge of how to perform the necessary rituals is often kept secret—it is esoteric knowledge—and passed on only to another authorized person.

Calendric ritual
A ritual performed on a regular schedule, such as Sunday church services, or Christmas mass, or Ramadan, or for good crops at the beginning of each planting season.

Crisis ritual
A ritual performed irregularly, as needed, such as weddings, prayers for rain, and healing ceremonies.

Priest
A religious specialist who may or may not directly contact the supernatural.*

In complex chiefdoms and kingdoms the religious specialists may be full-time retainers of the paramount chief or monarch. The chief or monarch uses tribute—food, clothing, and labor to build houses and temples—to provide for these retainers. Religious specialists of this type are called *priests*. It is their job to provide religious support services for the ruler, and they are usually themselves of high rank. They perform, or help the ruler perform, the rituals that ensure the well-being of the society. The performance of such rituals would make it very clear to the commoners that the aristocrats were needed, since only they had the 'blood' that connected them to the supernatural forces that controlled the forces of the universe. This could be seen as a form of reciprocity: the commoners give tribute; the aristocrats give back good crops or a return of the sun. Religion is thus performing its function of justifying the distribution of power in a society: the aristocrats deserve their position of wealth and prestige.

Origin Myth
Religious and semi-religious explanations about the origins and values of a society and its place in the world (see also myth).

Origin myths often give further religious explanation for the division between aristocrats and commoners. Myths are stories that deal with fundamental questions concerning the human condition from that society's point of view. Origin myths frequently tell how the gods or spirits gave the ancestors of a chiefly or kingly lineage certain powers or titles, giving them the right to their present position of power. By comparison, myths in egalitarian societies make it seem natural that people don't have power or authority over each other. The social control functions of religion also contribute to the position of the aristocrats. Believing that the gods, spirits, or ancestors will be displeased if you fail in your obligation to support your chief with gifts for redistribution or with tribute for your king helps keep you in line, as does the belief in the 'divine right of kings.'

Religious justification alone is not adequate in societies where so much is being demanded of ordinary people that there is widespread suffering. How stratification is maintained under such severe stratification is the topic of Chapter Seven.

WAR, THEFT, AND SLAVERY

The ability to use force effectively and consistently, and to prevent others from using force, is critical in distinguishing states, such as kingdoms or our own society, from chiefdoms. This applies to the ability to raise and control and provision an army or police force to be used internally, to put down rebellions and to enforce demands for tribute, and externally in wars of conquest. The presence of external enemies gives elites an excuse to maintain the military force they need and gives them an apparently critical role to play in organizing defense, furthering their claim to power and allegiance in the eyes of ordinary people (see also Chapter Seven).

War
The stealing from and/or killing of members of another group of people authorized, legitimized, and organized to do so by their own group.*

Legitimate
Seen by members of a group as correct, appropriate, and approved by people in positions of authority.*

• **Want more?**
Try *Oil Fuels War* http://www.theguardian.com/commentisfree/2015/dec/08/oil-fuels-war-terrorists-isis-climate-movement-peace-cop-21

War involves the purposeful gathering together and organizing of a group of men (and occasionally women), from one social or political entity to systematically kill members of another entity. This is usually under the direction of a leader with some degree of authority, and the participants are seen as *legitimately* authorized by their group and the institutions of their society to steal resources from, and if necessary kill, members of another group. Revenge for earlier thefts is frequently cited as the justification for aggressive war.

Theft, in one way or another, is always at the heart of war in all societies.

War takes quite different forms in egalitarian, ranked, and stratified societies. Since bands have little to steal there is no point in war. They have few material goods to steal, and since everyone has access to the means of production, people can generally get for themselves whatever they need. Bands usually don't defend "their" territory. They don't deny other people the right to forage on their territory, so a war is not necessary. You just need to go visiting to use other people's resources. And there is no point in stealing people, since there is no system for using other people's labor. Having a slave will do you no good; nor will stealing a woman and marrying her, since men have no way of benefiting from their wives' labor. Generalized reciprocity makes all this unnecessary. As a result, real warfare, as opposed to fights or quarrels between individuals or families, is uncommon. Individuals in bands do get mad at each other, and sometimes murder each other, but that is not war.

In societies that emphasize accumulating a surplus, such as farming societies, people's investment in land and other resources is large, so protecting your investment is extremely important. After all, if you have spent hours clearing and growing a garden that you depend on to feed you and your family, and now the crops are about ready to harvest, you don't want other people to come in and use up your crops. Unlike bands, you have good reason to keep other people out; you are likely to defend your territory. But in addition, the incentive for warfare increases: instead of producing your own surplus on which to base prestige or power, it may be possible to raid other people for their surplus or to take their ceremonial valuables, or, in pastoral societies, to steal from their herds. Or it may be possible to take over other people's land in order to produce a larger surplus for yourself. If population pressure becomes an issue, then warfare may also increase as one group tries to get control of a larger or more productive territory. This same principle is at work today in the long-standing disputes and frequent wars between India and Pakistan. Religious fanaticism is fuel for struggles to gain control of the glaciers that feed the rivers both countries depend on; who can 'steal' water from the other? Climate change will make this an even more burning issue that it is now.

In tribal societies with Big Men, the Big Man may lead raids and battles, but warfare may lead to few deaths and little land may actually change hands, although ceremonial valuables and food stores are often stolen. Rarely is a whole people conquered and made subject to the conquering group, since egalitarian redistributors gain their prestige by giving away, and having more people to give away to isn't going to particularly enhance your power. However, individuals may be captured and forcibly married or adopted into the winning group. Those additional wives add to a man's ability to raise his status, and adopted children enlarge a lineage or can replace dead members, often those who have been killed in war.

> *War may enhance the power of older men as compared to younger ones—but young men do eventually become older, making this quite different from gender inequality.*

Decisions made by older men about the conduct of a battle or about the conduct of policy with potential enemy groups may have an enormous influence on how long young men live. Warfare may give older men access to additional wives if young men have to spend their early years as unmarried warriors. However, in tribal societies no one can force you to join in a war or to follow orders. And, unlike our own wars, tribal leaders are out there along with everyone else, often taking bigger risks than others. Their high status doesn't give them the right to direct operations from safety, and their sons are as likely as anyone else's sons to be killed. If Big Men didn't put themselves on the front lines, they wouldn't be Big Men very long. Braver and more competent leaders would be followed, and people would stop making exchanges with them. This is quite different from stratified societies. Warfare is more common, more and more lethal, and on a larger and larger scale in societies that are more stratified.

> *Warfare usually means greater inequality—as it does in our own society.*

Warfare in chiefdoms has a different character from tribal warfare. It is generally on a much larger scale, is often more frequent, more formalized, more people die, it frequently involves the conquest of additional territory. This is because the aristocrats of chiefdoms, particularly of complex chiefdoms, have potentially far more to gain from war than do tribal leaders. Far more work has been invested in farmland and in storing food and making ceremonial valuables—there is much to steal and much to defend. But in addition conquering a territory makes sense: chiefs can let conquered people continue to live and work as before, except that now they have to pay tribute. Other members of the aristocracy can also benefit, by enslaving war captives.

Slavery
A system of forced labor in which people's ability to work, and in some cases their entire bodies, including their ability to reproduce, no longer belong to them. The value of the work they do is taken from them with no compensation at all.

> *Slavery makes it possible to gain additional workers without having to give them kinship rights.*

Slavery is common in chiefdoms and kingdoms since getting additional workers to aid one's own lineage in producing surplus makes sense in a society where it is possible to deny people basic rights. Most slaves were war captives or the children of enslaved war captives. Adult male war captives were generally killed, often with great ceremony, so it was captured women and children who were enslaved. Adult male slaves were generally people who had been captured as children, or who were born into slavery. It wasn't until the Atlantic slave trade in the 1600s began supplying enslaved Africans to the American colonies that there was much emphasis on enslaving adult men.

In tribes captured women and children were usually absorbed into the tribe through marriage or adoption, and are thereby given rights, which meant they were not enslaved. But in chiefdoms generally slaves could be ransomed or could work their way to freedom. As slaves their lives were often very similar to the lives of commoners. They lived in their owners' houses, were not seen as racially inferior, ate and dressed like other people. They did more grunt work than other people, and they couldn't leave, and their children, or they themselves, might eventually be absorbed into kin groups through marriage. As a slave you and your children were not property in the same sense that enslaved Africans in the United States were. Generally slaves in chiefdoms could have fairly decent lives. But although they generally did much the same work that commoners did, unlike commoners they themselves did not benefit at all from that work. Their ability to work belonged entirely to their owners. They did not need to be included in the familial system of reciprocity or in the exchanges of stratified redistribution. Thus their work provided a bigger surplus than did the labor of commoners, and it was this fact that made getting war captives an incentive for war.

But these are all reasons why aristocrats might be interested in conducting an aggressive war. These reasons don't apply to commoners, so why would commoners agree to go to war? They won't get tribute from conquered lands, and generally they didn't have slaves.

> *Commoners will have to be given a reason to think going to war and risking death or disablement or enslavement as a captive makes some kind of sense.*

It is true that chiefs, unlike Big Men, may have the authority to require men to join the fight. But people in chiefdoms can and do shift their allegiance if they believe a chief's demands are outrageous. Basically war in chiefdoms is made to seem reasonable in two ways. One is making it possible for you to get rewards, so that a man who is a good fighter can gain honor and raise his status, and sometimes the status of his family, above other commoners. Some societies have low-ranking titles that such a man can acquire through achievement rather than birth. Complex chiefdoms sometimes have an intermediate category of people between commoners and aristocrats; you can be born into the middle category or move from commoner into the intermediate category by achievement, usually in war, although not into the aristocratic category.

The other system of making war seem reasonable to commoners is to claim that war is required for religious reasons. This justification plays a role for some in the U.S., who believe that Islam is contrary to the will of God. Schools spend considerable effort, from the Pledge of Allegiance to the teaching of history, in producing patriotic citizens who believe in "My country right or wrong." And at times the state uses its policing power to use force to get recruits. When all else fails in keeping an adequate supply of soldiers conscription is backed by the threat of jail.

> *Most people in states do not have the political power to prevent others from taking away what they produce; the elites directly control the police and army or control them indirectly through their influence on the state judicial system and its laws about the protection of private property and labor contracts. A society that legitimizes the right to benefit from the labor of others is one with a system of ranking or stratification, not an egalitarian society.*

"FAILED STATES"

Failed States
A state that is unable to enforce the state's monopoly on the use of force and thus cannot guarantee the right to private ownership of the means of production, control their infrastructure, or enforce control of its borders.

States that have lost—or perhaps never really had—the monopoly on the use of force are referred to as *"failed states."* These are states that do not have adequate force to perform the policing and enforcing role of a state, and therefore are not able to control their own citizens. A failed state can't prevent unauthorized people from using force, for instance in rebellion or as strong men or warlords. This frequently results from the competition between local elites, some of whom support and are supported by the state, while others withdraw their support from the state in order to challenge the position of those connected with it. Much of this happens with the connivance of powerful outside entities, such as multinational corporations or foreign governments seeking leverage for their own agendas of neocolonialism or empire.

Nation-building
More frequently today it refers to the process of foreign military, economic, and political intervention in a failed state or newly formed state in order to create governmental institutions that will ensure stability, will control the use of force by unauthorized groups, and will act in the interests of the intervening foreign state.*

• **Want More?**
Try searching for video *"Military Industrial Complex from Eisenhower to Obama"* Or go to *Big Money Behind War…* http://www.aljazeera.com/indepth/opinion/2014/01/big-money-behind-war-military-industrial-complex-20141473026736533.html

Military-industrial complex
The economic and policy connections between defense contractors, the arms industry, the Pentagon, and the military.*

In other cases failed states result from revolt, sometimes of a nationalist or ethnic group seeking control of the state or to break away from it, sometimes of oppressed peoples seeking human rights. A failed state doesn't have adequate policing power to enforce the elites' right to the means of production, leading those elites to hire private mercenary forces, or to seek protection from, or themselves become, 'strong men' or 'warlords' or gang leaders controlling local militias. Nor does a failed state have the military or police power to defend its borders adequately. Borders become porous, allowing militias, refugees, and migrants to cross back and forth. ***Nation building*** thus becomes a priority to elites in the surrounding states or for outside elites intent on using the resources or labor of the local people. U.S. nation building in Iraq, for instance, has put a priority on access to oil.

Efficient exploitation through dependent development usually requires a local government that can prevent exploited people from revolting, and that can build and maintain an infrastructure for transportation and communication. Without this control an imperial occupation of the country is likely to be necessary. This occupation is likely to be described as nation-building, a euphemism implying that occupation is benevolent and temporary. That ordinary people in failed states suffer enormously is true; it is always ordinary people who bear the brunt of the catastrophes of war and hunger created by internal fighting between elites and by invasion and occupation. That local elites often become fabulously wealthy in the process is also true. What is not true is the benevolence of invasion and nation building, which to a large degree is designed to support the interests of the elites of the invading country, including the corporations involved in the ***military-industrial complex*** of which President Eisenhower warned as he was leaving office.

The human costs are staggering of what some anthropologists are calling the 'war machine'—a term that includes not just the military-industrial complex but also war budgets, environmental destruction, the legal and illegal international arms trade, the exploitation of workers, and the ideologies that justify the war.

CLIMATE CHANGE

There is another issue with which anthropologists are becoming increasingly concerned, one which at the moment is most catastrophically effecting people in failed states, but also in most states which have undergone colonialism or neocolonialism and have large numbers of very poor people. Many of these are societies in which many or most people are engaged in farming or fishing—in other words, highly dependent on weather patterns. Often their communities were once fairly egalitarian. However, the effects of colonization and neocolonialism have made it extremely difficult to maintain corporate groups, where all equally have rights to use resources. Now embedded in stratified societies, incorporation into the world economy, minus their former resources, has generally led to widespread poverty, especially when coupled with austerity programs. Others were societies already stratified, so that colonialism and neocolonialism simply made the situation of the people who were already oppressed even worse.

Climate change is beginning to wreak further havoc on these more vulnerable societies, partly because of their geographic location, where climate change is most advanced, and partially because of poverty, inequality, and environmental destruction such as deforestation that makes the environment less able to cushion the effects of violent storms. And perhaps starting with Hurricane Katrina, the US is beginning to feel it effects, but in any case the U.S. will surely be directly affected in the near future. As in other countries, as both Hurricane Katrina and Sandy demonstrate, although a storm may hit both rich and poor, it is the poor who suffer the worst long-term consequences.

Most scientists—97% of them—say that climate change is anthropogenic. It is human behavior that has lead to global warming. Many Americans don't know this, however, since massive funding has gone into promoting and in some cases actually paying the few scientists who back the fuel industry's claims that we do not need to change our behavior.

Greenhouse gases in the atmosphere trap heat, like a greenhouse does, so that far less of the sun's heat escapes back out into space. Added heat makes the polar icecaps and glaciers melt away, so they no longer reflect heat back out, compounding the problem. Deforestation, like the massive cutting of the Amazon, means CO_2 is no longer trapped in trees, and adds to the greenhouse effect. And as we burn more and more fossil fuels, more and more CO_2 is released; the greenhouse traps more heat, the glaciers melt faster. The process accelerates in a vicious circle. As glaciers melt away the many rivers they fed go dry or flood. The oceans warm, making massive tropical storms like Katrina more and more common, with resulting devastation, storm surges, and catastrophic flooding. Weather patterns become chaotic; rains don't come when they should, or come in deluges that destroy crops and communities and erode land. Rising temperatures, too much rain, too little rain, all brought on by global warming. And while global temperatures have changed before, they have taken hundreds, more often millions, of years to do it. The world has never seen anything like this before, and it has never happened in a world crowded with people.

• **Want more?**
Try *After Sandy…* http://www.theguardian.com/commentisfree/2013/oct/28/sandy-new-york-storm-inequality

Anthropogenic
Caused by human activity.

• **Want more?**
Try *Koch Industries: Secretly Funding the Climate Denial Machine* http://www.greenpeace.org/usa/global-warming/climate-deniers/koch-industries/

• **Want more?**
Try *Climate Refugees: The Human Face of Climate Change* http://www.climaterefugees.com/home.html

Climate change, particularly in the Global South, is arriving under conditions of poverty, inequality, exploitation, deregulation of the economy, privatization of public services and resources, and imposed austerity programs of structural adjustment. Precarity is already a condition of life. Because of those conditions, in addition to destroying livelihoods and inducing droughts, floods, desertification, and enabling the spread of new diseases, climate change has lead to famine and violence. Governments in failed states and in states undergoing structural adjustment or in states at war can't or won't distribute aid or access to resources. People struggle over resources like water. Many have to leave and migrate to cities in hope of work, which often proves to be non-existent or so low-paid or sporadic that malnutrition is rampant. Under those conditions some, especially young men, turn to militias, to gangs, to the drug trade, sometimes simply in hopes of an income, but sometimes also providing a form of law and order and services to their urban slum communities. Anger at government inaction or at action that makes things even worse builds, exacerbating already existing tensions.

Climate change thus can lead indirectly to chaotic civil wars, to even more chaotic wars between rival factions, and can inflame already existing differences between neighboring countries or within countries—religion frequently becomes a fanatical excuse for genocide as groups or countries fight to protect or to seize needed resources, particularly water. Wars lead to more famine, more deaths, more anger, and more desperate refugees. This is not to say that climate change directly causes desperation and violence; instead it makes already difficult tense situations of inequality even worse, so that violent reactions are more likely. It wouldn't have to be this way. In a just society food would be distributed from other areas in time of famine, water would be rationed. The conditions that make climate change particularly hard on the poor would not exist. Farmland would not be hoarded by a few huge landowners and worked by poverty-wage farm laborers. If most land is owned by only a few, that leaves only marginal land in many countries for everyone else, as is often the case where peasant farming is the livelihood for millions of people. These are the people who are most vulnerable to climate change, along with people in coastal fishing villages. Adequate taxation and land reform, financial aid for local water systems that would let water be stored during violent rains to be used later, aid in moving whole communities when necessary, in subsidizing low-cost small scale technologies—there is a lot that could be done to make a decent life possible, even with the effects of climate change. But climate change on top of existing tensions is indeed likely to escalate the scale of national and international violence. It wouldn't have to, though, with strong governments committed to social justice, and with an international commitment to end IMF and World Bank imposed austerity and structural adjustment policies and to limit the ability of corporations to mine resources and people. Unless we do this, catastrophes like the Syrian refugee crisis will become far more common. Syria's civil war is an example of a war that was exacerbated by climate change—years of drought raised already existing tensions and combined with other causes of the war. The refugees flooding into Europe in 2015 are driven partially by the war and partially by drought and economic breakdown, to the point where uprooting themselves and risking their own and their children's lives, risking life in refugee camps—all that becomes reasonable. As in most such situations, it is not necessarily the poorest who leave; it is people who have at least a little money or connections and whose family situation gives them the freedom to leave. The burden of war and climate change is thus borne by those who are left, those who are most vulnerable.

Ultimately, simply dealing with the consequences of climate change, if predictions are correct—and so far not only have they been correct, but they have been understated—will not be adequate. Climate change seems to be happening even faster than predicted. Climate change coming slowly, and with a small population, could be manageable. People would do as they have always done—they move to a more suitable location, migrating temporarily or permanently. But that isn't possible in a world with defended borders, where all land is already occupied, or at least claimed by somebody, and where farmable land is starting to shrink but population is continuing to grow.

• **Want more?**
Try *Katrina's Hidden Race War* http://www.thenation.com/article/katrinas-hidden-race-war/

So what are the options? It is easy to imagine a world in which all those who can afford it live in gated fortress communities and everyone else suffers in a world riven by continuous resource wars implemented by those who live in the gated fortresses, protected from angry mobs and able to ignore the suffering outside their gates. And that suffering is likely to be justified by propaganda enflaming racist definitions about who 'deserves' to suffer. Covert or overt race war in which whites defend their privileged position could well be the result.
Or, while alleviating the suffering caused by climate change, we can do something to halt the production of greenhouse gases.

If climate change is anthropogenic, caused by human behavior, then we can change our behavior. This would certainly involve tinkering with the workings of capitalism and the free market. Oil companies could not set foreign policy or domestic policy. Profit could not rule decisions; nor could individual desires for consumption. Just as people have learned not to smoke in public and much less inside their homes, we could learn not to think we need SUVs or well-watered green lawns, for instance. Jobs in coal-mining would need to be replaced, perhaps with jobs in the solar industry, and energy companies could not be allowed to monopolize solar energy in order to produce big profits. Local communities might run their own solar or wind energy systems.

Incomes around the world might drop for those at the top of the stratification system; CEOs might no longer make more in a year than ordinary workers would make in many lifetimes; the top 1% might have to pay the kind of taxes they did in the 1950s and 1960s. That tax money could be used to subsidize the invention of alternative technologies, which would have to be sold at prices people could afford or provided as a public service, as roads are now. Public transportation would need to replace most of the need for cars; bicycle lanes and sidewalks would make cars less necessary—and us healthier. Tax money could be used to alleviate poverty around the world, so the tensions that lead to violence and war would not do so as often. It could be used to resettle people who have become climate change refugees, emptying the refugee camps. But however it was done the bottom line would have to be, as quickly as possible, slowing and eventually stopping the use of the fossil fuels that produce greenhouse gases, before the earth reaches the 'tipping point,' when it will become impossible to stop the continued heating of the earth. This probably means major changes in the world's social, political, and economic systems. Otherwise our children and grandchildren will live in a very different world from this one, if they are not among the millions dead of disease, war, famine, or flooding.

I realize I've painted a pretty dire picture here. But if we don't know what is going on, we don't know we need to act. And it truly seems that we do need to act.

RECAP

Structural violence
Violence that is not a result of individuals or the state taking direct action to harm others. Structural violence generally results from inequality built into the social structure and results in deaths, maimings, malnutrition among those most seriously exploited. A death resulting from a society's refusal to commit adequate tax money to care for the poor is an example of structural violence. A death caused by murder is not.

Dealing with the issues raised in this chapter, issues that contribute to structural violence and human suffering, issues such as the 'war machine,' climate change, resource wars, failed states, and inequality generally, will not be easy. States are designed to protect the position of those at the top of the stratification system.

Elites contend with each other for power and dominance. Wealth, beyond a certain point, becomes meaningless in itself, except in relation to power struggles between elites. This means that serious contenders can never have 'enough;' the stakes are always rising. Consequently elite demands for labor and resources are, in the long run, insatiable. States are well organized to exploit their own people, but what is not available from inside a country must come from outside it.

It is the job of the state to make it possible for elites to meet their ever-expanding need for more. The rights of more people, in more places, will have to be denied. Rampant structural violence is a direct result.

REFERENCES/SUGGESTED READINGS

On stratified and somewhat stratified societies

Averkieva, Julia 1988[1971] The Tlingit Indians. In North American Indians in Historical Perspective. Eleanor Leacock and Nancy Lurie, eds. Pp.317-342. Prospect Heights, IL:Waveland.

Frazier, Kendrick 1999 People of Chaco: A Canyon and It's Culture (updated edition). New York: WWW Norton.

Gailey, Christine 1987 Kinship to Kingship: Gender Hierarchy and State Formation in the Tongan Islands. Austin: University of Texas Press.

Oswalt, Wendell and Sharlotte Neely 1999 The Natchez: Sophisticated Farmers of the Deep South. In This Land Was Theirs, 6th ed. Wendell Oswalt and Sharlotte Neely. Pp 477-500. Mountain View, CA: Mayfield Publishing Co.

Rountree, Helen 1989 The Powhatan Indians of Virginia: Their Traditional Culture. Norman, OK: University of Oklahoma Press.

Sunday, Peggy 2002 Women at the Center: Life in a Modern Matriarchy. Ithaca: Cornell University Press.

Stuart, David 2000 Anasazi America: Seventeen Centuries on the Road from Center Place. Albuquerque: University of New Mexico Press.

Weiner, Annette 1988 The Trobrianders of Papua New Guinea. Belmont CA: Wadsworth. Young, Bilione and Melvin Fowler

2000 Cahokia: The Great Native American Metropolis. Urbana: University of Illinois Press.

On modes of production

Patterson, Thomas 1993 Archaeology: The Historical Development of Civilizations. Englewood Cliffs, NJ:Prentice Hall. Pp 91-104.

Wolfe, Eric 1992 Europe and the People without History. Berkeley: University of California Press. Pp.73- 100.

On stratified redistribution

Harris, Marvin and Orna Johnson 2007. Cultural Anthropology, 7th edition. Boston: Pearson/Allyn and Bacon. Pp. 107-108.

On the organization of states, including their need for force

Diamond, Jared 2005 Guns, Germs, and Steel: The Fates of Human Societies. New York: W.W. Norton and Co.

Giddens, Anthony 1987 The Nation-State and Violence: Volume Two of a Contemporary Critique of Historical Materialism. Berkeley: University of California Press.

Greenberg, Stanley 1980 Race and State in Capitalist Development: Comparative Perspectives. New Haven: Yale University Press.

Patterson, Thomas 1993 Archaeology: The Historical Development of Civilizations. Englewood Cliffs, NJ: Prentice Hall.

On the creation of hunger

Bennett, Jon and Susan George 1987 The Hunger Machine: The Politics of Food. Oxford NY: Polity Press.

Dossani, Sameer 2008 Africa's Unnatural Disaster. Foreign Policy in Focus. June 26. Electronic document, http://fpif.org/africas_unnatural_disaster/,accessed June 28, 2008.

On climate change

Baer, Hans and Merrill Singer. 2014 The Anthropology of Climate Change: An Integrated Critical Perspective. New York: Routledge.

Biggers, Jeff. 2015. Call It What It Is: A Global Migration Shift From Climate, Not a Migrant or Refugee Crisis. Common Dreams August 28. www.commondreams.org/views/2015/08/28/call-it-what-it-global-migration-shift-climate-not-migrant-or-refugee-crisis.

Chew, Sing. 2007. The Recurring Dark Ages: Ecological Stress, Climate Changes and System Transformation. Lanham: AltaMira Press.

Climate Change Refugees: The Human Face of Climate Change (documentary video) http://www.climaterefugees.com/home.html

Crate, Susan and Mark Nuttall, eds. 2009 Anthropology and Climate Change: From Encounters to Actions. Walnut Creek, CA: Left Coast Press.

Crumley, Carole and Alf Hornborg. 2007. The World System and the Earth System. Walnut Creek, CA: Left Coast Press.

Fischetti, Mark. 2015. Climate Change Hastened Syria's Civil War. Scientific American, March 2. http://time.com/4024210/climate-change-migrants/

Not Just the Koch Brothers: New Study Reveals Funders Behind Climate Change Denial Effort. 2013. Science Daily. December 20. http://www.sciencedaily.com/releases/2013/12/131220154511.htm

Parenti, Christian. 2011 Tropic of Choas: Climate Change and the New Geography of Violence. New York: Nation Books.

Roberts, J. Timmons and Bradley Parks. 2007. A Climate of Injustice: Global Inequality, North-South Politics, and Climate Policy. Cambridge: MIT Press.

Singer, Merrill. 2013. Respiratory health and ecosyndemics in a time of global warming. Health Sociology Review 22(1): 98-111.

Zhang, David, Peter Brecke, Harry Lee, Yuan-Qing He, and Jane Zhang 2007. Global climate change, war, and population decline in recent human history. Proceedings of the National Academy of Science. December 4. www.pnas.org/cgi/doi/10.1073/pnas.0703073104.

On the "war machine"
Singer, Merrill and G. Derrick Hodge, eds. 2010 The War Machine and Global Health: A Critical Medical Anthropological Examination of the Human Costs of Armed Conflict and the International Violence Industry. Lanham MD: AltaMira Press.

On varieties of slavery
Campbell, Gwyn, ed. 2004. The Structure of Slavery in Indian Ocean Africa and Asia. Portland OR: Frank Cass.

Chatterjee, Indrani and Richard M. Eaton, eds. 2006. Slavery and South Asian History. Bloomington: Indiana University Press

Meillassoux, Claude, 1991 [1986]. The Anthropology of Slavery: The Womb of Iron and Gold. Alide Dasnois, tr. Chicago: University of Chicago Press.

Miller, Joseph 2012, The Problem of Slavery as History: A Global Approach. New Haven: Yale University Press.

CHAPTER 5
FACTORING IN GENDER

The next several chapters discuss the forms of inequality that have been invented to allow elites to get away with structural violence, so that the inequalities and the suffering they cause appear not to be caused by human policies and decisions. These inventions—the factors of race, caste, ethnicity, and class—define certain categories of people as "Other," so that denying them rights appears normal, a part of nature. They are added to gender, which exists in all societies, although not necessarily as a factor of inequality. In stratified societies these factors intersect with each other and with gender in various combinations, with several of them operating as factors of inequality in the life of one person or community and as factors that convey privilege in the lives of other people. We will start with gender in this chapter and add on other factors in the next chapter.

THE QUESTION OF GENDER

The general strategies for organizing equality and inequality are discussed in Chapter Three. What was not discussed there was the issue of gender equality and inequality. In fact, the use of the term egalitarian in that chapter can be somewhat misleading. Some of those societies are called egalitarian because rights are equally conveyed to all men, ignoring the existence of some gender inequality.

Gender
The learned behavior and attitudes associated with a particular sex in a particular society.

But before we can discuss gender equality, we need to be clear about *gender* itself. Sex and gender are different but interrelated concepts. Sex is basically biological—you are male or female, although you will see that even that is not quite cut and dried. Gender is learned behavior, behavior that you acquire as part of socialization in your own society. This means that gender is very flexible. There are on-going arguments about how much of a role sex—biology—plays in shaping men and women's behavior. For instance, is male aggressiveness taught to them? In our society it is easy to argue that men are naturally more aggressive than women, but perhaps they pick up aggressive attitudes from the glorification of violence in our culture, ranging from football to violent TV shows, to admiration for aggressive business practices, to assuming war is reasonable.

Division of labor
The performance of different tasks by different categories of people.

Sexual division of labor
The assignment of a society's tasks according to sex. In some societies the division between the work that men do and the work that women do is very clear. In others there is considerable overlap.

All societies have a *division of labor*—a system of deciding who is going to focus on what kind of work. All societies use sex as one of the deciding factors in assigning tasks. For some societies this *sexual division of labor* is very strict, and you would not think of doing something the other sex normally does. In others, the division is fairly flexible, with some tasks done mostly but not exclusively by one or the other sex. Some have a great many tasks that can be done by both men and women. Most band societies have a fairly flexible sexual division of labor and very little gender inequality. As in most societies where men hunt, egalitarian foragers expect men to do most of the hunting and women to do most of the gathering. But even this basic division is flexible. Women frequently hunt small animals; men returning empty-handed from a hunt may gather food they pass on the way. In some societies women may take on 'male' roles and engage in hunting, and there are even a few societies where big game hunting is not just a male role. And there are forms of hunting, such as net hunting or drives, which require the participation of everyone regardless of sex. In net hunting, although both sexes are involved, there is still a sexual division of labor, with men killing the animals that the women (and sometimes children and elderly men) drive into the nets.

However, beyond assigning big game hunting to men, there is an enormous variation in the roles played by men and women. In some societies it is men who carry heavy loads; in others it is women. In some it is women who build houses; in others it is men, or both. In some men make clothing; in others it is women. In some societies fathers or grandparents do a great deal of child care after a child is about three years old. In bands men and women do have different basic areas of responsibility, but also a great deal of individual freedom in who actually does how much of what. Men who are lousy hunters do a lot of gathering, for instance, and some women set far more traps for small animals than others. In most egalitarian foraging societies women actually bring in more food than men do, sometimes as much as seventy to eighty percent in areas where hunting is not very dependable. In most cases women bring in the staples, and a band can go for weeks at a time depending solely on this gathered food. However, meat is a very favorite food, and provides large amounts of protein.

The division of primary responsibility for hunting and gathering between men and women seems to be based on the fact that women's work in foraging societies must be interruptible.

In a society without bottles and in groups that have only a few adult women, who bear children only every three or four years, it is unlikely that several women will be lactating at the same time. Every woman must carry and nurse her own child—they can't take turns and nurse each other's child. So a woman would have to hunt with her baby and run the risk that the child might cry at any moment and scare the game that has been stalked for an hour. This isn't terribly practical, although it is done in a very few societies. The hunt may not be interrupted to care for a child, while gathering may. And notice that foraging women *do not* "stay home and care for children." Women go many miles from camp, carrying their nursing children with them (older children often stay in camp with older people and the men and women who are not hunting or foraging that day). Children get cared for along with gathering or other work; in farming societies children often accompany their parents, making a slow transition from playing to helping. Childcare is not done separately from the rest of life, as it is in most American families. It is also not true that women are too weak to hunt—they frequently carry much heavier loads than men do on their return from foraging or harvesting. Since both gathering and hunting require long years of education, teaching children primarily what they will do for most of their adult lives makes sense, rather than teaching girls to hunt in preparation for those years when they happen to be without children.

In addition, many societies have several options in their definition of gender and of gender roles. Women under certain conditions can take on a clearly recognized role, with its own norms of behavior, that is neither that of the typical man nor of the typical woman. Men have a similar set of options. This is particularly relevant for the people whose sexual organs are neither clearly male nor female—in all societies this is two or three percent of all babies. In other societies both men and women can essentially change sex, so that a woman who has done this is treated largely as if s/he were a man.

This *gender diversity* exists in all societies, but it is primarily in relatively egalitarian societies, and not in all of them, that diversity is treated as a normal part of the human repertoire. This means that in these societies even the sexual division of labor is not exactly a division between 'men' and 'women.' Instead it is a division between gender roles; who, biologically, is in those roles may include a few people who are not people we would think of as biologically male or female. And this diversity gives a different twist to gender equality; it might be more accurate to think of gender role equality. Bear this in mind as you read further about gender and gender equality.

Like all societies, in addition to the sexual division of labor, bands also have a *division of labor by age*. Different roles are assigned to people of different ages. Children often do not participate seriously in hunting or gathering until their late teens. They have a real childhood, unlike many children in stratified societies. They play, learn, care for younger children, and gradually prepare for adult roles. Generally this happens earlier for girls than for boys. The elderly play important advisory roles for younger adults, sometimes as leaders. They help with child care,

• **Want more?**
Try *The Two Spirit People of Indigenous North America* http://www.firstpeople.us/articles/the-two-spirit-people-of-indigenous-north-americans.html

Gender diversity
The definition in some societies of multiple sexes and genders beyond the two typically regarded in the U.S. as natural and biological; includes also acknowledgement of transgendered, bi-sexual, lesbian and gay identities.

Division of labor by age
The assignment of a society's tasks according to age, so that the elderly, the middle-aged, and the young adults are expected to focus on different tasks.

and are extremely important in the education of children, passing on religious knowledge, history, medical and biological knowledge, and the skills needed for foraging.

THE QUESTION OF MARRIAGE

• **Want more?**
For marriage around the world try *Defending Traditional Marriage: Whose Definition, What Tradition?* http://www.huffingtonpost.com/american-anthropological-association/defending-traditional-marriage_b_1460026.html

People in the United States usually believe that the only proper basis for marriage is that two individuals have fallen in love and have exercised their individual right to choose to marry. In most of the world, except in extremely egalitarian societies, that is an unacceptable basis for marriage. People do sometimes fall in love, and that is usually seen as a good thing if the person you fall in love with is already your spouse, and a bit of a tragedy if you fall in love with someone you can't marry. In most of the world, simply being in love is not a sufficient reason for a marriage. And as is perfectly obvious from looking at the U.S. divorce rate, falling in love is not a particularly dependable system for choosing your life partner. Decisions about marriage in most of the world are a family or lineage affair, not an individual affair, and the individual is expected to marry in a way that benefits the entire group. This is important in societies where the entire political and economic structure is based on kinship, making your marriage an important issue for everyone in the group. As we will see, it is even more important in ranked societies and those stratified societies where kinship is the basis for conveying rights to a few and denying them to others. So in most of the world, 'selfishly' following your individual preference isn't an option—unless you were lucky enough to fall in love with someone the group sees as an appropriate marriage partner.

Except in extremely egalitarian societies, marriage is usually more of a contract between groups (usually groups of relatives or corporate kin groups), than it is an arrangement between two individuals.

Marriage is frequently more important in the construction of kinship and of social relations between groups of in-laws than in creating a nuclear family, especially in societies where kinship, as the basis of a political and economic system, determines how surpluses are produced and distributed. Love in such marriages is a result of a good relationship between people who married for economic and political reasons.

This may sound like a pretty bleak basis for marriage, and often it is. But don't be ethnocentric about it: most likely a lot of the people you know are also in pretty bleak marriages. And there is another factor to consider. Cultural determination in the U.S. sets us up to expect to fall in love. We are carefully socialized practically from birth to find someone to claim as a boyfriend or girlfriend. Think of adults asking kindergarten kids, often in a rather teasing tone of voice, "So, have you got a little girl/boyfriend yet?" In societies where kin groups determine marriage choices, nobody would dream of saying such a thing. As a married adult you would expect your closest relationships to continue to be with your own relatives and with members of your own sex. Spouses are expected to live up to their obligations; they should be good husbands or wives, as that society defines them. If you both do this, you may well develop deep respect and caring for each other; you may experience what people in the U.S. call love. But if you don't, you would still have a good working relationship with your spouse, and your emotional support would come from friends and relatives. Nobody, including you, would think you had a bad marriage.

And generally in equalitarian societies there is yet another factor to consider: you usually can divorce, since you always have rights in your own lineage, although this may be a little harder to arrange in the less egalitarian patrilineal societies, where bride-wealth or dowry may have to be returned. On top of that, those societies that recognize gender diversity don't even require that you have to be a man or a woman, according to your biological sex. So you don't necessarily have to marry a person of the 'opposite' biological sex, although you do need to marry someone in a different gender role from yours.

• **Want more?**
Try *Musuo Walking Marriages* http://mosuoproject.org/walking.htm

Up to this point you have probably been reading along without questioning the idea of marriage itself. But really, what is the point of marriage?

Why does it matter whom you do or don't have sex with? Why don't women just continue living with their parents and the rest of their family, and when they have kids, those kids get taken care of by the family? Actually, there appear to be a few societies that do something along those lines. And, in fact, a pattern something like that is developing in the U.S. More and more unmarried women with children are continuing to live with, or stay close to, their parents.

The father of the child often has a continuing relationship with the mother and child, but he also stays with his own family. The father often contributes some financial assistance, so that the mother, her kin, and the father all jointly support the child. Given the recent shifts in our economy, it may well take an entire group cooperating to support the child, and it may be years before the child's parents can afford to marry, although they may eventually be able to live together. They may legitimize their situation with an engagement ring. Being fiancés has become a half-way house between boyfriend/girlfriend and marriage, carrying sexual rights, rights to children, and financial obligations, a formal status that was unrecognized in this way until the last twenty or so years. Or the father may be almost completely uninvolved. There are other societies that have had patterns something like this, where the biological father of the child is only peripherally involved, with few rights or obligations as husband or father in relation to the child, the mother, or the mother's family. Instead his obligations are primarily toward his sister's children.

Generally anthropologists say that *marriage* is universal: it exists in all societies. But some question that. It is certainly true that all societies have some system of regulating sexual behavior. Marriage generally gives the spouses priority for sexual access; however, it does not necessarily give the spouses exclusive rights to the other's sexuality. In fact in some types of marriage in some societies sex between the partners is not expected. Marriage as a sexual behavior regulator probably does cut down on squabbles within the group. But is marriage really only about sex? More usually marriage is defined as a socially recognized arrangement between (usually but not always) at least one man and one woman, that regulates the sexual relationship between the partners and other members of the society, gives the woman's children legitimate rights, assigns rights over the children, and assigns rights and responsibilities to both partners, to other spouses and their children who are also part of the marriage, and to the group of in-laws created by the marriage.

It isn't so obvious that marriage in this sense is universal. In egalitarian bands the whole group, not individual marriage partners, carries out many of these functions. For instance, responsibility for feeding the family and caring for children is held by the entire group. All children automatically have rights as human beings in a band. Who their parents are doesn't matter much. Or what about the societies where the father of a child may be the acknowledged father but has practically no rights or obligations as a result, and indeed may not even continue to have a sexual relationship with the mother? Instead his obligations may be to the people in the household where he grew up. And what about those societies that allow a woman (usually a woman without children or without sons) to legitimately 'become' a man, marry a woman who then has sex with a man who will have no rights as father or husband, while the female husband claims fatherhood of the children and makes them heirs?

One of the explanations often given for the existence of marriage is that it sets up men to provide necessary support to their children. But it is clear that groups of cooperating relatives can do this too. Men may be needed in raising a child, but those men can be uncles or grandfathers or surrogate men, and often are, even in the U.S. as our marriage system is changing. However, it is true that marriage doubles your kin, tying more people in to responsibility toward a child. But in a band you don't particularly need to double your kin, and in a tribe you have rights in your own lineage, although having ties to several lineages does give you more people to call on for assistance in trying to raise your status.

Another piece of the puzzle is that marriage in tribes is usually more formally organized than among bands and the more egalitarian tribes; it is even more formal in chiefdoms and states.

And the more egalitarian the society, the easier it is, and the more common it is, to divorce. This gives a clue about the reason for marriage as more than just a mechanism for regulating sex, as to a large extent it is in bands. But to see the point of this clue, we need to go back a minute to the fact that, unlike bands, tribes, chiefdoms and states do produce a surplus and do have a system for using other people's labor. It is women who do much of the work of producing a surplus, and in patrilineal societies in particular, wives' work is important in enhancing husbands' prestige.

Marriage, in other words, in patrilineal societies, is one way of laying claim to a woman's work. But even more importantly, marriage is the only way that men can lay claim to children. Marriage gives men a kind of biological right to children, similar to the biological right that women get automatically by pregnancy, childbirth, and nursing. It makes fatherhood and motherhood into parallel statuses.

If having rights to children matters (as opposed to loving a child, which anyone can do—you don't have to be married to love a child; you don't even have to be the mother's sexual partner), then marriage is likely to be relatively formal. In bands having rights to a child doesn't make much sense: you aren't better off (although you may be happier) with children. You don't need to claim them to enhance your prestige or to use their labor. But in other societies, claiming children does matter. A lineage wants to have lots of members; that is part of how lineages maintain their position, and in tribes how aspiring Big Men get the support they need. If the society is matrilineal, women in producing children are producing members for their own lineage. Who the father is doesn't matter as much, either to the members of the matrilineage or to the child, since the child's rights are conveyed by the mother. But suppose the society is patrilineal. The only way to get new members for a patrilineage is to set up some system that transfers a child to the father and his lineage, away from its mother and her lineage. Even the women who become husbands do it in order to be able to claim children. Women, in other words, have to produce children who will not belong to their own lineage. Marriage is the system for doing that. Without some such system patrilineages would all die out. So matrilineal societies typically are less strict about marriage, and divorce is more common, and who your father is matters less.

But notice: this makes marriage, especially in patrilineal societies, an expression of power, giving men, in a sense, the right to take women's children away from them. Or alternatively marriage can be seen as a system for making sure a child will have rights as an adult, in a society where only men have the power to convey rights.

This is where bridewealth comes into the picture. In giving a woman in marriage to a man in a patrilineal society, the woman's kin are transferring to the husband's group rights over the bride's sexuality, labor, and future children. This flow of rights is balanced by bridewealth going to the bride's kin—a transfer of something tangible in the other direction. This is not 'buying a wife,' but it does validate the marriage. The marriage may be only the beginning of a set of transfers between the two groups. For instance, there may be further transfers with the birth of each child. These marital exchanges are common in tribes and chiefdoms, but are of less importance in egalitarian societies and in matrilineal societies.

Bridewealth, especially in patrilineal societies, functions also as a system giving senior men control over younger men, since young men will most likely need help from their elders in amassing the goods needed for bridewealth, especially in their first marriage. It also gives senior men control over the allocation of women's fertility and labor by controlling the supply of brides, since they are making most of the final decisions (often with considerable input or influence from their wives, mothers, and sisters) about who marries whom. In fact, in most societies men can marry more than one wife, and the senior men may marry a lot of the available young women, leaving lots of young men unable to marry until they are fairly senior themselves. This is particularly important in societies that do not have a system of accumulating wealth in the form of money or investments, so that the only way you can raise your status is by controlling other people's labor and then giving away their surplus production.

In somewhat stratified societies this means that having a large household, lots of retainers, an impressive retinue is a mark of status in and of itself, beyond the importance of producing a surplus. Wealth meant 'wealth in people.' Lots of wives helps provide that large household, but so also can slaves. Enslaved women increase the size of the household, and as women they produce both work and children. Children whose fathers are lineage members can be incorporated as a junior branch of the lineage, growing the number of retainers and the influence and status of the family. This is why in Africa and Asia before the Atlantic slave trade women were more highly valued as slaves than men were, and it is also why, once the Atlantic slave trade took off, that it was mostly men who were shipped to the Americas—local elites had a better use for the women in their own households. If you can't pay people wages to work for you without some system of money, then one way of gaining control of labor is through kinship, marriage, and exchange obligations. Societies where surplus production is less important and where women's labor is not particularly important for creating male prestige, especially if they are matrilineal, often don't emphasize bridewealth or have as many formal exchanges, and almost all marriages are monogamous.

MARRIAGE TYPES

Monogamy means that a person has only one spouse at a time. Most societies around the world have not had a strict rule like ours requiring monogamy. But even in societies that permit *polygamy*, most marriages are actually monogamous. *Polygyny* is a form of polygamy in which a man has several wives. *Polyandry* is a form of polygamy in which a woman has several husbands at a time. Polyandry as the preferred form of marriage is quite rare. However, many bands and some tribes do permit polyandry; almost all permit polygyny. This is because it is generally important in such societies to be married, since the political and economic system is based on kinship. So if there is not a husband or a wife available for a monogamous marriage, people without spouses may marry into already existing marriages, making that monogamous marriage into a polygynous or polyandrous one.

In societies where women's labor is important for creating power and prestige, polygyny is more common.

Having several wives is often a status symbol among the elite in the stratified societies, as well as a source of labor and children. Co-wives in these societies are often expected to cooperate, usually under the leadership of the first wife. Together they are expected to be an important part of the labor force needed to keep an elite household producing enough, and providing enough hospitality, to maintain and enhance the position of the husband, and of the lineage as a whole. They may work along with, and direct the labor of, other women who are slaves in the household. If the first wife does a good job there may be very little conflict between the wives. In many societies the wives are sisters, a system called *sororal polygyny*, with the oldest sister in charge.

Polyandry involves one wife and several husbands, who are usually brothers. In this case it is called *fraternal polyandry.* Polyandry is frequently associated with land shortages and population imbalance (sometimes a result of female infanticide). Polyandry can help control population growth, because a woman can have only so many children, no matter how many husbands she has. Polyandry lets men in the society be married without needing as many wives as there are husbands. If many girls do not marry and have children as adults, fewer children are born, and all men have heirs, and all children have an inheritance—the comparatively few children of the one wife in a polyandrous marriage inherit all the land as a unit, rather than dividing it up among lots of children from many wives. The brothers in this new generation will again avoid actually splitting up the land they have inherited by making another polyandrous marriage.

Monogamy
Marriage to only one spouse at a time.

Polygamy
Marriage to more than one spouse at a time.

Polygyny
Marriage of a man to two or more women at a time; a form of polygamy.

Polyandry
Marriage of a woman to two or more men at one time; a form of polygamy.

Sororal polygyny
A form of polygyny in which the co-wives are all sisters.

Fraternal polyandry
A form of polyandry in which the co-husbands are all brothers.

• **Want more?**
Try *When Taking Multiple Husbands Makes Sense* http://www.theatlantic.com/health/archive/2013/02/when-taking-multiple-husbands-makes-sense/272726/

GENDER EQUALITY AND INEQUALITY

Having a fairly strict sexual division of labor does not necessarily mean gender inequality.

People in the United States tend to think that the only way men and women can be equal is if they do, or are free to do, exactly the same work—there is no sexual division of labor. That would be one way of getting gender equality, but it is not the only way, and it is not the way gender equality works in many of the societies where it exists.

Gender equality
A relationship between the sexes in which men and women have equal degrees of control over their own lives and have equal access to the resources they need to live in their society.*

Gender equality means that men and women have equal degrees of control over their own lives, and have equal access to the resources they need to live in their society. Gender equality can exist in societies where men and women have different basic tasks if both men's work and women's work is given respect, and if both men and women control what they produce and can make their own decisions about their own work and their own lives. This is typical of bands and sometimes of small farming societies, but not of stratified societies like our own.

You might be tempted to think that gender equality exists in bands because the work women do, bringing in the staples and often the largest proportion of the food, is extremely necessary and important. But in many societies doing the hardest and most necessary work doesn't bring equality. What does seem to bring equality is controlling what you produce.

Think about low paid daycare workers or aides in nursing homes. Or think about how dependent slave-owners were on their slaves; their wealth came from the work done by enslaved Africans, but that very important work certainly didn't bring equality. If you work in a factory making chairs, you don't control what happens to those chairs. The factory owner does. And the owner has far more control over his or her own life than you do. You probably can't even decide that you will start work at nine o'clock each morning so that you can see your kids off to school. The owner decides that for you; nobody makes and enforces such decisions for the owner.

GENDER EQUALITY

• **Want more**?
Try *Ju'hoansi* http://www.peacefulsocieties.org/Society/Juhoan.html

Among egalitarian foragers both men and women control their own work and decide what to do with what they produce. An individual man won't benefit by getting more work out of his wife: because of generalized reciprocity, on days when a woman stays in camp other women share with her the food they gathered that day. On days when she gathers, she shares with the women who shared with her. Each woman decides for herself what she will give to whom, and she gets the respect that often goes to a gifted and generous gatherer. Men do the same thing with the food they bring back. Whether or not your particular sexual partner or parent brings in food on any particular day makes very little difference in what you eat or in whether you have the things that are considered necessary in your society.

For the same reason, controlling the labor of other men or other women would do you little good, so there is little inequality between members of the same sex. There is no way that you can raise your status or become wealthy by getting other people to work for you. If you have extra stuff, the only thing you can do with it is give it away—and if you keep it all for yourself, you are going to be pretty disgusted with yourself the next time the band moves and you have to carry it all with you.

Marriage in egalitarian foraging bands tends to be fairly informal; marriages break up fairly easily, and remarriage is very common for both men and women. It may take several marriages before you find one that works, and then you will probably remain in that marriage for the rest of your life. But you stay because you choose to, not because you have to, or because you are dependent on your spouse.

Since women aren't dependent on their husbands for food or other necessities, women find it far easier to leave a husband than they do in our society.

For most American women, divorce is a financial disaster, at least for a number of years. Men typically earn far more than their wives, and child support, even when it is paid, rarely replaces that lost income. And in the United States you don't automatically have the right to food and shelter, as to some extent you would in a more socialist society, or as you would in an egalitarian foraging band, where all people have foraging rights in a large number of places. If you join a different band after a divorce, you and your children are not a burden on the people you have joined. In the U.S. having a divorced daughter return home may mean financial hardship or crowding for her parents. None of this applies to egalitarian foragers, making it easy for a woman or man to leave an unsatisfactory marriage. It also means that there is relatively little spouse abuse, and what abuse there is goes both directions.

The relative ease of divorce is related to the fact that there is no property to be divided up if a couple splits up. Nor is there property or rights or privileges to pass on from one generation to the next, so heirs—biological property and privilege receivers—are non-existent.

This makes it possible to avoid placing huge importance on biological fatherhood. Nor is it important to make sure that wives produce lots of children—children are not needed as a labor supply and bring no wealth and very little prestige in an egalitarian society. Children are loved, but they don't raise your status.

Men take responsibility toward the children born to their wife, and in a band all the men are involved in providing the meat for all the children in the band. Who your father is makes no difference to the child's access to resources. So whose semen might have been involved in a conception is relatively unimportant. Social fatherhood, fathering because of love of the child or because of love or obligation to the mother, is far more important. If what matters most is women giving birth and if there is no reason for one to care much who the biological father is, then women retain rights, and the question of controlling women's bodies and their reproduction does not emerge, or is of little importance.

> *This is another aspect of gender equality. Women have as much control over their sexual lives as men do: there is no double standard.*

So husbands do not loose out economically or in status as a result of divorce, although they, like wives, may be deeply unhappy or angry if a spouse chooses to leave. Since bands don't produce a surplus and therefore you can't get power for yourself by getting your wife to work harder to produce a big surplus for you, your wife and children are not a labor force for you. So divorce does not mean the husband is losing either heirs or his labor supply. Divorce is a much bigger threat to men's power and status in more stratified societies.

MILD GENDER INEQUALITY

We can apply the principles that make for gender equality in hunting and gathering societies to see how they apply to small scale farming societies, where your rights come to you through lineage or clan membership, rather than automatically as a member of a band.

Before we can talk about the role of gender inequality in tribal societies, we need to go back a minute to talk about the kin-ordered mode of production as it operates in many tribal farming societies. In these societies who uses what resources is regulated by your lineage. But everyone belongs to a lineage and has rights in their own lineage resources and in the resources of their spouse's lineage. These lineages may be rather competitive, and may cooperate only when an external threat pushes them to do so. But within the lineage there is a great deal of cooperation. In a patrilineal society men of a lineage usually work together, often under the leadership of the lineage elders, both in clearing land for cultivation, in assembling gifts for egalitarian redistribution, and in their political relations with other lineages, clans, and tribes. Their wives farm the land the men have cleared. Usually there is relatively little cooperation between the wives. Each raises food to feed her own family and to contribute to her husband's and often brother's gift-giving. The wives, in other words, are

• **Want more?**
Try *'Tribal Women's Work in Madya Pradesh'* for a society with a fairly egalitarian sexual division of labor, but no mention is made of control of decisions and money.
http://www.ifad.org/gender/learning/role/workload/in_1_2.htm

doing much of the work of producing a surplus that will be used by men in equalitarian redistribution to enhance their own prestige. Nevertheless, this is all work done within the kin-ordered mode of production—both men and women are working to fulfill kinship obligations and with people who are determined by kinship. They are using resources that belong communally to the lineage as a whole.

> *Despite the fact that this system conveys rights, it also sets up the possibility of using other's labor for your own benefit. Men can benefit from getting their wives to work harder, because wives play a significant role in producing the surplus men will then give away.*

This is particularly true in patrilineal societies because it is not balanced off by men's contributions to their wives' and sisters' competitive efforts to raise their own status, as it often is in matrilineal societies. And you can also benefit from the work done by others of your own sex, usually younger members of your lineage who need your support in their own endeavors and will probably ultimately benefit themselves if you are successful. If you can talk them or manipulate them into turning their surplus over to you, and talk your spouse into producing more, then you have that much more to give away. So there is some reason in such societies to try to control the production and labor of other people, particularly of women.

War usually enhances the power of men as compared to women.

Another factor contributing to gender inequality is war. Men as warriors gain an importance that they don't have in bands. They are the defenders (or aggressors), a role not available in bands. Women, who are usually not trained as warriors/soldiers, are dependent on men as the protectors. They don't want to be stolen themselves, either to be married or to be enslaved. Nor do they want their crops or animals to be stolen, or the ceremonial valuables they have themselves acquired or helped men acquire. This increase in gender inequality is particularly noticeable in patrilineal societies, where men also control access to the means of production. In matrilineal tribes and chiefdoms men and women are often fairly equal, especially in those matrilineal societies where women control access to the means of production, while men control issues related to war and diplomacy. In patrilineal societies men control two important areas—access to the means of production and war. In matrilineal matrilocal societies men control one, women the other, leaving them more or less balanced.

Nevertheless in tribal societies this does not amount to serious exploitation. Nobody (including spouses) can force you to do anything, and allowing someone else to use your surplus does not leave you in trouble. In most horticultural societies the work-load is not especially heavy most of the time; producing a small surplus does not work you to death. Even in patrilineal tribal societies women do their own manipulating, often to benefit their own lineage. They are far from helpless in relation to their husbands, and can leave or quit cooperating if they are really dissatisfied. And frequently if a member of the lineage does well, the other members also gain a little prestige, and feel that their honor has been upheld – rather like how a small town feels when its football team beats the neighbors.

DENYING RIGHTS: GENDER INEQUALITY AND MARRIAGE IN RANKED SOCIETIES

In more stratified societies the emphasis is on conveying rights to a few and denying them to others. Gender, marriage, and gender roles in such societies are important in making sure that rights are conveyed only to the right people.

All of the conditions that lead to mild gender inequality in small scale farming societies are considerably more pronounced in ranked societies, particularly in patrilineal ones.

The whole system of rank is based on kinship: you get your position as commoner or aristocrat based on who your parents are. Privilege is conveyed 'in your blood;' privilege is believed to be literally a part of you. The denial of rights to privilege is also believed to be inborn. This distinction between categories of people is seen as natural, just as it is seen as natural that Elizabeth is queen—she has the right 'blood' and nobody else does. It is believed to be necessary to keep that bloodline 'pure,' so that the next generation will also carry the inborn right to privilege and to the title of king or queen. To ensure purity, the privileged category in a ranked society is *endogamous*—children have to marry other children in the privileged category. So the British royal family is expected to marry other members of the aristocracy, preferably from the ranks of other royal families. Recently that rule has become a little less strict, as Kate Middleton becomes the first commoner to marry an heir to the British throne in hundreds of years.

Endogamy
A pattern, preference, or requirement to marry a person who is a member of one's own social group or category.

In chiefdoms and most complex chiefdoms, as opposed to kingdoms, everyone is part of a lineage—that is, part of a corporate group—and lineages are often headed by someone with an inherited title. Some lineages rank higher than others, and have higher-ranking titles to pass along. This means people of high rank are relatives of the commoners in their own lineage. In a kingdom, however, the aristocratic families are entirely separate. Everyone in an aristocratic family is an aristocrat. Everyone in a commoner family is a commoner. They have no joint ancestor. In extremely stratified kingdoms commoners don't have lineages: they don't have corporate groups of kin that jointly control resources. All the resources are held by the aristocrats, leaving the commoners very much at the mercy of the aristocrats.

In a ranked society the aristocracy is generally endogamous, although there are some exceptions to this rule. In a kingdom parents in aristocratic lineages will arrange marriages for their children with members of aristocratic lineages. In a chiefdom endogamy works slightly differently, since there are high ranking people in many different lineages, rather than in just a few aristocratic lineages that are set off from the commoners: aristocratic parents arrange marriages for their children with children of comparable rank in other lineages or clans. Generally in chiefdoms and especially in complex chiefdoms a great deal of effort goes into making marriages that are as advantageous as possible, particularly in trying to make sure that the children of the marriage will be in line to inherit high-ranking titles. Marriage decisions also take into consideration the amount of wealth that will be given as dowry or bridewealth and in later marital exchanges—is the lineage a strong one with lots of commoners who can produce the surplus needed to enhance your child's and your own status? Marriages are also the basis of alliances between lineages, so a great deal of political maneuvering goes on.

Marriages may even be used to cement the relationship between a paramount chief and the chief of a conquered territory. If the paramount chief marries a daughter of the conquered chief, the conquered chief's grandchild in a patrilineal system will be in line for very high-ranking titles. Actually the paramount chief may marry many wives and cement many conquests in this way; extra titles may gradually be invented to accommodate more children. In a matrilineal society, the child of the paramount chief will be in line to inherit high titles in the conquered group. Either way, conquered and conqueror are now joined by kinship. The top ranks in the two groups will be relatives and children of the conqueror will be inheriting the right to control the conquered group.

Commoners are also endogamous, marrying within their category. However, very little is riding on their marriages. There are no titles to inherit, no position of authority within the lineage, no possibility of gaining wealth. Dowry or bridewealth are much smaller considerations. So commoners in ranked societies are far more likely to be allowed some choice in choosing a spouse. Generally there are rules for commoners, as there are for the aristocrats, about marrying outside your lineage and clan, and your elders may exert some pressure on you. Technically they may arrange your marriage, but they may arrange it with the person you pick. Your marriage will convey to your child rights to lineage resources, but at the same time will deny to your child rights to privilege.

This means that ranked societies need to control women's sexual behavior in order to keep commoners' children from inheriting privileges. Men's sexual behavior is rarely subjected to as strict restrictions as those imposed on women.

> *In actuality the whole system of ranking depends on regulating marriage and regulating women's sexual behavior.*

In ranked patrilineal societies a wife is frequently expected to have sex only with her husband, particularly if they are members of the aristocracy, to make sure that the children she has are actually of 'pure' blood. If marriage is a way of enabling men to claim children for their own lineages, then in ranked societies, where privileges are passed on from father to child, being sure that the child has a 'blood' right to that privilege is going to be important. In a tribe, where lineage and birth do not carry privileges, ensuring biological fatherhood is much less of an issue. This matters far more in patrilineal ranked societies than matrilineal ones, since in matrilineal societies the child's rights come from the mother.

Thus the whole system of marriage in ranked societies is generally more formally organized than in bands and small scale farming societies, and divorce may be much less common. This is partly because of the importance of keeping privilege in the family or lineage; commoners cannot be allowed to marry in and have their children inherit privilege. This formality is also associated with the greater importance of controlling people's labor and with the exchanges made based on kinship obligations.

In addition to the control of women to maintain pure bloodlines, and to the use of woman's labor, there is another important factor contributing to gender inequality in ranked societies. Warfare is common in chiefdoms, and far more is riding on the outcome of a war: both aristocrats and commoners have good reason to dread losing a war. Consequently, war brings even greater importance to men as soldiers than it does in tribal societies. Taking these conditions altogether, gender inequality is far more pronounced in patrilineal ranked societies than in tribal societies.

In some ranked matrilineal societies female control of resources may mitigate these conditions, although often not to the point of actual gender equality. However, in ranked matrilineal societies that are also matrilocal, a woman may actually be the head or co-head (with her brother) of a lineage. Such societies may include many ways in which a woman can gain a certain amount of power—but only if women control what they produce, and control the redistribution of what they produce. This right is considerably more likely for women in matrilocal, matrilineal societies, because they may hold the right to use land and houses as a group of related women; men in this case gain the right to farm a particular piece of land because of their relationship to the women, as sons, brothers, or husbands. In some such societies women are chiefs in their own right. In that case some titles with the rank of chief may be held only by women, while others must be held by men. In others, women may determine who among the eligible men will be chief or have the power to depose chiefs. As chiefs or other titled aristocrats women, like men, benefit from and create power on their own from the labor of women and men in other lineages. In societies with well-developed systems of gender diversity, where women can become men, they may purchase slaves and give bridewealth to marry wives, thus making for themselves a large household and retinue. Building wealth in people this way can make it possible to take on titles that are reserved for men. Or they may remain women but build a household through purchase of slaves and through paying bridewealth for men in their lineage. Paying the bridewealth conveys rights to children, so children from the marriage are hers, rather than the husband's. Women can reach positions of considerable power this way, sometimes even in patrilineal societies. This is a bit different from most patrilineal societies, where women who are part of the more powerful lineages also benefit from the labor of other people, but only through their relationships with men; rarely can they create their own personal power base.

STATES: FAMILY AND GENDER

In states where the means of production is held privately by individuals or families, rather than by larger kin-based corporate groups, the family tends to be a more formally recognized and bounded unit than in more equalitarian societies. The *family* in such societies is an economic unit, responsible for the care of children and other dependent members, and it has to adjust itself to the economy it has to deal with. Families can be very large, with several generations living together, called an *extended family*. *Nuclear families* include only parents and their children. In most societies some form of extended family is common, and often seen as ideal. Having numerous adults means a sharing of work and responsibility, providing greater security for the members, although often less individual freedom.

Polygyny and polyandry, like extended families, are also ways of forming larger families. As in other societies, polygyny may be a status symbol for elite men in states. But even where it is permitted, it may be fairly rare in states unless women are a major source of labor as they are in many chiefdoms, adding to a family's wealth or productivity. However, in many states the ideal wives' work is primarily to raise children who are well-trained in elite ways, to produce meals for guests, and to maintain a household in a way that upholds the family honor. In that case more wives mean more expense, and only the elite can afford polygynous families. Most commonly in states each wife does not have her own household, and it is frequently the responsibility of the first wife to manage the entire household. The position of head wife often carries a great deal of prestige, and families trying to arrange marriages for their daughters will place great value on

Family
An intimate kin-based group, consisting, usually, of at least a woman and her children.*

Extended family
A family consisting of three or more generations living together.*

Nuclear family
A family consisting only of parents and their children living together.

getting a position as head wife. However, being a minor wife to an extremely rich man also has its advantages over being the only wife of a poor man. The wife is less likely to be worked to death, she will probably be well fed, and the children will grow up with advantages and the possibility of inheritance.

The *dowry* system, rather than bridewealth, is common in patrilineal states, where the control of private property is at stake. The bride's family gives her share of the family estate to her at marriage. In some societies the dowry actually is supposed to belong to the bride, and is seen as a form of insurance for her, to be sold to benefit her and her children if necessary. However, instead of keeping it as insurance, the bride is sometimes made to hand over the dowry to her in-laws. But in other societies the dowry really is meant to go directly to the husband or husband's family. Unless she has no brothers, the bride's dowry usually does not include land. The husband may use the wealth in the dowry to buy land to extend the family estate. The bride's brothers will inherit their own family's land. They may use their own brides' dowries to add to their share of the land.

Because the family is an economic unit, and because stratification determines a family's access to resources, family structures in a society vary according to the family's position in the stratification system. All families in states have to deal with the effects of stratification, but some families have far more options than others do.

Members of the elite frequently claim that the family and household system of those at the bottom of the stratification system is immoral—they have too many kids, or mothers don't stay home to take care of them, or they do stay home when they shouldn't, or there are too many or too few men involved, or they have too few or too many people living in the same household. Such patterns are attributed to inferiority, not to economic structures and policies.

Nuclear families and single-parent families, dependent on just one or two adults, run into serious trouble if one of the adults gets sick or dies. Nuclear families are more able to move, however, which is why most nomadic foraging bands are composed of several nuclear families. The band can easily split when necessary. It is also why economic circumstances may cause extended families to break into smaller, more mobile units, even in societies where the extended family is the ideal. When a society industrializes and more people become dependent on wages and on individually getting an education and a job, nuclear families also become more common, particularly among the well-off. Nuclear families that have been successful may separate in order to keep their income themselves, rather than contribute to the large extended family. The extended family operates as a single unit in which individuals are expected to put the needs of the whole fam-

Dowry
Wealth transferred from the bride's family to the bride, or more frequently to her husband or his family. In some societies this wealth is seen as giving the bride her share of the family property, transferred at marriage rather than as inheritance on the death of her parents.

• **Want more?**
On economic changes affecting family patterns in the US try *The New Instability* http://www.nytimes.com/2014/07/27/opinion/sunday/the-new-instability.html?_r=0

ily ahead of their own individual desires or needs. Extended families may remain common among people living on dying wages—they often can't afford to live separately.

Both the very poor and the very rich tend to have large families, and for similar kinds of reasons: family is who you can count on. The poor see children as the best investment they can make in their future and in the future of their other children. In both agricultural and industrialized society there are many people with very little besides family to fall back on. This includes the people who do not own the means of production or who have been denied access to an education and therefore have difficulty selling their labor at decent prices. For them, sickness, unemployment, and various kinds of crises mean you had better have a large group of relatives; one of them may be able to help you out. People who are better off have more options. They can have servants, or can fall back on health insurance, hire daycare, get help in seeking employment, buy homes instead of rent them. A large family is not so critical if you have other resources.

Even in significantly industrialized societies agricultural workers such as sharecroppers, as well as peasant families, often have very large families, and landlords often look for large families. Since large families provide more labor for the farming family, it is usually considered to be women's duty to produce many children, as well as to work on the land. With many children the chances are better that some of them will be in a position to take care of their parents in old age. Both men and women work far more hours than they do in egalitarian or ranked societies, and have to deal with the stresses and uncertainties caused by poverty and dependency. Women often work several hours a day more than men.

Landowning families, particularly if they are well to do in a less industrialized state, may also have large families. Children are assets: their marriages can be used to cement alliances with other landowning families. And the rich need heirs who can be trusted to prioritize family interests because they themselves benefit if the family investments and business enterprises do well. Among landowning families physical labor is often looked down on, especially for women. Having women who do little physical work becomes a status symbol, proving that you have people to do such work for you. Men in ordinary landowning families may do physical work, but if they are really wealthy they, like their wives, typically do little physical work. They may even have overseers or supervisors who relieve them of the need to deal with the agricultural workers at all. Women in elite families may not work much harder physically than do the men, since servants do much of the work of raising children and dealing with the house and food preparation. However, managing a large household labor force may take a great deal of time and managerial talent. Women are also responsible for making sure that children learn behavior and knowledge appropriate to elite status, and, like women in poorer landowning families and in agricultural laboring families, they may be expected to be more or less continually pregnant.

As a society industrializes, the requirement that a good wife produce many children is often eased in better off families. Instead of investing in many children, they are now expected to make a heavy investment in the education of just a few children, with the expectation that the education will pay off in middle class status and a good income for the children. But for those families that regularly experience the roadblocks that deny their children a good education and good enough medical care so that they can all be expected to live, having a very few children does not make sense.

> *Families become smaller only when poorer people are able to force their society to convey rights to them that provide them with security. They limit family size when they can believe that if they have only two children both will live to adulthood, that they will get a decent education, that education leads to decent pay, and that there will be money for their care in their old age.*

The lowering of wages in the U.S. has forced changes in many working class families by requiring that they have two wage earners. It is rare that women 'stay home and just take care of the kids.' It is true that this pattern was common in the U.S. among middle-income White families for a fairly brief period after World War II. Women from the more exploited parts of our population have generally worked outside the home throughout our history, and except for that brief period, non-elite women at home workplaces worked hard at productive labor on farms, or at other enterprises such as running boarding houses or weaving.

GENDER INEQUALITY IN STATES

> *The control of women reaches its extremes in patrilineal states that are both severely stratified and where inheritance, birthright or rank determine whether you have rights to the means of production.*

Remember that in mildly stratified societies, such as chiefdoms, biological fatherhood is important, particularly if the society is patrilineal? This was because privileges were being passed from aristocratic father to son, and kept commoners from being able to inherit privileges. But remember also that commoners had access to the means of production, and that they were not being severely exploited. You could have a good life as a commoner. Things are quite different in a severely stratified society. The rights that are being passed along are not just perks; instead they matter deeply in terms of very basic things like whether you have enough to eat, whether you are old at thirty-five, how many of your children die, and whether you live in a state of permanent exhaustion. If position is inherited and matters at the basic level of life and death, then a family with high position will be deeply concerned with making sure that the children who inherit that position are the legitimate heirs.

Being a legitimate heir requires two things. First, simply being the child of a particular man is not enough. For you to be legitimate, your mother must be a licensed 'heir-bearer.' In most states that means that she must be married to the man.

• **Want more?**
For rules governing US marriages until fairly recently try *Women and the Law* http://www.library.hbs.edu/hc/wes/collections/women_law/

The marriage license is a contract giving her the right to have children he fathers biologically, and giving her the right to expect that he live up to the social expectations of fatherhood—she and the children have the right to at least minimal financial support and the children have the right to inherit from him. The contract gives him the right to expect sexual and support services from her, and gives him the right to claim authority over her children. The legitimacy of children—that is, the licensing of a woman to have children because she is attached to a particular man who claims both biological and social fatherhood—is not of great importance in bands and tribes, and often not among the commoners in a chiefdom, or among the most exploited groups in a state. This is because there is nothing to inherit; who your father is does not make a big difference.

Second, being a legitimate heir requires that the mother's husband is really the father of the child.

This is also true in many chiefdoms and complex chiefdoms, but there it is rarely seen as so important that a woman can be killed if she is believed to have violated this rule or is believed not to be a virgin at marriage. This is because much more is at stake in a state, and it is not obvious who the father of a baby is. Biological motherhood is never in question, but biological fatherhood is. Nobody asks, "Are you really the mother of the baby you gave birth to?" Asking, "Are you really the biological father of the baby your wife just gave birth to?" does make sense. The only way for anyone but the mother to be absolutely sure—at least before DNA testing—is to be absolutely positive a woman never has even the slightest chance to have sex with someone else.

So a rigidly enforced double standard is usually associated with severely stratified societies where the property is passed through the male line.

A rigid double standard means that women can't have sex with anyone but their husband, and sometimes can't even be seen near other men. Men have the exclusive right to sex with their wives, and wives generally do not have the right to say no. Men, on the other hand, can have sex with other women because children he might father with them will never be heirs: they are illegitimate because their mothers are not licensed. The only real restriction on men is that they can't have sex with some other man's licensed heir-bearer—that would be trespassing on the other man's right to legitimate children.

If inequality is so highly developed that the elite can afford to support women who are prevented from doing many kinds of productive labor, then women may be prevented from leaving home on their own.

If a woman cannot go out, or cannot go out without a chaperon, it is much easier to be sure that the husband is actually the biological father of any children she may have.

Purdah
The isolation of women from men in public (Arabic term); in some societies this means that women live their lives almost entirely within the household.

• Want more?
Many Muslim women are comfortable with head coverings; try *Muslim Women Uncover Myths about the Hijab* http://www.cnn.com/2009/US/08/12/generation.islam.hijab/

Purdah is one way of controlling women's movements and keeping them protected, both from other men and from their own supposedly insatiable desire for sex, which causes them to tempt men. Binding upper-class girls' feet in China was another way of accomplishing this control, by making it difficult for the woman to go anywhere without help. Before you get too ethnocentric, notice that high heels are bad for backs and feet and also make it difficult for women to move around freely, making women much more vulnerable to attack. Control of women's movements in some rural subcultures in the U.S. was achieved into the 1970s by the belief that women shouldn't learn to drive. The belief that it should be men who take women places lingers on in patterns that say it is more manly for the man to be the driver, and that men are better drivers than women. And it continues to be far more reprehensible for a woman to spend a great deal of time away from home than for a man to do the same thing.

Rape is generally common in societies where controlling women's sexuality and behavior is important.

The U.S. has a high rape rate, and fear of rape and harassment frequently prevents women from going places or doing things alone. This reaction is reinforced by blaming the woman for getting herself raped. Blaming the victim this way means that gossip and blame focuses mainly on the woman, taking attention off the behavior of the man who raped her.

Generally it is the families with rights to pass on who are most insistent on following these rules, such as purdah, for controlling women. Others may follow them as much as they can because they mark high status and because they are often enforced by religion. However, poorer families may need to have women working in the fields or involved in marketing the family's produce, or doing other activities that take them out on their own. Consequently, the lives and behavior of women in landowning and elite families may be much more rigidly controlled than are the lives of peasant women or workers. This gives the elite and collaborator class an excuse to claim that the people being exploited have immoral families and therefore benefit by being controlled by the people above them.

In societies with a market economy and a class-based social structure there may be a gradual shift away from such tight control of women. In such societies inherited position is not the only way to own the means of production, and owning the means of production is not the only way to get enough money to support your family. If your position is not rigidly fixed at birth and if you can buy the means of production, or if you can sell your labor, then who your father is becomes somewhat less important. This is particularly true when there is little to inherit. Family honor may still demand the double standard, but it is no longer a matter of life and death, and eventually the concept of legitimacy can become irrelevant, as it is rapidly becoming in the U.S. Nevertheless, upper class families continue to work hard to make sure their children fall in love with, marry, and have children by, people they define as appropriate for the production of heirs.

> *The shift away from the rigid control of women doesn't necessarily bring with it real gender equality, although inequality may be less pronounced.*

• **Want more?**
For a film that includes the effects of development on women try searching *"Ancient Futures: Learning from Ladakh"* (Note: this is a polyandrous society.)

On the other hand, as described in the section on gender inequality in Chapter Two, the shift to a market economy in societies where women previously had some autonomy very frequently leads to greater gender inequality. Women in some societies have recently been more thoroughly incorporated into the workplace in situations where they regularly interact with men. Previously women had worked almost entirely in situations like sewing factories or nursing which excluded men, partly so that fathers and husbands would allow them to work there. Nevertheless, most women in the U.S. and around the world who work away from home or farm still work in situations where nearly all the people they come in contact with are women. But even women who have broken away from that gender-segregated pattern are subject to the glass ceiling when it comes to promotions, and may be subjected to sexual harassment, frequently by men who feel their manhood is threatened by having to treat a woman as an equal. Sexual harassment is a means of maintaining the traditional male right to the better jobs. And simply working outside the home doesn't necessarily gain power for women. If what they produce, or their paycheck, is taken away, either by father or husband, then they are simply working harder without any increase in their power to determine their own lives or to influence the decisions made by others. And they are in addition, like most men, experiencing the inequality of the class relationship between the owner of the means of production and the worker.

There is an added consequence of gender inequality added by climate change itself in the context of the war machine. Because the war machine profits from providing more and more weapons, small scale conflicts are far more lethal. Women suffer all the obvious common consequences of civilians in war—death, dismemberment, starvation, death of loved ones—but in addition they are often targeted specifically as women. Rape, for instance, is rampant during wars, and is often performed in front of husbands, fathers, and sons, and is a statement of dominance over the men who are unable to provide protection. It is a form of one-upsman-ship which is particularly potent in patriarchal societies where gender norms mean that the woman is no longer an appropriate heir bearer—men's property rights have been damaged, as well as causing emotional turmoil for both the woman had her family. Climate change is arguably making such conflicts more common; wars become more likely as shortages of basic resources such as water and farmable land exacerbate existing tensions. Since it is primarily women who do the difficult work of holding a family together, of feeding people, and of caring for the sick, injured, and emotionally stressed, women carry more than their share of the burdens imposed by both war and climate disasters. Statistically, since women make up far more than half the world's poor, they are also more vulnerable to the poverty-related consequences of droughts and floods. But in addition, gender norms which restrict women to homes or that make women reluctant to seek help mean that women are more likely than men to die during climate disasters. And it is often women who deal with the day to day drudgery of coping with the less dramatic consequences of climate change—water shortages, lack of fuel, lack of food, caring for those sick from new diseases spreading with rising temperatures.

LOOKING AHEAD: PATRIARCHY

Attitudes about gender and gender inequality in stratified societies are important ideological building stones of patriarchy, which is itself critical in maintaining elite hegemony. Consequently gender plays a role in racial and class inequality; gender inequality is about more than inequality between men and women. Chapter Seven discusses how patriarchy works with other ideological constructs to maintain stratification.

• **Want more?**
Try *War Hits Home When It Hits Women and Girls* http://www.unicef.org/graca/women.htm

• **Want more?**
For consequences of the burden on women in the US scroll down in *The Uncounted* http://www.cnn.com/interactive/2014/03/us/uncounted-suicides/

• **Want more?**
Try *Women Are More Likely lo Die* http://www.smh.com.au/national/women-more-likely-to-die-in-natural-disasters-20151120-gl420j.html

REFERENCES/SUGGESTED READINGS

Ethnographies focusing on gender

Bonvillain, Nancy 1980 Iroquoian Women. *In* Studies on Iroquoian Culture. N. Bonvillain, ed. Man in the Northeast, Occasional Publications in Northeastern Anthropology 6: 47-58.

Endicott, Kirk and Karen Endicott 2008 The Headman was a Woman: The Gender Egalitarian Batek of Malaysia. Long Grove IL: Waveland Press.

Jensen, Joan 1995 Native American Women and Agriculture: A Seneca Case Study. *In* Unequal Sisters: A Multicultural Reader in U.S. Women's History. Vicki Ruiz and Carol DuBois, eds. Pp 70-84. New York: Routledge.

Murphy, Yolanda and Robert Murphy 2004 [1974] Women of the Forest. New York: Columbia University Press.

Perdue, Theda 1998 Cherokee Women: Gender and Culture Change, 1700-1835. Lincoln: University of Nebraska Press.

Sanday, Peggy 2002 Women at the Center: Life in a Modern Matriarchy. Ithaca: Cornell University Press.

Strathern, Marilyn 1972 Women in Between: Female Roles in a Male World. New York: Seminar Press.

Analysis and illustration of theory related to gender equality

Bonvillain, Nancy 2006 Cultural Anthropology. Upper Saddle River, NJ: Pearson Prentice Hall. Pp.198-203.

Brown, Judith 1976 Economic Organization and the Position of Women among the Iroquois. *In* Toward an Anthropology of Women, R Rieter, ed. Pp 235-251. New York: Monthly Review Press.

Draper, Patricia 1975 !Kung Women: Contrasts in Sexual Egalitarianism in Foraging and Sedentary Contexts. In Toward an Anthropology of Women. R. Reiter, ed. Pp. 77-109. New York: Monthly Review Press.

Kugel, Rebecca and Lucy Murphy 2008 Native Women's History in Eastern North America before 1900: A Guide to Research and Writing. Lincoln: University of Nebraska Press.

Lamphere, Louise 2001 The Domestic Sphere of Women and the Public Sphere of Men: The Strengths and Limitations of an Anthropological Dichotomy. In Gender in Cross-Cultural Perspective, 3rd ed. C. Brettell and C. Sargent eds. Pp.100-110.   Upper Saddle River NJ: Prentice Hall.

Stark, Jill 2015. Women more likely to die in natural disasters. Sydney Morning Herald 11/22. http://www.smh.com.au/national/women-more-likely-to-die-in-natural-disasters-20151120-gl420j.html. Accessed 1/8/16

On gender diversity

Achebe, Nwando. 2005. Farmers, Traders, Warriors, and Kings: Female Power and Authority Authority in Northern Igboland 1900-1960. Portsmouth NH: Heinemann.

Amadiume, Ifi. 1987. Male Daughters, Female Husbands: Gender and Sex n an African Society. London: Zed Books.

Jacobs, Sue-Ellen, Wesley Thomas, and Sabine Lang, eds. 1997 Two-Spirit People: Native American Gender Identity, Sexuality, and Sprituality. Urbana: University of Illinois Press.

Martin, M. Kay and Barbara Voorhies 1975 Supernumerary Sexes. In Female of the Species. Kay Martin and Barbara Voorhies, eds. Pp.84-107. New York: Columbia University Press.

Nanda, Serena 1990 Neither Man Nor Woman: The Hijaras of India. Belmont CA: Wadsworth.

Williams, Walter 1992 The Spirit and the Flesh: Sexual Diversity in American Indian Culture. Boston: Beacon Press.

Varieties of Marriage

Hua, Cai 2001 A Society without Fathers or Husbands: The Na of China. Cambridge MA: Zone Books/MIT Press.

Levine, Nancy 1998 The Dynamics of Polyandry: Kinship, Domesticity, and Population in the Tibetan Border. Chicago: University of Chicago Press.

Mencher, Joan 1965 The Nayars of South Malabar. *In* Comparative Family Systems. M.E. Nimkoff, ed. Pp. 162-191. Boston: Houghton Mifflin.

Oboler, Regina Smith 1980 Is the Female Husband a Man? Woman/Woman Marriage Among the Nandi of Kenya. Ethnology 19:69-88

Slavery and gender before the Atlantic slave trade

Campbell, Gwyn, ed. 2004. The Structure of Slavery in the Indian Ocean Africa and Asia. Portland OR: Frank Cass.

Meillassoux, Claude. 1991 [1986]. The Anthropology of Slavery: The Womb of Iron and Gold. Alide Dasnois, tr. Chicago: University of Chicago Press.

Miller, Joseph. 2012. The Problem of Slavery as History: A Global Approach. New Haven: Yale University Press.

CHAPTER 6
FACTORING IN RACE, CASTE, AND CLASS

In states the systems for denying rights to the people who are most seriously exploited—and at the same time for conveying rights to those who most benefit from exploiting people—include gender, birthright, race, caste, and class in various combinations. The resulting stratification systems thus cover a fairly wide range of possibilities. As systems for denying rights in states, feudalism and capitalism use significantly different combinations.

In some ways feudalism and capitalism may seem quite different, but there is one basic underlying similarity. Both use a system of stratification to set up two categories of people, those who own the means of production and those who don't. Those who don't own have no choice but to provide labor to create surplus, and therefore wealth, for the small group of owners.

This system can be shown in a simple diagram (diagram 2). It may help to keep this diagram in mind as you read. Notice that the value going to the owner is greater than that being given in compensation. If this weren't so, if the owner gave back as much as the owner received, no wealth would accumulate in the owner's hands. In a capitalist system the difference in the size of the two arrows will generally be greater than in a feudal system. In other words, capitalism is the more effective system of wealth accumulation. But in both cases, the society is organized as a system for allowing surplus to accumulate in just a few hands—which is the whole point of a stratification system. Having such a system is one of the necessary underlying conditions of inequality. In states, both kingdoms and republics, as compared to complex chiefdoms, ordinary people have few rights to counteract that accumulation. Having a really efficient accumulation system is the mark of a state. And such efficient systems are necessarily accompanied by *structural violence*—those at the bottom of the stratification system really suffer, and some die, from the consequences of inequality, even if the elite they are directly in contact with are not particularly greedy or bear any particular ill-will towards them. They suffer because the denial of rights is seen as perfectly normal, so very hard labor, hunger, dying children, early death are all also seen as perhaps unfortunate, but perfectly normal. Bear in mind that this is what many Americans think about immigrants to the US. Bear in mind also that climate change is predicted to bring far more immigrants to the U.S., particularly if

Structural violence
Violence that is not a result of individuals or the state taking direct action to harm others. Structural violence generally results from inequality built into the social structure and results in deaths, maimings, malnutrition among those most seriously exploited. A death resulting from a society's refusal to commit adequate tax money to care for the poor is an example of structural violence. A death caused by murder is not.

austerity programs imposed to service debt make it impossible for governments such as Mexico's to sustain even minimal social services to desperate people. Will the U.S. enforce the suffering there with a 'Fortress America' ideology, using razor wire, walls, and tanks along the borders?

While both feudal and capitalist societies are divided into these two basic categories, the categories themselves can be divided. Not all capitalists are rich, for instance. Many family farmers own the means of production but are deep in debt and have a lot of trouble paying their bills. So do the owners of many small businesses. Many feudal fief-holders, while far better off than their serfs, were also far from rich, especially when compared to higher-ranked people with better fiefs and with fief-holders of their own.   And if you don't own the means of production you are not necessarily poor. Retainers in the king's courts, for instance, were often wealthier than many fief-holders. Managers of factories and businesses are selling their managerial abilities to the owners of those businesses, usually for a great deal of money, and often are wealthier than many small business owners.

• **Want more?**
Explore website *U.S/ Mexico Border Militarization* http://afsc.org/key-issues/issue/us-mexico-border-militarization

> *Both the capitalist and feudal modes of production require people who have little choice, so that they will 'agree' to be cheap labor. Therefore in both systems some people must be selected to end up in that situation and then denied the rights that would give them choices.*

Diagram 2: Basic Organization of a Stratified Society

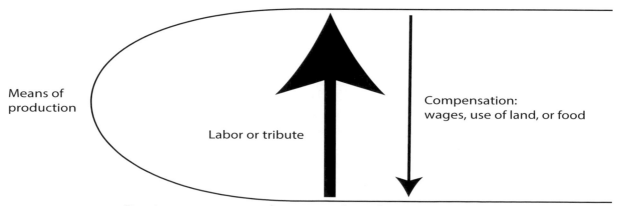

Own or control means of production
- Class: capitalists, including small farm and business owners
- Feudal: feudal lord, independent craft and merchants
- Caste: landowning castes, business castes

Means of production

Labor or tribute

Compensation: wages, use of land, or food

Don't own or control means of production, provide labor
- Bureaucrats, managers, supervisors, retainers
(manage & control rest of workers)
- Working class, serfs, slaves, sharecroppers, laboring castes
(provide labor)

CASTE

Caste
A hereditary endogamous occupational social group in a society in which everyone is a member of such a group and the groups are arranged in a hierarchy of purity, prestige, and power.

• **Want more?** For the caste system generally and the role of colonialism in caste try searching "Cataracts of Silence: Race on the Edge of Indian Thought."

The *caste system* was originally a way of organizing a feudal-like mode of production, particularly within the numerous small kingdoms which now make up India. It has now been adapted to the capitalist mode. As a factor on which to base inequality, the caste system is the tightest of the systems for assigning position by birth. There is no flexibility, even in the middle. Each occupation has its own caste, although today many new occupations are not tied to caste. In a caste system, all individuals are born into their family's caste, work at the caste occupation, marry within the caste, and follow caste rules for interacting with other castes. Castes are ranked one above another, and those at the top are believed to be purer or holier than those at the bottom. Caste is a permanent system of stratification: you can't change your caste. However, a caste as a whole is sometimes able to raise its status.

India is the classic example of a society with a full-blown caste system. Nevertheless, there is significant evidence that the system was somewhat less rigid before the British conquered India. Colonial bureaucrats appear to have tightened the system because it gave them more control and simplified management problems. They found shifting, flexible, or ambiguous categories of people hard to understand and so they legally defined castes and caste membership. So the 'classic' caste system may be to some extent the product of imperialism. In any case, caste in this classic sense has been a dominant feature of India's social structure for at least several hundred years.

The vast majority of Indians are members of a caste. Caste is rejected by Indian Muslims, but it does apply to Hindus and to many Christian denominations in India. Caste was the basis for a very complex division of labor and power, and to some extent still is, although discrimination based on caste is now illegal. There are many people who, while acknowledging the existence of caste, deny that it is relevant to their own lives or to their interactions with other people, and do not follow many caste rules.

A classic caste system generally defines caste occupations very specifically, and ranks all occupations one above another. Being a member of a low caste does not guarantee that you will be poor. Someone who is a member of the potter caste might perhaps run a large pottery business and do quite well financially. However, a wealthy potter is still a potter, and will be seen as an inferior person by most members of higher castes. Such a potter would have to marry another potter, since castes are endogamous, and their children would be potters, since caste is hereditary. But being in a lower caste does make it far less likely that you will be well off, even though it is possible. And being in the highest castes doesn't mean you will be wealthy. Those castes that own the means of production are the most likely to be well-to-do. However, in many parts of India those castes, the land-owning and business castes, were not the very highest. The highest castes, the

Brahmin castes, were typically priests, teachers, and administrators for the local kings and big landowners, and later for the British. Some were extremely poor; nevertheless, they were perceived as ritually purer and therefore superior to even the landowning castes.

Women in poorer families worked in the caste occupation in addition to generally doing all the childcare and housework for their family. Women in wealthier or high caste families generally did an enormous amount of housework, or supervised servants, but did not work in the caste occupation. So a wife in a poor potter family might spend most of her time doing jobs defined as women's work in pottery making, and care for her children at the same time. Children would also be assigned tasks at a very early age. But a wife in a better off potter family would not do pottery tasks. Instead those tasks would be done by other very poor potters who were attached to the family as laborers and servants.

Most people in India were, and still are, involved in agricultural work. In the classic system large landowners of the land-owning castes owned most of the land or held it in a fief-like arrangement—the system appears to have varied considerably in different places and over India's long history. And in some areas, particularly mountains, a more egalitarian system apparently held sway.

In most of India most people without land in each village worked on the landowner's land as laborers. The owner or his representative directed their work. When the crop was harvested each laborer was given a specified number of bushels of grain. There were also religious festivals when agricultural workers were given clothes. They had the use of land on the edge of the village for building a very small house and sometimes a very small plot to cultivate for their own use. Other people without land did their caste occupation, making the village's pottery, or doing the laundry, or taking care of cows. Like the agricultural workers, they were given a specified amount of grain by each landowner when the harvest was brought in, as well as clothes and space for a house. All of these landless people were being seriously exploited by the landowners, but they did receive, in most cases, enough to just barely survive. However, the very lowest castes, the Dalit (formerly called untouchable) who cleaned streets and latrines and dealt with dead animals (and in some areas also were agricultural workers), did work that was considered so polluting that they were not supposed to touch members of the higher castes. They had to live outside the village, and were seen as barely human by many people in higher castes. Their exploitation was severe—and in many cases still is. Once India gained its independence from England in the 1940s more agricultural people, including some Dalits, were able to own their own land. The new Indian government passed laws forcing the break-

• **Want more?**
Try *India's Dalits Still Fighting Untouchability* http://www.bbc.com/ news/world-asia-india-18394914

up of the old big estates; the land had to be given to the people who did the work on it, although the landowners were allowed to keep enough to ensure an adequate income for themselves. Landless Dalits in rural India now often receive wages instead of part of the crop, but the wages are so low that it is totally impossible to survive on them—in many cases they are actually worse off than before. Desperate Dalits often become bonded laborers, essentially selling themselves as permanent laborers to the landowners in return for handouts of food and some kind of roof over their heads.

Who can get which jobs today in the newer industrialized capitalist sectors of the economy in India is based on a combination of class (which we will discuss next) and caste. Caste is still more important than class in jobs that existed before industrialization. For instance, there is a caste whose traditional occupation is washing clothes. It still helps to be a member of that caste to get a job in the laundry industry. Each occupation had its own caste, and that caste still has a traditional right to those jobs. However, it is now possible for members of any caste to get jobs that were not part of the old caste system, such as nuclear physicists or college presidents or factory workers. In fact, however, it is easier for members of the higher castes to get the better paid positions since it is easier for them to be in the middle- or upper-income groups, due to their traditional control of the means of production or to caste occupations that were likely to bring greater income. With larger incomes, on average, the higher castes have an easier time getting an education and are more able to pull strings, and are thus more likely to be able to get the jobs that depend on an education and provide a middle class wage.

CLASS

Republics, and industrial societies in general, are organized to assign rights or deny them through a class system instead of through caste or ranking. Class is another of the factors on which inequality is based. In a class system there are two basic classes, an idea introduced in Chapter One. In the capitalist mode of production the means of production are privately owned (not controlled by hereditary right through the authority of a chief or king). Unlike the tributary mode, capitalism makes it possible to buy and sell land. But there are other means of production too—factories, mines, bulldozers, ships, warehouses—everything (except labor) that is needed in producing the goods needed in a capitalist society.

A relatively small number of people own the means of production. This is the capitalist class.

But to actually produce anything, they also need labor—the working class. Family farmers, mom and pop businesses, small con-

• **Want more?**
Try *Bonded Labor in India* http://www.indiacelebrating.com/social-issues/bonded-labour-system/

• **Want more?** Try *Caste is not Past* http://www.nytimes.com/2013/06/16/opinion/sunday/caste-is-not-past.html?_r=0

tractors all own very small amounts of the means of production and therefore are able to supply most of their own labor. But people who own much larger amounts of the means of production, or who are selling a very *labor intensive* product, can't possibly do all the work themselves. Unless they can get additional labor, owning a huge factory or a fast food franchise won't do them any good.

CLASS AS A FACTOR FOR PRODUCING INEQUALITY

In the capitalist mode of production most people don't own the means of production. Consequently they don't, on their own, have the resources to feed, house, and clothe themselves. They are denied the right to farm or mine or make hamburgers using the means of production belonging to someone else. If necessary, force will be used to protect the rights of the property owners, and trespassers find themselves in jail—putting you in a cage is an effective way of denying you access to the means of production. So if you aren't an owner, then all you do have is your ability to work. You will need to find someone who needs your labor. So you sell your labor—your ability to work—and the person who buys your labor owns what you produce. The owner then sells what you produce, trying to make as big a profit as possible. The profit is what is left above the costs of production, including the cost of materials and your wages. The profit belongs to the owner, not to the people who did the work of production.

This is the class system, which is associated with capitalist societies. Class systems divide people into economic strata based on their position in the labor market. When you look for a job at a fast food place, you are looking for an opportunity to sell your labor (remember the fast food workers in Chapter One?). You are in the working class because you sell your labor in the labor market.

Your employer does not own you. You can't be bought or sold, as you could be if you were a slave, and after you leave each day your ability to work belongs to you again. And you aren't a serf, either.

> You may feel like your job makes you a slave or a serf, but it really doesn't. It is just a lousy job.

You aren't tied to the fast food place; you can quit and work somewhere else. But since you aren't a serf, the owner doesn't have to give you lots of holiday meals or provide you with fuel for your home.

The owner of the fast food joint is in the capitalist class because he or she owns (or rents and therefore controls) the means of production—the tools and building. The manager of the fast food joint is in the working class like you, but in the professional/managerial part of the class. The manager is also selling his or her labor, but in a better paid part of the labor market than you are.

Labor intensive
A crop or product that requires proportionately more hours of work than most others.*

Diagram 3 illustrates the relationship between classes. Notice that this diagram is an expansion of diagram 2, which illustrates stratification in general. Diagram 3 shows how stratification operates in a capitalist society.

The professional/managerial class consists of managers of businesses, architects, accountants, engineers, teachers, social workers, tax collectors, government officials, judges, police, military officers, prison wardens, nurses, the president, members of Congress, and many others. Together it is their job to make labor profitable. Part of their job is making the workers themselves productive, which requires educating, supervising, and controlling them so they work hard and don't revolt or threaten the power of the capitalist class, or fight among themselves so much that conditions for business are insecure. Others in this class design the machinery and technology and production processes so that the workers' labor produces as much as possible. The class as a whole forms an intermediate buffer class between the people who are being exploited and the people who become wealthy from exploitation. Many, but not all, are very well paid for their services to the capitalist class. Some are paid by the capitalists directly; others are paid by government agencies, using tax money.

Diagram 3: Class Structure in a Capitalist Society

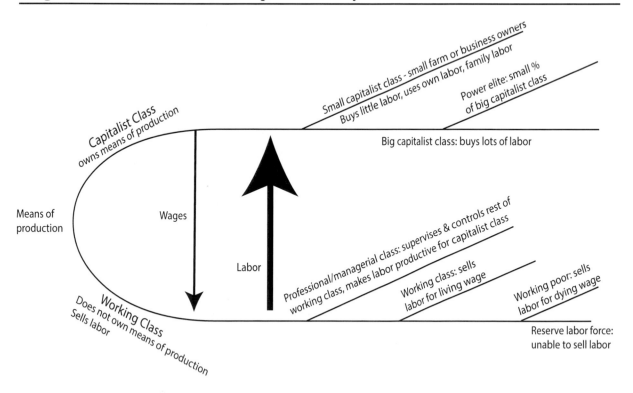

> *In a class system you are supposed to earn your position, not inherit it. In reality, most children 'inherit' advantages or disadvantages from their parents, and children of the owning class also inherit wealth and property.*

In a class system it is possible to change position. Technically it is possible to shift from the very lowest to the very highest positions. In reality most shifts are quite small, and most children end up in much the same position as their parents were. The capitalist class and those in the professional/managerial class who sell their labor for a good price are usually able to give their children advantages, either through education or inheritance, which allow the children to have positions similar to those of the parents. Similar advantages are denied to the children of people who sell their labor under poor conditions, or who can't find people to buy their labor at all. Their children are also likely to end up living and working under conditions similar to those of their parents. However, despite the advantages given to some and the denial of those advantages to others, some do change class. Class systems in some states make it relatively easy to change position; in others, it is much more difficult. Changing position is much harder in societies with high degrees of inequality, such as the US, where, since the 1980s, more and more people go through their lives in the same position as their parents. But in Canada, for instance, with greater equality than in the US, more people who start out poor are able to get an education and then a good job.

> *Denying some children decent educations, enough to eat, or adequate health care means there will be a supply of workers in the next generation who have little choice but to work for low wages.*

• **Want more?** Try *Back to School, and to Widening Inequalities'* http://robertreich.org/post/95749319170

Class systems include road blocks, such as poor educations, to make sure that a large number of people are prevented from making the choices that would place them in well-paid or ownership positions. Various combinations of race, religion, ethnicity, and gender often determine which people are given road blocks and which people are given a glide-path for making such choices. In a caste system or a feudal system the decision about who will have the least desirable positions is already determined by birth. Who gets the glide-path is an issue of political power; political power usually results from control of resources. So we are back to conveying or denying rights. Those with resources use their political power to enforce their right to benefit from other people's labor.

As a society industrializes, it is likely to shift toward a class system. Rules that ascribed status at birth are gradually modified. India, for instance, still has a caste system, and marriage and many other interactions are determined significantly by caste, but it also has a class system. Caste is no longer the formal and legal system for determining your occupation or in determining whether you are someone who owns the means of production, whether you are in the intermediate group, or whether you provide labor for very low wages. In a similar way in the U.S. race is no longer legally the single most important factor in predicting which group someone is in. However, people who own the means of production in both societies continue to need very cheap labor, and caste and race are now significant in informal systems for denying rights and creating people with few choices. So caste and race are important in creating the class system.

> **In a class system there is a more or less constant struggle over who will have to take the least desirable positions.**

RACE AS A FACTOR FOR CREATING INEQUALITY

Race has served two different but related functions in the U.S. It has been an important factor on which to base the inequality needed to create a cheap labor force. Equally important it, along with gender, has been critical to the ideology that helps to keep capitalism going, despite the fact that the majority of the working class is damaged by capitalism. In this chapter the focus is on race as a factor for creating inequality in the U.S.—a capitalist society in which the capitalist class has lost its right to own slaves but still needs to have a supply of people to assign to the most exploited classes.

In the U.S. *segregation*, a form of *apartheid*, was upheld in various forms by state legal systems for nearly one hundred years, from the end of Reconstruction after the Civil War until it was overthrown by revolt in the 1950s and 1960s. In the U.S. during that time, Whites were the dominant race. This definitely did not mean that all Whites were well off, or that all Whites owned the means of production. There were desperately poor white people, who were differentiated from wealthier Whites by class, but they nevertheless had rights as members of the dominant race that Blacks did not have. And by many they were considered, and many considered themselves, different from and superior to the other category, the people who were defined as Black because they had known Black ancestry (even though both so-called Whites and so-called Blacks were mostly mixtures of both). White violence backed up state laws that, while not outright denying Blacks the right to vote or hold political office, made it extremely difficult to do so. Many poor Whites were also kept from voting when segregation was established in the 1880s and 1890s. Whites also had a near monopoly on land-owning. Interracial marriage was illegal.

Race
An artificial grouping of people invented to fill ideological needs in situations of massive inequality.*

Segregation
The legal separation of two or more segments of a population, based on an ideology claiming that certain kinds of contact with a subordinate group is damaging or demeaning to the dominant group.*

Apartheid
A legal policy of maintaining separation between racial or ethnic groups, with favorable working and living conditions and ownership of the means of production reserved for the group in power.*

• **Want more?**
Search for the trailer for the documentary *Slavery by Another Name*

Sharecropping
A social and economic arrangement in which non-landowners farm land, often under the direction of the owner, and give the owner a portion of the crop, usually half.

Terrorism
The systematic use of violence designed to terrify an entire population or group within a population into submission.*

• **Want more?** Try *Lynching in America: Confronting the Legacy of Racial Terror* http://www.eji.org/files/EJI%20Lynching%20in%20America%20SUMMARY.pdf

Each race had its own professionals, who served only members of their own race. So there were Black teachers, ministers, and midwives, for instance. There were some who were self-employed, such as carpenters, cabinet-makers, and seamstresses, and in some areas there were a few landowning farmers. Some combined farming with working for wages away from home during the week. Whites owned most, but not all, businesses, so that profits from the purchases of both Blacks and Whites went to those Whites who owned the means of production. Blacks did most of the physical labor for businesses and for big landowners, along with the poorer Whites. They also provided services to the dominant race as servants, nannies, and yard workers. The agricultural labor of the South was largely provided by *sharecroppers*, people, both Black and White, who farmed small sections of land for a big landowner in return for half the crop. They were being super-exploited, since their half of the crop was barely enough to keep them alive; malnutrition was common, and there was a high infant mortality rate. We will discuss the sharecropping system in the section on intensive agriculture.

The legal 'justice' system, run by the wealthier White people, protected White rights and privileges and protected those Whites who owned the means of production from both Whites and Blacks who didn't own the means of production. The legal 'justice' system even provided a partial replacement for slavery. Black convicts were leased for a comparatively low fee to some large plantation owners, mine owners, and factory owners, who took on the responsibility for feeding and housing the prisoners. Conditions were generally abysmal, and the death rate was extremely high, a result of overwork, malnutrition, crowding, and contagious illnesses. The illegal 'justice' system, enforced by groups like the Ku Klux Klan and by informal groups of Whites, used harassment and *terrorist* tactics such as lynching to fill in what they thought were "loopholes" in the legal 'justice' system. Legally, for instance, both Blacks and Whites could own land or run businesses. The illegal 'justice' system ensured that in fact Whites owned almost all land and businesses. While the North did not have a legal system of apartheid, poverty, harassment, and terrorism produced similar conditions in the North. Many anthropologists argue that although segregation was legally dismantled in the 1960s, its remnants have been revised into the racial inequities of today and continue to play an important part in providing the cheap labor capitalism requires.

> *A similar system of legal and illegal restraints maintained the power of White people over other groups besides those whose ancestors had been enslaved. In each section of the U.S. various restraints were applied to whichever groups provided the cheap labor, so that they could be seriously exploited or super-exploited.*

This included, at various times and places, Irish immigrants, people of Native American and Spanish ancestry who lived in the Southwest—land which the U.S. took by conquest—Chinese laborers who were brought here to provide almost free labor building railroads, and people coming as immigrants from Mexico and Latin America. Almost everyone in the United States has ancestors in at least one of these groups.

STRATIFICATION AND SUPER-EXPLOITATION

Dominant group
Those people in the category that includes the major power holders in a society, whether that group is based on race or class or gender.

Many stratification systems include the idea that members of the *dominant group*, which controls the means of production, have a minimal responsibility for the survival of those members of the categories of people who do most of the actual work that enriches them. This is a form of stratified redistribution. In Indian villages, for instance, landowners were responsible for giving part of the crop to the lower caste families who were attached to them, working their land, washing their laundry, making their jewelry, cleaning their latrines, etc. If a crop failed, the landowner still had that responsibility, and had to use grain stored from other years. Although not all landowners lived up to their responsibilities, there was enormous religious and social pressure to do so. Landowners in the U. S., particularly in the South, often felt and still feel some social and religious pressure to be 'good' landlords to their 'good' sharecroppers, and to play a paternalistic helping role in times of illness or other crises. This paternalism, nevertheless, left the sharecropping family in abject poverty, did not strain the resources of the landowners, and created a feeling of loyalty, obligation, and gratitude which kept the sharecropping family tied to the landowning family. Those same feelings meant that the sharecropping family often provided tremendous help during crises in the landowning family. Bad landowners were not repaid with such a loyal workforce. On the other hand bad landowners could easily replace sharecroppers who left them because there were so many unemployed people, an enormous reserve labor force of desperately poor Black and White families looking for some way to keep themselves fed and housed.

All stratification systems are, by definition, systems of exploitation, removing the value of the work done by ordinary people and placing it in the pockets of the elite, and making that relationship seem natural.

Regardless of the responsibility taken by the dominant group, none of the systems of stratification require an end to exploitation, and in many cases barely provide for the survival of the people who do the most difficult work in creating the wealth of a society.

When so much value is taken away that people can't cover the costs of maintaining themselves and their families, you can talk about super-exploitation. In capitalist societies where some people are paid extremely low wages, you can also use the term dying wages to talk about super-exploitation. This term doesn't apply to people who are not compensated with wages, although the same basic principle applies: serfs are super-exploited too.

> *'Dying wages,' a form of super-exploitation, is a term implying that if these low wages were truly all people had to depend on, some people would die. Working for minimum wage and no benefits in our society is working for a dying wage if you have a family.*

Although less than in more socialist societies, in the U.S. we have some protection from the consequenses of super-exploitation. Redistribution of tax money in various programs, often called 'welfare,' means that we are not totaly dependent on the market economy and the sale of our labor for survival. If you had no help from government redistribution programs like food stamps, subsidized day care, medical cards, and Pell grants, and worked for a minimum wage, you really could not make it unless you had several people with such jobs in the same household, or unless you had parents or other friends or relatives who let you live with them, or you had a good network of people who helped each other out through a system of generalized reciprocity. In fact, it can be argued that non-capitalist transactions, like reciprocity and redistribution, are a major part of the economy even in capitalist societies, and that without them super-exploitation would kill off even more of the people who do much of the work of creating wealth. Both the capitalist mode of production and the feudal mode of production are absolutely dependent on super-exploitation of a fairly large portion of the population, and on significant exploitation of a large number more. It is their work that provides the wealth that 'trickles up' to the few and is used to pay the bureaucracy and administrators and supervisors who keep the workers working. This is the wealth created by the free or very cheap labor of serfs in feudalism, or by enslaved Africans for nearly 400 years of colonial and then U.S. history, or today in the U.S. by agricultural migrant workers, prisoners, nursing home aides, low-paid factory workers, fast food workers, low-paid members of the military, and many others, including people working in corporations outside the U.S. for even lower wages than people in the U.S. can legally be paid.

We can probably agree that no one would want to be super-exploited, or even severely exploited. After all, given a choice, you wouldn't just volunteer to be one of the people who works for minimum wage. You wouldn't say, "Oh, I'd rather have no benefits." If you are working for minimum wage, or close to it, it is probably because you had no choice in the matter. And a state depends (unless it is truly socialist) on having a large number of people with little choice but to allow most of the value they produce go to benefit the elite. You may be thinking, "Well, I made

• **Want more?**
For consequences of racial inequality try *New Report says US Health Care Violates UN Convention on Racism* http:// www.colorlines.com/ articles/new-report-says-us-health-care-violates-un-convention-racism

the choice to go to college so I can better myself; if you don't like minimum wage that is what you should do." It is true that you may succeed in getting a better job—although you should be aware that many of those better jobs involve making sure that workers work hard or are kept under control, so that as much wealth as possible will end up in the hands of the elite. If you do get a better job, that may cure your financial problems, but it doesn't change the fact that lots of very cheap workers are needed if profits are to be large, so someone else will now be flipping hamburgers instead of you. And if everyone had a Ph.D., and hamburgers still needed to be flipped, we'd have very low-paid Ph.Ds. doing the job. If there really were enough high-paying jobs for everyone in the United States, there would still be exploited and super-exploited people doing the work that creates the basic wealth in the American economy. They just wouldn't live in the U.S. But the system would not have changed.

> *Education may help you, but only if others don't get an education; education doesn't fix the system itself.*

Super-exploitation is somewhat limited in most republics. Generally the sale of people as commodities is illegal. Nevertheless, there are numerous instances around the world where slavery does exist, even though it is illegal. In the U.S. actual slavery is rare. Nevertheless, there are many people forced to work under conditions that are not truly free, and their compensation is not in the form of wages, or is so low that the person is totally dependent on the business owner.

People in this situation include nannies and maids whose employers take their passports and expect them to work in return for a room in the house and access to household food. Such women are often required to perform sexual services as well. Without their passports they are at the mercy of the employer. Others are here without the permission of the U.S. government and work in sweatshop conditions for far less than minimum wage, producing and processing much of the food we eat, cutting tobacco, working in back alley small factories. If they protest their low wages they can be reported to Homeland Security. For some, particularly trafficked laborers, this comes close to a new form of slavery. Others are held in *debt peonage*: they owe an exorbitant sum to the labor contractor who brought them to the U.S., and are in addition charged for 'room and board'—which sometimes amounts to baloney sandwiches and housing in an old chicken house or run-down trailer or barn, so crowded that people have to sleep in shifts or sleep on the floor. We also have corporations operating industries in prisons; prisoners 'volunteer' to work, and are either paid perhaps $.50 an hour or have their minimum wages taken back to pay for 'room and board.' What is left pays

• **Want more?** Try *The Invisible World of Domestic Work* http://inamerica.blogs.cnn.com/2012/11/27/the-invisible-world-of-domestic-work-report-documents-abuses/

Debt peonage
A system of involuntary servitude that allows employers to force people who owe them money to work for the employer until the debt is paid off.*

for toothpaste and other small items, as well as phone calls, all charged at exorbitant rates. We have people on welfare—some of those people in the reserve labor force in Diagram 3—who, if they can't find regular employment, are now expected to work for the state or volunteer at local businesses in return for their welfare check. This works out to much less than minimum wage, and, like prison labor, provides employers with an exceedingly cheap labor force of people who have no right to protest. Lastly, although we don't buy and sell people, a black market in body parts is developing for medical purposes. And some argue that surrogate mothers are renting out their wombs, and that babies brought into the U.S. for adoption are in some sense being bought from super-exploited mothers living in societies where neocolonialism, often in combination with war, has created massive poverty.

PRODUCTION AND LABOR IN STATES

Specialization is an important characteristic of stratified societies, and in effect contributes to stratification in societies dependent on market exchange. Such societies generally have a complex division of labor, with many people specializing in producing goods other than food. Others provide services instead of making things. Some of those who specialize may not produce any of their own food. They make market exchanges for their food with people who farm, and with other specialists for other necessities. The farmers themselves often depend on the specialists for tools, cloth, and other specialized products. Market exchange makes all these transactions possible. People sell what they produce and use the money to buy other necessities from other specialists. People doing this kind of work may own their own means of production—the tools they use, the building they work in, and the resources they need, such as clay for making pottery. Other people may sell their labor or be apprenticed or enslaved, providing labor to a specialist who owns the means of production. Everyone's work—their specialization—is not given equal value, so the compensation they receive may leave some suffering the ravages of poverty, while others are very well off indeed. The caste system and feudalism were both systems, as is capitalism, for organizing the complex division of labor that is typical of states.

As in other severely stratified societies, in industrialized societies the vast majority does not own their own means of production. Since industrialized societies have market economies, most people therefore sell their labor for wages. Very few people are directly involved in farming in industrialized societies, since generally the farming itself is mechanized. Instead, many work for large corporations, often in factory settings, where their work has been *deskilled*. Much of the creative thought that went into the production of goods in non-industrial craft production has been removed—the process has been reorganized so that less skill is required. In craft production individuals made an entire prod-

Specialization
A detailed division of labor, in which some people specialize in producing one good or service, while other people produce different goods or services.

Deskilled
Tasks that have been deskilled have been organized so that they require less skill; this can be done by dividing the job into a number of smaller discrete operations that can be performed by people with relatively little training, or by using technology, such as cash registers that make it unnecessary for cashiers to know how to make change.

• **Want more?** Try *How Technology is Eliminating Higher Skilled Jobs* http://www.npr.org/2011/11/03/141949820/how-technology-is-eliminating-higher-skill-jobs?sc=fb&cc=fp

uct, performed a wide variety of tasks, and made decisions about design and about the production process itself. Assembly-line work removes the need for the old type of skill, because an individual performs over and over one small portion of the overall process of making a product such as a car or a can of soda. Considerable dexterity may be required, and some training, but the years of training and experience that went into becoming a master craftsman are no longer required. This means that many workers in industrialized societies are relatively easy to replace, or increasingly can be replaced by robots, an extreme form of deskilling. If you quit or are injured on the job, it won't take long to train your replacement. This means that employers can get away with paying low wages, or with shifting the burden of the cost of health care onto the employees, or with requiring involuntary overtime, or with hiring mostly 'temporary' and 'part-time' workers, or with disabling safety mechanisms. After all, if you quit in disgust or are disabled, the company won't particularly suffer from losing you. You don't have irreplaceable skills. So long as there is a large reserve labor force out there, waiting for jobs, there will soon be someone else sufficiently desperate to agree to work under the conditions that you have rejected—or that disabled you.

This means, of course, that it is to employers' benefit to have a lot of unemployed people waiting in the wings to take your job. When that supply runs low, employers and their political allies may pressure the state to provide more desperate workers.

Creating desperate workers can be done by pushing people off welfare, cutting food stamps, cutting state funding of health care, and generally reducing the social safety net, so that people have little choice but to agree to work for dying wages. Labor camps such as those run by big corporations in Nazi Germany were an extreme example of the state providing such workers. Legalizing slavery was another way. So is legalizing corporations' right to use prison labor, or giving corporations the legal right to bring in workers under contract from other countries. Alternatively, for work that does not have to be done in the country itself, such as making car parts or underwear, employers can move production plants to countries that already have lots of desperate people. But work such as flipping hamburgers or cleaning nursing homes or changing diapers in day care centers or picking lettuce or construction work does have to be done locally. If the supply of local cheap labor is inadequate, desperate people from other countries can be brought in, legally or illegally.

Agriculture

Agriculture
Intensive cultivation of crops; this is a type of farming that uses various technologies, such as plowing or irrigation, to grow much more in a given area, generally using both human labor and energy supplied by animals or machines and generally meant to produce a large surplus (compare with horticulture).

Stratified societies generally depend on some form of intensive *agriculture* in order to produce a surplus large enough to support a non-producing elite and an urban population which is producing specialized goods and services but frequently is not producing enough food to feed itself. Since food production is the world's most basic economic endeavor—without it people can't survive—it also has been the original basis of the world's social structures. Just as in bands foraging is basic to social organization, in stratified societies elite needs for enormous numbers of people to serve as laborers in labor intensive non-mechanized agriculture has been basic. The systems of categorizing people to provide that labor—race, caste, slavery, serfdom, gender—then became the basis for the entire society, and as other forms of specialization and industry developed, that basic structure was adapted to the new context. Even those categories, like serfdom and slavery, that apparently disappeared with capitalism and class, cast their shadows over class structure.

Intensive agriculture produces more food per unit of land than do extensive forms of farming. Making the same amount of land produce far more means that people involved in intensive agriculture have to work far harder than do most foragers and horticulturists. Flooding rivers provide fertilizer every year in some places, but elsewhere a lot of work is needed in such activities as working animal and human wastes or some sort of green manure or other fertilizer into the soil. In industrial societies chemical fertilizer may be used—easier, but expensive and dangerous to the humans applying the fertilizer, as well as to the environment and those who live nearby.

Mechanized agriculture
Agriculture that depends on the heavy use of machinery, fossil fuels, and artificial fertilizer.

Some crops (such as tobacco or cotton or rice) are far more labor intensive than others (such as corn or wheat). But in either case, agriculture produces more per unit of land by using the land more continuously and by planting crops closer together. Many, but not all, forms of intensive agriculture supplement human with non-human forms of energy. For instance, oxen or horses may provide both fertilizer and some of the necessary energy. Wind and water energy may be used. In *mechanized agriculture* fossil fuel energy is used. The term refers to the application of technologies that make it possible to grow far more food than does horticulture on a given piece of ground. Agriculture produces more by using technologies that make it possible to farm land more continuously and to plant crops closer together.

One big problem to overcome in agriculture is getting nutrients into the soil so that it can be used over and over without the long fallow periods that most horticultural systems require. One of the reasons the use of domestic animals is so common in agricultural systems is that the animals provide fertilizer as well as providing food or energy. Human wastes may also be returned to the soil, or flooding or systems of green manure can bring in nutrients. Other intensifying technologies include weeding, which removes plants which compete with the crop, transplanting, which allows spacing each plant for maximum yield, and irrigation, which makes it possible to grow far more plants in an area than the normal soil moisture would permit.

People making the major investments in money or labor that agriculture requires want to be secure in their control of the land. Otherwise they can't be sure that they will benefit from their investments. For this reason agriculture is generally associated with either private ownership of property or with a secure system of landholding such as that provided by a feudal system. In a severely stratified society, where the means of production—in this case farmable land—is owned by only a few people, the benefits of private property are restricted to the few. If you own little, you have little to protect, and the rights of private property make it very hard for you to get land. This means you are likely to find yourself needing to provide labor to the property owners in return for some form of compensation. And this, of course, is handy for the property owners, since they need a labor supply.

This right of private ownership or control is guaranteed by the state and is backed up by the legal use of force by the state. Private ownership or control is generally associated with significant inequality between landowners and non-landowners.

Providing a Huge Labor Supply for Non-Mechanized Agriculture

Energy efficient
The fewer calories of energy needed to produce a calorie of food, the more energy efficient that method is.

Non-mechanized agriculture is extremely *energy efficient*. It allows the production of approximately fifty calories of food energy for one calorie of energy expended. This means that farming families may produce large surpluses. It is also extremely labor intensive. In a highly stratified society this means that people who own large amounts of land, more than they can work themselves, will want a system for providing themselves with lots of cheap labor so that they can profit from the land they own. In somewhat less stratified societies many families may own small farms and need only small amounts of labor beyond what the family itself can supply.

In highly stratified societies the ability to produce a large surplus often does not benefit the people who grow it.

Non-mechanized agriculture is frequently organized by large landowners who allow landless families to farm in return for a large portion of the crop or a return made in labor, as we saw with caste in India and with feudalism. Sharecropping in the U.S. was another system for providing labor. Or landowners may hire people to do farm labor, as is frequently done now in the U.S. In highly stratified societies in which lots of individual farming families do own or have use rights in land, representatives of the state or members of the elite may require large amounts of tribute or tax. In any case, the people who do the actual work have little or no control over what they produce. The landlords or other elite take all but what is needed to keep most of the farming family alive. Much of the remainder of the farmer's production goes to pay for other necessities, since producing fifty calories of food for one calorie of energy expended requires growing grain and often very little else.   Producers are often poor and undernourished, despite the huge amount of food or other crops they grow.

> *The division between those who provide the labor and those who take control of the surplus they produce is generally marked by widespread beliefs about the inferiority of the exploited group. Such beliefs are justified by ideas about difference: caste, race, ethnicity, or religion, language, or designations such as white trash. This pattern is characteristic of non-mechanized agriculture wherever rights to the means of production are conveyed to one set of people and carefully denied to others: otherwise the owners would have no labor force to create wealth for them.*

We have already talked about how caste, feudalism, and slavery accomplished a system of denying rights to some and conveying them to others. But there were also other systems. We will talk here about some of the other systems that have been used in what is now the United States.

Encomienda, hacienda, and slaveryNative American were all systems used in the U.S. Southwest. Much of the U.S. Southwest was part of Mexico until the U.S. military conquered it in 1848 after nearly two years of a war of aggression.   Spanish armies, along with disease, had conquered the Aztec rulers of Mexico in the 1500s. The monarch in Spain gave high-ranking conquerors the right to use huge land grants, much like feudal estates. These grants were called encomiendas. The Indians living on that land were included in the gift, and forced to work for the grantee. Haciendas, by contrast, were privately owned and worked by Indian sharecroppers, who, like those on encomiendas, had no longer any right to their own land.

• **Want more?**
Try I*ndian Slavery in the Americas* http://www.gilderlehrman.org/history-by-era/origins-slavery/essays/indian-slavery-americas

> *On many of the large landholding missions in California and much of the Southwest, thousands of native people were virtually enslaved during the 1700s. They worked as servants, laborers, and farmers.*

The mission and hacienda systems remained in effect after U.S. conquest, in some cases well into the early 1900s, although actual slavery was illegal by that time and systems of peonage had replaced it. Many of the Spanish-speaking people in California and the Southwest now are the descendents of Native American-

Native Americans who had been in what is now the United States far longer than any English-speaking people. The fact that English is the national language is a reflection of power and conquest, including the power of English-speaking East coast elites over West and Southwest Spanish-speaking elites, who frequently prided themselves on their 'pure' Spanish ancestry and imposed their language by force on native people, just as English-speakers imposed English by force on Native AmericanNative Americans in the areas they controlled. Once the most powerful group had established their language as the national language, they continued to impose it by somewhat more subtle methods on later newcomers.

Sharecropping, which we have mentioned several times in this chapter, was instituted as the replacement for slavery on plantations. Since the Southern elites were, for the most part, allowed to keep their plantations after the Civil War, the plantation owners still needed a large cheap workforce if they were going to profit from their landholdings. Large farms and plantations were divided into many small sections, and then sharecroppers were contracted to farm each section and allowed to use a house. Frequently the houses were so poorly constructed and maintained by the landowner that snow sifted in through the cracks in the walls. In return, all the sharecropping families had to hand their crop over to the landlord to be sold; after the sale they were to get half the money from their own crop, while the landlord got halves from many crops. Since the sharecroppers were paid only when the crop was harvested, they had nothing to live on while it was growing. So the landlord gave them very minimal supplies on credit. Very often the sharecroppers' half barely covered what they had gotten on credit during the year.

So the whole family, including little kids, had worked for an entire year for nothing but a leaky roof over their heads, barely enough food to keep them alive, and perhaps a dress piece or two. Malnutrition was common, and many landlords did not even allow sharecroppers to raise a garden on their land.

The laws that made this all legal were passed very quickly after emancipation. The landowners wanted laws that would make their former enslaved workers stay on and work for tiny wages, almost as if nothing had changed. The freedpeople resisted this idea. They thought that they should have greater rights than that, and many believed that the country, and their former owners, owed them some compensation for the generations of enslaved labor that was the foundation of U.S. wealth. They thought that the right to small farms should be conveyed to them. Landowners resisted that idea, and with the help of state legislatures laws were passed that largely confined Blacks to sharecropping and work as domestics. Being unemployed was a crime, but

• **Want more?** Try Farmers Without Land, describing poor white farmers: http://mshistorynow.mdah.state.ms.us/articles/228/

enforced only against Blacks; changing employers if you were a sharecropper was illegal except during a brief period every January. In many areas you still needed a pass to leave the land-owner's land. Although the laws enforcing this during Reconstruction didn't last too long, laws about debt and vagrancy performed the same function. Debt peonage laws made it illegal to leave if you owed your employer money, and landlords often juggled the books to keep sharecroppers in debt. By the early 1900s most of these laws had been repealed, but nevertheless terrorism kept the system going with little change into the 1960s, under the legal and illegal enforcement of segregation. Although it was legal to own land, Blacks who did were in danger of lynching through the illegal 'justice' system run by landowners and business people in the Ku Klux Klan and others whose intent was to maintain privilege for Whites and deny rights to Blacks.

> *Although this system was instituted as a way to maintain white supremacy and as a replacement for slavery, keeping race as a factor for inequality and therefore profit, in fact by the early 1900s there were large numbers of poor Whites who were also sharecropping.*

The system was not quite as vicious for Whites as it was for Blacks. They were not likely to be lynched or castrated or raped if they challenged the landlord's bookkeeping—but they were also unlikely to get their money. If they did get out of sharecropping and bought land or started a business they were not risking their lives. Nevertheless, their children, like Black children, suffered high rates of malnutrition and infant mortality, and women had high maternal mortality rates and looked decades older than they were. Both Black and White sharecropping men and women died, on average, at a much younger age than did the landowners.

Peasant

A member of a farming category of people in a state who use non-mechanized agriculture to raise crops for their own subsistence and pay tax, rent, or tribute to the elites who control the land. Their payments may be specified to be in the form of crops, money, or labor.

Usufruct (Use right)

A traditional right to the produce of a certain piece of land (to use the fruits of the land), generally in a society that does not have a system of private property.*

Peasant farming is a more indirect system for producing profits in non-mechanized agriculture on marginal farm land. **Peasants** are farmers in states who have some access to land on which they practice non-mechanized agriculture. They grow food for market as well as for their own use. However, outsiders dominate the society and deny peasants' rights. This means elites can control processing and distribution of their produce, resulting in large profits for outsiders and low income for peasants. They have little control over their lives and little influence on political and economic policies that affect them. One could argue that the small family farmers who didn't sharecrop and instead owned or rented marginal land in the U.S., particularly in the South, were actually peasants, although that word is never used in reference to people in the U.S. In some cases peasants own small amounts of land, but more frequently have a traditional right to use a piece of land. This right is called **usufruct**. The peasant may be required to pay a fairly small amount in kind to the actual landowner to keep that right.

Cash crop
A crop grown for sale rather than to feed one's family directly; often a luxury crop such as sugar, flowers, or tobacco that is grown for export.*

Other peasants are basically squatters on unused land. Peasant farming is usually possible only on land that is of poor quality or is so distant from major marketing centers that it is of little use to large landowners for *cash crops*. Despite the poor quality of the land and distance from markets, peasants are often better off than farmers who work directly for a landowner on better land. They usually grow a wider variety of crops, and much of what they produce goes to feed themselves. If the land should become a possible source of profit, for instance if a road to market is put in, peasants are often driven off and the landowner turns to more profitable crops for sale, such as soybeans or flowers for the international market. Peasants now are among the most vulnerable to climate change, and are likely to become more and more caught up in migration to cities or to become climate refugees.

Industrial and Mechanized Agriculture

In industrialized societies most farming is mechanized agriculture, needing far less field labor than non-mechanized agriculture. Mechanized agriculture makes heavy use of energy through machinery, fossil fuels, artificial fertilizer, herbicides and pesticides. High yields per acre are common because of massive energy inputs, although not necessarily higher than very labor-intensive non-mechanized agriculture. In terms of energy use, mechanized agriculture is very inefficient: approximately 10 calories of energy are required to produce one calorie of food energy. This means that it is an expensive form of farming if energy costs are high, as well as contributing heavily to the greenhouse gases of climate change. But if energy costs are low, a big landowner may make a bigger profit by shifting from non-mechanized to mechanized agriculture. This means getting rid of the former labor supply by kicking sharecroppers or peasants out. Their little fields that were farmed by lots of people working with hoes or with plow animals are combined into one big field that is farmed with just a couple workers and tractors. With a shift to mechanized agriculture may also come a shift in attitude: local elites no longer feel quite such a strong need to maintain the existing system of denying rights. They no longer need quite so much cheap labor and may not fight quite as hard to uphold the rigidities of inferiority based on factors such as caste or race or religion or language. So the shift to mechanized agriculture has sometimes meant that movements for social justice among the super-exploited have been able to make some headway. The U.S. Civil Rights Movement, for instance, finally began to make headway in the late 1950s, just as tractor farming became common in the South, and especially a bit later as mechanical cotton pickers came on the market.

However, in most cases no such advantage is evident for the displaced farm laborers, and even if there is, there are other massive problems resulting from the shift to mechanized agriculture.

> *Shifting from non-mechanized to mechanized agriculture often leads to greater poverty and increasing inequality for large segments of the population.*

That shift can have an effect much like closing down all the factories in a town. There are no jobs. Desperate people flock to the big cities, and soon there are no jobs available there, either. Discrimination against the newcomers keeps the old factors of inferiority alive as people in the dominant group try to keep what jobs there are for themselves. Ideas about 'those people' abound as the dominant group justifies its right to good jobs. Even many small farm owners do not benefit from the shift to mechanized agriculture, because land becomes concentrated in fewer and fewer hands. Only the already well-off can afford tractors and chemical inputs, so big landowners become bigger as they buy up the land of small farmers who go bankrupt and become landless laborers on the big farms or migrate to cities, where they form part of the reserve labor force or work for generally low wages. This process can be seen at work in the U.S. as bigger family farms go bankrupt and are bought up by agribusiness corporations for *industrial agriculture* or by sub-division developers. Interestingly, Amish farmers, by refusing to mechanize, are among the few groups of family farmers who are actually increasing in numbers

The shift to mechanized agriculture does not produce more leisure for most people, nor does it use fewer people to produce the food we need. While it is true that fewer people are working in the fields, farm families typically need at least one person with a job off the farm in order to make it. And instead of lots of people in the fields, we have lots of people still involved in producing food, but doing it in factories producing fertilizer and tractors, doing jobs that used to be done on the farm itself, or in processing and transporting food. Even industrialized societies that have shifted to mechanized agriculture are still dependent on labor-intensive techniques for crops that don't lend themselves to mechanized farming, such as burley tobacco, sugar cane, or many vegetables. These crops are usually produced by family labor in peasant or sharecropping situations or in plantation-type settings using hired or contracted labor. The family or hired labor is usually composed of people who have been denied rights: racial or ethnic minorities or the poorer segments of populations within the industrialized nation or in other countries around the world.

• **Want more?**
For contrasting pictures search "Amish Farmers Images" and "Industrial Agriculture Images"

Industrial agriculture
The factory-like production of crops or animals for slaughter, done on a huge scale, and highly mechanized.*

Industrial Production

Industrial
Producing goods using
mechanization fueled by
non-human and non-
animal forms of energy,
usually fossil fuel or
nuclear energy.

Industrial societies continue to be just as dependent on agriculture as are other states. Since much of that agriculture is mechanized, however, fewer people are directly engaged in farming. But
if you fly across the United States, you will see that the vast majority of land in the U.S. is still devoted to agriculture, either in crops
or in pasture for meat animals. In fact, agriculture is one of the few
economic sectors that produces a trade surplus, and is important
in keeping our trade deficit from being even bigger than it is. And
although it won't be obvious in your flight, the U.S. is also dependent on agriculture that is carried out in other countries. Just
because it is done elsewhere and imported, or because fewer
Americans are out in the fields, doesn't mean the U.S. has in some
way moved beyond agriculture. Likewise, people often talk about
the U.S. as being a 'post-industrial' society—that we are now a
service and information society. This is just as inaccurate as thinking agriculture is no longer important to the U.S. economy. However, it is true that much of the manufacturing that used to be
done in the U.S. is now done by U.S. owned or subcontracted
companies in other countries where people are desperate enough
to work for even lower wages than in the U.S.

After World War II unions in the U.S. forced most large-
scale industries, such as the automobile, steel, and mining industries, to pay living wages for a forty-hour week and provide benefits such as paid health insurance. As a result, up into the 1980s
there were lots of good jobs. This was true in much of Europe also,
except that in many European countries the working class had
succeeded in pushing a more socialist agenda than in the U.S., so
benefits there were greater than in the U.S.

*However, in both the U.S. and Europe these benefits and good wages
were limited to certain categories of people and depended on the
exploitation of other people, either within the country or in countries
that had previously been colonized.*

Even now industrial work for the exploited categories,
particularly in the Global South, pays very little, in many cases
barely enough to keep the worker fed, with very little left over to
provide for other members of the family. These are the people
who provide the cheap labor or cheap resources that keep the
whole system running.

Most industry and much agriculture around the world is
organized through the capitalist mode of production and depends
on exploited categories for its source of cheap labor. Corporations
are privately owned. They may be owned by a group of people,
although one person or family usually owns a controlling share—
and receives most of the profit. A few other people or families
may own sizable chunks, and if the company sells shares on the
stock market thousands of other people may own miniscule por-

• **Want more?** Try
exploring
Executive Pay Watch http:/
/www.aflcio.org/
Corporate-Watch/
Paywatch-2014

tions and receive miniscule portions of the profits. There are also a few worker-owned cooperatives, such as Mondragon in Spain, where workers themselves own the means of production, profits belong to the workers, and there is no one who makes vastly more money than other people. We will discuss these more in Chapter 8. In socialist countries all or some industry may be owned by the state and the profits are not accumulated by a few individuals but are redistributed back to the citizens through health care, housing, free education and other forms of public welfare, and relatively low wages. The bureaucrats running the state industries, as well as the rest of the state bureaucracy, are well-paid compared to the rest of the population, but not nearly as well paid as they are in many capitalist countries. The U.S. has the world's largest gap between the wages of ordinary workers and their CEO. CEOs in U.S. major corporations in 2007 made an average of $10.8 million, an increase of approximately 45% since 1997. By 2013 their average pay had gone up to 11.8 million, while the average worker's pay was $16 per hour, or about $35,000 a year. The average worker, in other words, would have to work 337 years to make what the average CEO makes in a year. On minimum wage, that would be 774 years, and minimum wage has not even keep up with inflation, so those wages bought less than they did in 1980, when CEO made only about 40 times the average worker. Minimum wage would be $31.45 if it had merely kept up with the pay raise of the top 1% in the U.S.

Although good jobs in the U.S. began moving rapidly out of the country in the 1980s, there had never been nearly enough of them to go around. For most of the twentieth century those good jobs were reserved for men who were White. Good jobs for White women and for women and men of color were scarce, and even some White men could not find jobs that paid a living wage. Some of the jobs that did pay a living wage, like unionized mining, were so dangerous that you risked death, illness, and disability on a daily basis. But many other dangerous jobs didn't even pay a living wage; women who worked in cotton factories, for instance, suffered high rates of brown lung, a disease like miners' black lung, which causes you to slowly suffocate to death. Other low-paying jobs are physically or emotionally difficult, like being an aide in a nursing home or waiting tables or unloading trucks and railroad cars. These low-paid and difficult jobs are held mainly by White women and men and women of color. This was, and still is, a system for providing employers with a low-wage work force without angering White men, whose support the elite need to keep the whole system going.

However, confining White women and men and women of color to low-paid, dangerous, or exhausting work required the massive denial of rights on a national, state, and local level. It was perfectly legal to pay a woman teacher less than a man, for instance. Until the 1950s it was legal to put White kids in good schools and children of color into separate poorer schools. Even

• **Want more?**
For video try searching "Triangle Shirtwaist Fire" and search "Women in Cotton Factory 1990s Images".

• **Want more?** Try
Root Causes of Immigration: NAFTA http://www.weareoneamerica.org/root-causes-immigration-nafta

after the law changed after a prolonged battle, it was still perfectly legal to under-fund schools in poor White and minority neighborhoods so drastically that the bathrooms didn't even have toilet paper. Until the 1960s it was perfectly legal to discriminate in jobs and housing on the basis of race and gender. However, as affirmative action laws—meant to reverse some of the effects of generations of the denial of rights—began to take effect in the 1970s, White men found that they no longer had an exclusive right to the better jobs. There was widespread anger as they found that there was now more competition for good jobs since employers could no longer consider only other White men—this despite the fact that in reality White men continued to have the easiest access to good jobs. This anger intensified in the 1990s after the passage of NAFTA created so much poverty in Mexico that far more desperate people began crossing the border to take mainly low-paying jobs in the U.S. At the same time better paying jobs went south in even greater numbers, causing massive job loss in the U.S. Anger at job loss was often directed at immigrants, to the point that a referendum in California passed because so many people, mainly White, were in favor of denying, among other things, prenatal care for the unborn babies of people without government permission to be in the U.S. This is, of course, anger directed at the wrong people. It was the corporate elite causing job loss, not immigrants. Similar kinds of anger have greeted even mildly successful demands for equality all over the world, such as the gains made by Dalits and others of low caste in demanding equality in India.

THE OBVIOUS QUESTION

This denial of rights to some categories of people—creating and using factors of inequality—makes sure that there will be plenty of people with no choice but to work for low wages. It is typical of industrial production around the world, and, as in the U.S., is justified by ideas about the inferiority of the people being most seriously exploited. However, very few people are members of the elite, so very few of the people who have these ideas actually benefit from them. Even those who are better paid are under the direction of those above them, and their work goes to increase the wealth of those who own the means of production. Few people, even in the dominant group, get to make their own decisions about the work they do. Those who do have some decision-making rights are still answerable to those above them. Insurance policies may even tell doctors what kinds of surgeries, tests and medications are appropriate.

Stratification means that to those who have, more is given. Since those who don't have are in the majority, this raises a fundamental question: Why doesn't the majority revolt? We will address this question in Chapter Seven, where we will take a look from a different perspective at the role of race and gender as they are used to reinforce the other factors of inequality in order to maintain a stratified society.

> *Actually it takes a great deal of work to get people to put up with severe inequality.*

REFERENCES/SUGGESTED READING

Ethnographies, ethnographic discussions, and ethnographic films

Brooks, James. 2002. Captives and Cousins: Slavery, Kinship, and Community in the Southwest Borderlands. Chapel Hill: University of North Carolina Press

Buck, Pem Davidson 2001 Worked to the Bone: Race, Class, Power and Privilege in Kentucky. New York: Monthly Review Press.

Davidson, Osha 1996 Broken Heartland: The rise of America's rural ghetto. Expanded edition. Iowa City: University of Iowa Press.

Gray, Joe Jr. 1983 Lord and Father. 45 min. Whitesburg, KY: Appalshop Films.

Kingsolver, Ann, 2011, Tobacco Town Futures: Global Encounters in Rural Kentucky. Long Grove, IL: Waveland Press.

Kopple, Barbara 1976 Harlan County USA. 103 min. New York: Cabin Creek Films.

Lewis, Anne 1991 Fast Food Women. 28 min. Whitesburg, KY: Appalshop Films.

Skurnik, Jonathan and Kathy Leichter 2002 A Day's Work, A Day's Pay. 60 min. Harriman, NY: New Day Films.

Stack, Carol 1975 All My Kin: Strategies for Survival in a Black Community. New York: Harper Torchbooks.

Ethnographic novels and biography

Arnow, Harriette 2003[1954] The Dollmaker. New York: HarperCollins.

Bama 2002 Karukku. Chennai, India:Macmillan India.

Buck, David and Kannan M., eds.2011. Tamil Dalit Literature: My Own Experience. David Buck tr. Pondichery India: Institut Francais de Pondichery.

Menchu, Rigoberta, Elisabeth Burgos-Dubray, and Ann Wright 1987 I, Rigoberta Menchu: An Indian Woman in Guatemala. New York: Verso.

Moody, Anne 2004 [1968] Coming of Age in Mississippi. New York: Laurel Book/Dell Publishing.

Steinbeck, John 2002[1937] The Grapes of Wrath. New York: Penguin.

Umrigar, Thrity 2005 The Space Between Us. New York: Harper.

Valmiki, Omprakash 2003 Joothan: A Dalit's Life. New York: Columbia University Press.

Jadhav, Narendra 2007 Untouchables: My Family's Triupphant Escape from India's Caste System. Berkeley: University of California Press.

Ethnographic history and discussion of caste and social structure in India

Buck, David 2005 Introduction: Poetry in Stone. IN Melagaram Tirikutarasakppa Kavirayar's A Kuravanji in Kutralam: A Tamil tale of love and fortunes told. David C. Buck, translator. Chennai, India: Institute of Asian Studies.

Mencher, Joan 1974 The Caste System Upside Down: Or, the Not So Mysterious East. Current Anthropology 15:469-478.

Mines, Diana 2005 Fierce Gods: Inequality, Ritual, and the Politics of Dignity in a South Indian Village. Bloomington: Indiana University Press.

Oldenburg, Veena 2002 Dowry Murder: The Imperial Origins of a Cultural Crime. New York: Oxford University Press.

Prakash, Gyan 1993. Terms of Servitude: The Colonial Discourse on Slavery and Bondage in India. IN Breaking the Chains: Slavery, Bondage, and Emancipation in :Modern Africa and Asia, Martin Klein ed, pp.131-149. Madison: The University of Wisconsin Press.

Prashad, Vijay. 2001. Cataracts of Silence: Race on the Edge of Indian Thought. Geneva: United Nations Research Institute for Social Development.

On the history of race in the U.S.

Adelman, Larry 2003 Race—The Power of an Illusion. 3 episodes, 56 min. each. San Francisco: California Newsreel.

African Burial Grounds Website. http://www.gsa.gov/portal/content/101077.

Allen, Theodore 1997 Invention of the White Race, vol. II, The Origin of Racial Oppression in Anglo-America. New York: Verso Press.

Baptist, Edward. 2014. The Half Has Never Been Told: Slavery and the Making of American Capitalism. New York: Basic Books.

Bennett, Lerone 1993 [1975] The Shaping of Black America. New York: Penguin Books. Pp.1-109.

Blackmon, Douglas 2008 Slavery by Another Name: The Re-Enslavement of Black Americans from the Civil War to World War II. New York: Doubleday.

Daniel, Pete. 1972. The Shadow of Slavery: Peonage in the South, 1901-1969. Urbana: University of Illinois Press.

Du Bois, W.E.B. 1935 Black Reconstruction 1860-1880. New York: Russell and Russell.

Jones, Jacqueline. 1992. The Dispossessed: America's Underclass from the Civil War to the Present. New York: Basic Books.

Linebaugh, Peter and Marcus Rediker 2000 The Many-Headed Hydra: Sailors, Slaves, Commoners, and the Hidden History of the Revolutionary Atlantic. Boston: Beacon Press.

Smedley, Audrey 1993 Race in North America: The Evolution of a Worldview. Boulder: Westview Press.

On resistance and non-capitalist economy

AFP 2007 Descendants of Sitting Bull, Crazy Horse break away from U.S. Dec. 20. Electronic document, http://people.tribe.net/prayoga/blog/4c1150f0-1699-45e4-89e9-0b0cec75fdbc.

Gibson-Graham, J.K. 2006 A Postcapitalist Politics. Minneapolis: University of Minnesota Press.

Grossman, Roberta 2005 Homeland: Four Portraits of Native Action. 57 min. Oley, PA: Bullfrog Films, produced by The Katahdin Foundation.

McLeod, Christopher and Malinda Maynor 2001 In the Light of Reverence. 73 min. Oley, PA: Bullfrog Films.

Robinson, Cedric and Robin Kelley 2000 [1983] Black Marxism: The Making of the Black Radical Tradition. Chapel Hill: University of North Carolina Press.

Zinn, Howard 2005 A People's History of the United States: 1492-Present (revised and updated). New York: Harper Perennial Classics.

On mechanized vs. non-mechanized agriculture

Harris, Marvin and Orna Johnson 2007 Cultural Anthropology, 7th ed. Boston: Pearson/Allyn and Bacon. Pp.72, 76.

James, Randall 2007 Horse and Human Labor Estimates for Amish Farms. Journal of Extension 45(1), Article No. 1RIB5. Electronic document, http://www.joe.org/joe/2007february/rb5.shtml, accessed June 12, 2008.

On the organization of inequality in the U.S.

AFL-CIO. Executive PayWatch: High-Paid CEOs and the Low-Wage Economy. http://www.aflcio.org/Corporate-Watch/Paywatch-2014

Alexander, Michelle. 2010. The New Jim Crow: Mass Incarceration in the Age of Colorblindness. New York: The New Press.

Buck, Pem Davidson 1994 'Arbeit Macht Frei': Racism and Bound, Concentrated Labor in U.S. Prisons. Urban Anthropology and Studies of Cultural Systems and World Economic Development 23(4):331-372.

Fuentes, Annette 2003 [1997] Guiliani's Workfare: Slaves of New York. Baltimore Chronicle. Electonic document, http://www.baltimore-chronicle.com/workfare.html, accessed June 10, 2008.

Goode, Judith and Jeff Maskovsky. 2001. The New Poverty Studies: The Ethnography of Power, Politics, and Impoverished People in the United States. New York: New York University Press.

Kozol, Jonathan 1992 Savage Inequalities: Children in America's Schools. New York: HarperCollins Wilkinson, Richard and Kate Pickett 2009 The Spirit Level: Why Greater Equality Makes Societies Stronger. New York: Bloomsbury Press.

Maskovsky, Jeff and Ida Susser, eds. 2009. Rethinking America: The Imperial Homeland in the 21st Century. Boulder: Paradigm Publishers.

Reiman, Jeffrey and Paul Leighton. 2012. The Rich Get Richer and the Poor Get Prison: Ideology, Class, and Criminal Justice, 10th ed. New York: Routledge.

CHAPTER 7
MAINTAINING STRATIFICATION

Having laid out basic aspects of stratification, we are now in a position to return to the question posed at the end of Chapter Five. Why do people put up with positions toward the bottom of the stratification system and with the very unequal division of resources between the haves and the have-nots, and with control by the people above them? People who are being exploited greatly outnumber the elite, so why don't they revolt? After all, have-nots do not necessarily accept their situation, and since they are the majority in a severely stratified society, the dominant group could easily be overwhelmed in a revolt. In this chapter we will talk about the ways people are kept from revolting—but bear in mind that this doesn't always work. People do resist stratification and they do revolt, quite frequently.

> *Maintaining a stratified society, so that the elite continues to keep its hold on the resources of the society, keeps its hold on the means of production, and can continue to benefit from the work of the have-nots, is extremely difficult.*

Collaborator class
In a stratified society, a group of people whose function is to control ordinary people and to manage their production in order to extract wealth from them for the elite, with whom they are allied.*

Divide and rule
The strategy of getting people to fight each other rather than to fight those who are controlling them.

So a number of basic principles are at work in societies that remain stratified, maintaining the position of the elite:

1. The dominant group controls the resources of the society.

2. There is an intermediate *collaborator class*.

3. The dominant ideology of the society justifies stratification, so that it appears natural or inevitable.

4. Systems of *divide and rule* keep the people being exploited busy fighting each other instead of getting together to change the system.

5. The dominant group controls the legal use of force and often gets away with the illegal use of force.

The first two of these principles you have already seen at work, so they will be briefly summarized here, and then we will go on to talk in more detail about the other three.

The dominant group controls the resources of a stratified society.

This means that the elite control the means of production and therefore control people's ability to make a living. This alone gives huge leverage. Both the tributary mode of production and the capitalist mode depend on this fact. In kingdoms the monarch, perhaps with the advice and consent of high-ranking aristocrats, makes and enforces the laws that guarantee that the elite continue to control access to the means of production. The monarch generally also controls the state religion—another resource—that tells people what is right and wrong, and revolt, they say, is wrong. In republics laws—made by legislators who are mostly allies of the elite—guarantee the right of private property and inheritance of wealth. Enforcement of these laws means that those who own the means of production have the right to continue in possession. In both kingdoms and republics, in other words, the elite conveys rights to itself and denies them to others. Their control of other resources, such as the state religion in kingdoms, backs up their rights. In republics, they and their allies control resources such as access to the news media, so they can determine whose version of events will be publicized. They control printing companies and therefore can determine what books get published. They provide funding for religious organizations, museums, foundations, and research. And they control a society's system of government and the military and justice system. This means they can write laws as they see fit and determine to a large extent what will be considered a crime and who will be punished.

• **Want more?** Try On corporations controlling information try *"…Exxon 'misled' public on Climate"* http://www.theguardian.com/us-news/2015/oct/30/exxonmobil-climate-change-environmental-groups-federal-investigation

There is an intermediate collaborator class.

You met the concept of the collaborator when we talked about the manager of the fast food joint. These are people who buffer the elite from having to deal with the people they are exploiting. They are given some privilege and decent living conditions in return for doing the job of managing the people who do most of the work of creating a surplus and therefore are most damaged by the stratification system. This is the job of the retainers and administrators in a kingdom and of the professional managerial class in a capitalist republic (see diagrams 2 and 3). Collaborators act as allies of the elite. They generally buy into the system and believe that exploitation is right, and that they and the elite are doing a good thing for society. If they don't believe this they are unlikely to have been picked as retainers in a kingdom or as supervisors of estates, or as bureaucrats in a republic, or even as fast food managers. Think what would happen to a fast food manager who decided to share out all the profits from the business with the employees. Newspaper editors, in another example, are likely to find themselves fired if they publish material that seriously challenges the rights of the elite. Or if U.S. social workers seriously challenge the need for poverty in the richest nation on earth, rather than simply apply band-aids to people suffering the consequences of poverty, they also are likely to be pushed out of their job. Tribute collectors in kingdoms are another example, as are military officers and judges. All work to keep stratification going; although they themselves don't own the means of production they help the elite maintain their grip on the society's resources. They collaborate with the elite and are rewarded with relatively good or excellent wages, or with prestige, or with the belief that what they are doing is good for society.

> *At times collaborators disagree with and even seriously challenge particular policies, or may favor one set of elites over another, thereby forcing reform of the system. Such reforms often benefit ordinary people and make them less inclined to revolt. But such reforms don't challenge the basic principles of stratification.*

IDEOLOGY

• **Want more?**
For a news program that questions the hegemonic ideology try *The Real News* http://therealnews.com/t2/. For a list of alternative new outlets, scroll down in *Media Reform Information Center* http://www.corporations.org/media/

It may be becoming obvious to you by now that an awful lot of people are going to have to avoid questioning the elite's right to control the society's resources. And at least the collaborator class is going to have to actively support the social structure that keeps those resources in the hands of the elite and be willing to make sure the workers work hard so that the elite can make big profits or collect lots of tribute. Ideology plays a critical role in making this happen.

> *Stratified societies have to be built on the ideological assumption that it is natural that there will be haves and have-nots.*

This is the assumption of our own society. We may think it is too bad that some people don't have decent nutrition or decent schools or decent wages or decent medical care, but most of us don't think this situation is immoral or unnatural. We don't think of decent schools as a human right that belongs to everyone. We as a society are perhaps beginning to think decent medical care is a human right. If so, we are moving a bit toward the values that underlie egalitarian societies and the communal mode of production as well as those of more socialist societies.

Bear in mind as you read that ideologies alone are not sufficient in extremely stratified societies. In states the differences in wealth are so enormous that which group you are in—whether you are in the group with rights or the group denied rights—can be a matter of life and death. But if ideology fails, then the state, as an organized political and economic system, can provide force, putting down *revolts* and punishing those who don't cooperate. This force supplements the various ideologies that get most people most of the time to accept, or at least put up with, the right of

Revolt
An organized attempt to overthrow established power relations.

Secular
Not having to do with religion.

the elite to their position of privilege. Nevertheless ideology is effective most of the time in keeping people from seriously questioning inequality. And since it appears so natural, we need to take a long look at it.

Ideology can be religious or *secular*—that is, not having to do with religion. Or an ideology can have both religious and secular elements, as patriarchy does. Secular ideologies that help maintain inequality are beliefs such as "Somebody has to do the dirty work," "Doctors deserve to be rich because they save lives and spent a lot of money on their education," "People are poor because they are lazy." The dominant religious dogma in a society generally reflects and supports a society's distribution of power, and so acts as ideology. Both religious and secular ideologies discourage people from trying to increase equality, and encourage them to see those who do as 'troublemakers' who just want a handout. Members of the collaborator class will promote this interpretation, using ideology to turn public opinion against them.

Beliefs such as "The poor will always be with us," or "Indians were primitive people," or "Dalit women are sluts," or "Women go crazy once a month or at menopause, so you certainly wouldn't want one for president," or "People on welfare are lazy," or "People make bad choices so of course they are poor" all are examples of ideologies in our society which justify the continued existence of inequality. These are examples of blaming the victim, a concept you met back in the fast food example. If people in the collaborator class believe these ideas, then they will not feel guilty about their management or social control role in helping to make wealth flow to the dominant group. Nor will they be inclined to support moves toward social justice for the *subordinate group*, although they may well support increased charity to the 'deserving poor,' those who are properly grateful for the aid they receive or appear to be in the subordinate category only by accident.

Subordinate group
Those people in the category that is excluded from most positions of power in a society, whether that group is based on race or class or gender.

If people in the subordinate group believe these ideologies about themselves and about people like them, they are said to have *false consciousness*. False consciousness is like blaming the victim, only you yourself are the victim. A classic example of false consciousness would be a woman who believes it is her fault when her husband beats her. Or if you believe that your own stupidity in having a kid before you went to college is the reason you can barely make it from paycheck to paycheck, that is another example of false consciousness. The reason you are having trouble is that your employer is getting a bigger profit by paying you as little as possible, and you are having to put up with that because the U.S. government has not insisted on a living wage, has withdrawn support for affordable housing, has not made free daycare or college a universal right, has made going to college on welfare extremely difficult, and your family is unable or unwilling to help you out. Had you been born into a wealthy family it is quite likely

False consciousness
The attitude of a person in a subordinate group who believes the ideologies that claim subordinate people are truly inferior or truly deserve to have limited access to resources or power.*

that having a child would not leave you struggling from paycheck to paycheck. It is true that you had the kid, and that things might be easier without a child, but that isn't the cause of your difficulties. Your difficulties are caused by life in a stratified society.

Notice that both false consciousness and blaming the victim shift the focus of attention away from the basic causes of a problem and onto the behavior of the individual involved. If the problem is the individual's fault, then nothing appears to be unfair, and no one is likely to develop the *class consciousness* that might lead to revolt. That is why blaming the victim and false consciousness are so important as ideology in maintaining stratification.

> *People with false consciousness are not likely to rise up in revolt because they believe that in some sense they deserve the situation they are in. And if they do, people who blame the victim are unlikely to help them.*

False consciousness and blaming the victim are examples of some of the easiest ways to control people. They help to get people who are being exploited to believe that stratification is perfectly fine. This is one of the functions of ideology.

> *The dominant ideology of the society says that inequality is right, or at least natural and inevitable.*

In the rest of the chapter we will look at some of the most powerful forms of ideology, all built on forms of social structure that are foundations of most severely stratified societies. We will look at some of the ideological systems that do this, including patriarchy and the set of beliefs we call 'race'—looking at the gender factor and the race factor as they function ideologically in states.

MAINTAINING STRATIFICATION THROUGH IDEOLOGY: PATRIARCHY AND THE GENDER FACTOR (AGAIN)

Severely stratified societies tend to be *patriarchal*. This is related to the fact that in both the tributary and capitalist mode of production, most men are under the control of other more powerful elite men. Patriarchy is part of the system that keeps ordinary men from revolting against the demands of the elite. It surely controls women as well, but to see why it is associated with stratification, it is the control of men that is critical.

Class consciousness
Awareness that one's difficulties are due to one's membership in a class that is oppressed, rather than to one's own bad luck, poor decisions, or inadequate effort. Can lead to class conflict, in which members of an oppressed class attempt to force the oppressing class to be less exploitative.

Patriarchy
A society in which some men have power over others, who in turn have power over women in their families and see themselves, and are treated as, superior to women in general.*

A patriarchal society is one in which some men have power over others, who in turn have power over women in their families and see themselves as superior to women. Conveying these rights over some women to relatively powerless men is in a sense a payoff from the elite in return for their submission. Patriarchy conveys to men the right to control 'their' women, but at the same time denies most men direct rights to the means of production and to the resources they would need to compete with the elite for power and position.

To explain this, we need to look again at the production of a surplus. An individual's power is related to whether or not you control what you personally produce, as well as to how much of other people's surplus you control. In egalitarian societies much or all of what you produce is under your own control, and this leads to gender equality in bands and to relatively minimal gender inequality in many tribes. But no matter how productive you are in a stratified society, most people, men as well as women, are going to have limited power because you don't control what you produce.

Simply being productive does not give you power—as proven by the fact that the productivity and profits of the U.S. South were at one time based on the productive labor of enslaved Africans, who certainly did not gain power as a result of their productivity.

In a stratified society, by definition, most men can't control a great deal of what they produce. Nor can they control what happens to the value produced by their families, including the women and often the younger men. You are going to have to provide tribute or labor to the elite. If you pay tribute by giving part of the crop you and your family raised, or part of the cloth you or your wife has woven, or if you pay tribute by working on your lord's land, or if you work in a factory and make chairs, in all of those cases you have lost control of what you produced. If this doesn't happen you are not in a stratified society—or else, of course, you are an owner of the means of production.

Even some matrilineal societies are actually patriarchal if power is passed matrilineally from uncle to nephew, bypassing the women in the family. In that case men are still holding power within their families, even though it came from their mother's line. In both matrilineal and patrilineal societies, if a lineage head or aristocrat can demand surplus in the form of labor or tribute, that means they have greater power than other men. But patriarchy means that those commoner men who have to hand over tribute nevertheless have control over the women in their families. This control was, and in some parts of the world still is, upheld legally. Typically women could not own property except under certain circumstances; men were not held accountable legally for beating wives; a woman could not accuse her husband of rape; if she left she forfeited her right to her children; and women were without public political power and thus had no control over laws and public policy. What went on behind closed doors was determined by right by the husband. Although in the U.S. this pattern is no longer legal, the attitudes behind it are still evident. "A man's home is his castle" is a way of restoring honor to a man who, outside his home, has to be obedient. And it allows him to identify with other men, even if they are elite, because after all, they are all rulers of their own castles. He does not have to see himself as inferior to other men, and can see himself as superior to all women.

Patriarchal societies also tend to be heavily militarized. Obedience to military authority is defined as manly, and military action gives men importance as honorable warriors—not just controlled members of the working class. This is particularly important in societies like ours, where it is not clear that men can do anything that women couldn't also do. The idea that it takes a 'real man' to be a warrior helps explain why there has been such resistance and harassment of both women and gays in the military—they threaten a last bastion of manhood. As in other societies, the need to organize defense gives elites an important role, and helps to keep workers identifying with their elites. War—defending and transgressing boundaries—is a central business of a state, which means that it is important to have enemies. Many anthropologists would argue that the War on Terror has taken over the role once played by the Cold War, and that both the ideology of war and the profitability of war are critical to maintaining stratification.

As you can see, ideas about gender inequality and appropriate behavior for women are very compatible with ideas about patriarchy; they work together to uphold male supremacy, and male supremacy is part of the ideology that helps to keep elite men in control of other men. Ideas about gender and female sexuality and need for protection help both men and women to see patriarchy as natural. And both ideas underwrite the elite right to pass their wealth on to their children and to deny resources to other people's children.

• **Want more?**
On rape and harassment by US military try *The Roots of the Military's Rape Epidemic* http://www.alternet.org/world/roots-militarys-rape-epidemic Or watch the trailer for *The Invisible War* http://www.invisiblewarmovie.com/

MAINTAINING STRATIFICATION THROUGH IDEOLOGY: INVENTING RACE TO DIVIDE AND RULE

However, people often see through these ideologies or ignore them to some extent. If that happens a further tactic is needed to prevent revolts. The strategy of 'divide and rule' is frequently deployed to keep the people who are damaged by stratification under control.

> *The basic principle of divide and rule is to find some way of splitting up the people in the group to be controlled. You find something you can claim is a difference between them that truly matters and exaggerate its importance. Having created or exaggerated the perception of difference, you then claim that difference is a reason that one group should have slight privileges, causing the privileged group to take steps to protect its privilege and deny it to the others. Almost inevitably the groups come to hate and fear each other, and thus can't get together to revolt effectively.*

• **Want more?**
For an example of divide and rule try searching for the video *A Class Divided*.

The difference used is often one that people previously had not thought mattered all that much. Or it could be one that they did think mattered, but were not incensed about. This dividing wedge can be language, or ancestry, or what we call race. Religion can be used as another wedge issue, as the British government of colonial India did, pitting Muslims and Hindus against each other. The White South African government followed a similar course of divide and rule by encouraging fighting between tribes and political organizations which opposed White rule, making it difficult to join together in effectively challenging apartheid. Policies such as the so-called War on Terror, welfare reform (the so-called Personal Responsibility Act), and the attention paid to 'reverse discrimination' rather than to making *all* jobs pay enough to live on, have this effect. Issues such as abortion, evolution, homosexuality, school prayer and denial of climate change are also effective wedge issues in our society, emphasized by the media and by conservative religious and political organizations to the point where it is almost impossible for people on opposite sides of the issue to get together on anything else. As a result it is far more difficult, for instance, to fight effectively for the system of universal health care that polls show the majority of Americans want. Once this dividing wedge is active, the subordinate group is going to have a much harder time getting together to fight for changes that would benefit all of them. If they are busy directing their anger and fear and frustration at each other they are unlikely to work well together, and may even spend their time going after each other. If this works, then they can't challenge the dominant group, which will be able to continue or initiate exploitation policies.

INVENTING RACE IN THE U.S.

Race has been one of, if not the single most, powerful wedge tool for controlling all workers in the U.S. since the late 1600s.

And it was carefully invented for exactly that purpose, as I will explain in a moment. But first, since we mostly believe that race is real, even if we think people should not be treated differently according to their race, I need to explain the idea that it was invented.

• **Want more?** Try *Race: Are We So Different?* http://www.understandingrace.org/ and try searching for the video series *Race: The Power of an Illusion*

There are no separate biological groups of people—there is no biological reality to what we call race. There are no groups whose members are all more similar to each other than to members of other groups. There is definitely a socially constructed reality to race, but it is unrelated to biology. Think back to the Thomas Theorem from Chapter One. If enough people think something is real, it can have real consequences even if it is a flat out lie. That there are separate biological races is one of those lies that have real consequences; what race you are defined as makes a huge difference to your life in the United States. In reality, the earliest ancestors of every human on the globe came from Africa. As people spread out across the globe they continued having sex with the neighbors, who had sex with their neighbors, who had sex with theirs, and so on. So there were kids constantly being born here and there whose parents came from different groups. And their kids did the same thing. So a gene that started out, say in Central Asia, could show up generations later in Africa and Europe. We are all tightly interrelated.

However, as you well know, people from different parts of the globe do look different from each other. This is largely because, for instance, people with darker skins do better around the equator; their melanin protects them from skin cancer. Most likely all people originally were dark, but as they spread north dark skin became a disadvantage: it is hard to get enough Vitamin D from the sun if you are all bundled up trying to stay warm. It helped if what skin was exposed was lighter. As you go north from the equator at any point around the globe, on average, people's skin gets gradually lighter and lighter. If you make that trip, you will never cross a line at which you can say the people on one side are dark skinned and on the other are light, a point at which you can say you have switched from one race to another. Similarly people whose ancestors spent many generations near the tropics are more likely to carry the gene for sickle cell anemia, because that gene conveys protection against malaria. It doesn't matter whether your ancestors came from the African tropics or the Asian tropics; and if you came from South Africa, far from the tropics, you are not likely to carry the gene, despite being African. It has nothing to do with 'race' and everything to do with whether there were lots of the right kind of mosquitoes around.

So how come we have these ideas about race? To answer that we have to go back to colonial Virginia in the 1600s.[1] The colonial elites had been given huge land grants there by the English monarch. This gave them the right—if they could get the land away from the Indians who already lived and farmed there—to use the land to make their fortunes. You could literally grow money, since tobacco was used to buy and sell things. But to grow a lot of money, they needed a labor force; like other large land-

---

1. The following account is adapted from Buck, 2001, *Worked to the Bone: Race, Class, Power and Privilege in Kentucky.* New York: Monthly Review Press.

owners around the world, they wanted that labor force to be cheap. And to be cheap, it would have to be made up of powerless people who would have no choice —and people with no choice had to be created, as they have been all over the world. That took some doing.

The planters first tried enslavingNative American Powhatans and other native Nations in the Chesapeake area, but that didn't work well. Too many died of European diseases to which they had no immunity, and too many ran away. Their friends and relatives were not powerless, and helped them escape, and frequently fought back or avenged the capture. And since the enslaved Native AmericanNative Americans had been part of corporate groups before they were captured, they had rights to food, shelter, and protection if they got away. Enslaving Native AmericanNative Americans was usually successful only if they were shipped far from home. There was a massive and extremely profitable Indian Slave Trade conducted by the English and Spanish, who claimed it was legal to enslave war captives taken in fights between enemy native nations—even if it was the Europeans who instigated the war. These captives were generally shipped to the Caribbean and to Europe, but that didn't help the local Virginia planters.

So they turned instead to England for cheap labor. People who were defined in England as criminal were shipped to Virginia and other English colonies and sold as indentured servants. This meant the servant didn't own him or herself for a specified period of time, until they had worked for free long enough to pay back their owner for the cost of their passage to the colonies. Some people came voluntarily, but most came at the point of a gun, especially as the indenture period was made longer and longer. Lengthening the indenture gave the landowner more for his investment, and it put off the day when the freed servant was supposed to be given land. Meanwhile, in England, laws were passed to create more criminals for shipping. For instance, it became a shippable offense to be without a job (unless of course you were from a wealthy family that provided for you); stealing so much as a loaf of bread could get you sent; and so could being an orphan (unless of course you weren't from a poor family). Whole shiploads of little kids arrived to be sold in Virginia. And young women were sold as wives. At first the death rate was so high that few lived through to the end of their indentures. But as conditions improved, more became free. However, they were no longer given the land they were supposed to receive. Needless to say, there were a lot of very poor and furious former indentured servants. And those who were still indentured were also inclined to anger—they were likely to be severely overworked and underfed, and the indenture period was far longer than would be needed to pay back the cost of passage.

The first people from Africa arrived in the colonies along with the first Europeans. Some were free, some were enslaved or

• **Want more?** Try *Indian Slavery in the Americas* http:// www.gilderlehrman.org/ history-by-era/origins-slavery/essays/indian-slavery-americas

in some form of indenture. For several decades the labor force in Virginia was primarily European, but as England began running out of people to make into criminals, the planters imported more and more captured Africans. Africans in the colonies provided not only labor, but knowledge of various forms of cultivation. Plantation rice farming, for instance, was based entirely on African know-how, including the engineering and managing of the complex irrigation and water control systems rice required. Contrary to what you have probably been taught, the North also depended heavily on African labor. New York City, for instance, had more people enslaved than any other city except Charleston in the 1700s: Africans made up between 14% and 20% of New York's population.

• **Want more?**
For slavery in New York City, try *African Burial Grounds Website* http://www.nps.gov/afbg/index.htm

In Virginia in the 1600s there was not a clear distinction between working people of African ancestry and those of European ancestry. Slavery was not clearly differentiated from indenture, and indentures were growing longer and longer, so that indenture was more like slavery. Ancestry did not clearly differentiate who was enslaved, who was indentured, and who was free. People were identified by language or by European or African country of origin. Race, and the idea of whiteness, didn't really exist. Africans and Europeans lived and worked together, rebelled together, ran away together, married each other, and squabbled together. And during Bacon's Rebellion of 1676 they took advantage of the opportunity to rise up against the elite together.

> But after Bacon's Rebellion whiteness was invented to drive a wedge into the labor force. It was designed to prevent African and European people, people suffering varying forms of unfree and semi-free labor or who were 'free' but desperately poor, from ever again uniting to threaten landowners' rights to monopolize property and to create an immense, powerless, landless labor force.

Creating whiteness from a relatively undifferentiated mass of workers of varying and mixed ancestry, who initially did not distinguish among themselves by race, was a long process. New laws were passed about ancestry, marriage, and inheritance, tightening indenture into slavery for those identified by African ancestry and loosening it slightly into relative freedom for those able to claim European ancestry. The free group was given the earliest of a continuously evolving set of white privileges, including the (frequently unrealistic) hope of landownership. Massive propaganda encouraged White fear and hatred of Blacks. Those Whites, as well as Blacks, who didn't buy into the system, were severely punished and sometimes killed. It is worth quoting Lerone Bennett's analysis of how the early differentiation between Black and White was accomplished:

The whole system of separation and subordination rested on official state terror. The exigencies of the situation required men to kill some white people to keep them white and to kill many blacks to keep them black. In the North and South, men and women were maimed, tortured, and murdered in a comprehensive campaign of mass conditioning. The severed heads of black and white rebels were impaled on poles along the road as warnings to black people and white people, and opponents of the status quo were starved to death in chains and roasted slowly over open fires. Some rebels were branded; others were castrated. This exemplary cruelty, which was carried out as a deliberate process of mass education, was an inherent part of the new system (Lerone Bennett cited in Buck 2001: 26).

• **Want More?** Explore Whitney Plantation http://whitneyplantation.com/

Thus divided, the entire labor force was so weakened that the elite could maintain control of both Blacks and Whites. And whiteness has served that function ever since, although the forms of exploitation and the specific organization of whiteness itself have been modified.

> *Toward the end of the Civil War for example, the role of whiteness was critical in snookering people who were identified as White into consenting to policies that facilitated their own exploitation, as well as the even greater exploitation of people of color.*

Proposals were made in Congress for the confiscation and redistribution of enormous Confederate plantations. This could have provided very cheap land for poor White Southerners and free land in payment for generations of unpaid labor for people coming out of enslavement. Blacks and poor Whites would both have benefited. But that policy was never advocated by most Whites, at least partially because they believed the elite who said white supremacy would disappear if Blacks gained landownership, and they thought white supremacy mattered. W.E.B. Du Bois described this belief as a *'psychological wage,'*—the belief that although you are poor, at least you are White, and therefore a superior person—that belief is substituted for a real improvement in your life. It is rather like settling for being selected as employee of the month with your own parking place instead of being given a raise. So most Whites didn't protest elite efforts to keep Blacks in semi-slavery. The result was the sharecropping system for many Whites as well as Blacks. If Whites had stood up for Black rights, both Blacks and poor Whites would have been far better off.

Psychological wage
W.E.B. Du Bois' term for 'compensating' people psychologically for accepting inferiority by giving them someone over whom they can feel superior.

Segregation was invented in the late 1800s for the same reason, in order to suppress the Farmer's Alliance and People's Party revolt against elite control. Once again Blacks and Whites had managed to cooperate on the basis of their class position, to some extent ignoring whiteness and race. So the various state legislatures passed laws more thoroughly separating Blacks and Whites and equally importantly denying the vote to most Blacks and to many poor Whites.

• **Want more?** Try *Farmers' Alliance* https://tshaonline.org/handbook/online/articles/aaf02

White and Black voting dropped precipitously as a result, and has never fully recovered. So those most likely to vote to control elite behavior were largely unable to vote. And because racism, blatantly promoted by politicians, newspapers, and many White ministers, led not just to discrimination but also to the violence of lynch mobs, Blacks and Whites frequently hated and feared each other. Poor sharecropping Whites and Blacks, poor White mill workers and poor Black laborers and domestic workers, although all suffering, couldn't get together to fight back. They were divided and ruled. This system made it possible to control an enormous Black and White pool of desperately poor labor, damaging both Blacks and most Whites.

Race in the U.S. provides a classic example of all the principles involved in maintaining stratification.

The resources—the means of production and thus jobs, as well as the media and the power to enact and enforce laws—were all under elite control. Segregation laws, keeping Blacks and Whites from living and working together as equals, were a result of the exercise of that power. There was an intermediate collaborator class—White people who bought into whiteness and participated in hate-mongering, or supported the elite as small business owners or factory managers, or helped run the justice system that enforced it all. There were Black collaborators as well, although not nearly as many, for instance some preachers and teachers who advocated patience, or even believed that Whites truly were superior. Others weren't true collaborators, but were afraid, for good reason, to 'cause trouble.' The dominant ideology, believed by many in the dominant group, said that Whites were superior, and that they therefore needed to run the country, and that Blacks couldn't think well enough, or were too lazy, to run their own affairs. That ideology infected some Blacks with false consciousness. Divide and rule kept Blacks and Whites from getting together to get better conditions for everyone.

Race has been regularly used in the U.S. to help prevent the working class from joining together to form a broad coalition that might have the power to force changes that would benefit all members of the working class, regardless of race.

• **Want more?**
For understanding the role of white privilege, try exploring Tim Wise's website: http://www.timwise.org

Racism is subtly promoted by some politicians and some parts of the media, as well as by more overtly racist organizations. It is being used now to split the labor force over immigration, directing anger at people who speak Spanish and preventing the Latina/o, Black, and White segments of the working class from coming together to require the enactment of broader rights for all, such as universal health care and secure retirement. At this point even Social Security, Medicaid and Medicare are under threat. Anger at Muslims has been carefully promoted to do the same thing—the 'War on Terror' is cited to explain why the U.S. can't afford to provide these rights. Providing those rights would, after all, deprive employers of the cheapest of their labor force. The election and re-election of Barack Obama, significant as it is, has not changed this racial structure. His election may, however, have sparked a racial backlash by Whites who feel threatened by his election and by the erosion of their confidence in the economy and security of the U.S. post 9/11.

• **Want more?** Try
Black Churches Are Burning Again in America http://www.theatlantic.com/national/archive/2015/06/arson-churches-north-carolina-georgia/396881/

That backlash may be the source of the apparent upsurge in police killings of unarmed Blacks and of the burning of Black churches. The failure to bring justice for the murder of black teenager Trayvon Martin in 2012 led three young black women to form BlackLivesMatter, and with the murder of Michael Brown in Ferguson, Missouri in 2014 the movement grew dramatically. It has become a national and even transnational movement working for racial justice generally, but with an emphasis on the criminal justice system and police killings and sexual violence directed toward black men and women as well as toward other people of color. It reaches across gender and gender identity lines, and challenges capitalism's dependence on exploited labor. Anthropologists are both involved in the movement and challenging anthropology to address the ways in which white supremacy and white privilege continue to structure the US and international economic and political systems. Racism is none too subtly used by conservative talk show hosts and politicians to imply that the Blacks who were killed deserved it and the whole movement is composed of whiners who want a handout. It is also implicated in the push to effectively disenfranchise a large number of Black and Hispanic voters in many states by inaccurately claiming that undocumented immigrants are voting fraudulently, thus justifying rules that make registration and voting more difficult for poorer voters. Preventing the poor from voting, as we have just seen, is an effective way for elites in a democracy to keep their grip on power.

• **Want more?**
Explore *Savage Minds* http://savageminds.org/?s=black+lives+matter.
Also see *Black Lives Matter: A Critique of Anthropology* http://www.culanth.org/fieldsights/691-black-lives-matter-a-critique-of-anthropology

Racialized
The ideological process of designating certain categories of people as biologically separate and different from the dominant group. This process of race-making generally occurs to justify and enable super-exploitation.

• **Want more?** Try *Irish Americans, Racism, and the Pursuit of Whiteness* http://www.racismreview.com/blog/2010/03/17/irish-americans-racism-and-the-pursuit-of-whiteness/

Ideas about race have been used over and over to create an extremely cheap labor force. In fact, any group that is being severely exploited in the U.S. is racialized. Racialization is a process that has nothing to do with biology and everything to do with the definition and control of a cheap labor force.

The Irish, for instance, were once defined as an inferior race. They were not White people. Neither were Jews, or Italians, but all now are—because they are no longer a significant source of cheap labor. People coming from Mexico mostly aren't seen as white right now; might they be fifty years from now?

Race and race-like designations such as language and religion have been used as factors to create inequality around the world for these same purposes, justifying colonialism, empire and neocolonialism. Its continuing role is largely ignored in many discussions of globalization. The role of race is summarized in the following list.

The Uses of Race and Race-like Designations:
1. Defines the group of people to be super-exploited as different from and inferior to less exploited groups.
2. Provides a wedge for dividing and ruling the entire working class, not just those in the race or races defined as inferior.
3. Helps the collaborator class avoid feeling guilty about pursuing the policies that benefit the elite but cause the working class to suffer.
4. Provides an ideology (the psychological wage) that convinces members of the dominant race, regardless of their class, to identify with the elite and to believe that they themselves may some day join the elite.
5. Convinces some in the subordinate group to accept their position as natural or inevitable (false consciousness).

MAINTAINING STRATIFICATION THROUGH FORCE

But even divide and rule is sometimes inadequate to maintain stratification. So all stratified societies rely at base on the use of force and violence.

Legal force
The use of force that has been legitimized by the authorities of the institutions of a society and carried out by legitimate agents using specified types of force.*

This is just as true of our own society today as in any other stratified society. Since the dominant group controls the government, they can use force legitimately, through the 'justice' system, police, militias, or military. This *legal force* is used to put down revolts, and is also used on a daily basis on 'misbehaving' members of the subordinate group. If you look at the sharecropping system, for instance, the legal system directed this force against Whites as well as Blacks. Neither could challenge a sharecropping contract; neither could demand medical care or get employers thrown in jail for paying dying wages. Neither could decide to make a garden and pasture animals on a big landowner's unused back forty acres. Neither could accuse an employer of murder for deaths due to unsafe working conditions. That some of this is now changed has been due largely to revolts that have forced new laws and new employer policies, revolts orchestrated by the Civil Rights movement and by union organizing that crossed racial lines.

Despite these changes, however, some argue, with good evidence, that the racial bias, which leads both to the U.S. imprisonment of a far greater percentage of its people than other nations, and to the disproportionate imprisonment of people of color, has effectively created a revised system of segregation in the U.S. The prison system, along with the laws that limit access to housing, jobs, voting, and many other rights of citizenship for people released from prison, has institutionalized a system of second-class citizenship that most White Americans are unaware of or take for granted. People of color in the U.S, particularly Blacks, Native AmericanNative Americans, and Latino/as, however, are largely aware, and even those who have had no direct contact with the criminal justice system nevertheless deal daily with its consequences.

'Misbehavior' of people in the dominant group is generally not punished as severely, and much elite behavior that might be considered criminal is not defined as such, despite the death and destruction it causes (like lies about weapons of mass destruction or like taking away funding for medical care, or raising gas prices after a hurricane, or polluting the air and ground so that people die, or failing to provide funding for levees so that floods cause death and enormous destruction.) Some forms of elite behavior that are called criminal and do cause death are not defined as murder—such as refusal to follow safety regulations, as was done at West Virginia's Upper Big Branch Mine where in 2010 twenty-nine miners died in an explosion.

In addition, since the elites control the resources and also control the legal use of force (the army, the police, and the 'justice' system), they have more resources to use *illegal force* (such as hiring thugs). They can make it legal to buy labor to apply force (such as hiring private guards or a private military force like the Pinkertons who were hired in the U.S. legally as guards but also acted illegally to terrorize or kill union advocates in steel mills and coal mines). This use of illegitimate force is a form of terrorism. Illegal force is violence that is not exercised through the 'justice' system. It is usually led, as lynching was in the U.S., by members of the dominant group who are in the collaborator class or who are small-scale landowners or business people. Their followers in carrying out terrorism are often members of the dominant group who are being seriously exploited themselves, and want to protect the little privilege they receive from being of the same race, religion, or language as the people who actually own

• **Want more?**
On the legal use of force try *The New Jim Crow* http://prospect.org/article/new-jim-crow-0

• **Want more?** Try *Black Lives Matter: Eliminating Racial Inequity in the Criminal Justice System* http://sentencingproject.org/doc/publications/rd_Black_Lives_Matter.pdf

Illegal force
The use of force that has not been legitimized by a society or by the legitimate authorities of a society.*

the means of production. Their violence frequently goes unpunished.

These processes are very much alive and well in the U.S. today. Militarized policing is becoming routine. Police use tactics much like those used in situations of urban guerilla fighting during war, outfitted with surplus military equipment, including tanks, against U.S. citizens. The handling of the massive protests in Ferguson is just one example. The southern U.S., is now a militarized zone where, according to many analysts, to all intents and purposes the Constitution and the rights it conveys to citizens no longer apply, particularly if you appear Latino/a. This has all been accepted as a legal use of force. Police killings of unarmed civilians in situations where there was no reasonable reason to believe the shooter's life was in danger is still illegal; but the definition of what is reasonable fear when the victim is a person of color seems to be expanding dramatically. Combined with racial profiling and the long standing pattern of violence against Blacks, the result is what some see as a return to the 1940s. BlackLivesMatter has succeeded in bringing these issues at least to the edge of public consciousness.

• **Want more?** Try *The Militarization of the Police* http://www.slate.com/articles/news_and_politics/politics/2014/08/police_in_ferguson_military_weapons_threaten_protesters.html

RELIGION AND THE MAINTENANCE OF STRATIFICATION

Religion in stratified societies plays all the same functions that it plays in other types of societies. But just as the functions show up differently in chiefdoms as compared to tribes, so stratified societies put their own twist on the functions of religion. Those twists have largely to do with the often enormous difference between the lives of the haves and the have-nots. Having to deal merely with status differences is quite different from having to deal with differences that can be matters of life or death. Religious beliefs can form a framework that provides meaning for lives of hardship and misfortune or for lives made comparatively easy by wealth and privilege. These beliefs can act as an ideology that explains and justifies the entire stratification system, giving people living in it a sense of comfort, despite the dramatic injustice of the system.

All religions, including your own, have aspects that appear irrational to outsiders.

You have encountered this idea before, but it is worth repeating as we begin to talk anthropologically about a topic that may be deeply personal and important to you. Remember that anthropology is not trying to determine whose religion is right. Instead, it is trying to understand how and why religions function as they do in different kinds of societies. You have seen this in operation in societies quite different from yours. But it may feel very different to you when this same way of thinking is applied to your own religion. As you have seen, religion reflects the structure of the society. Since life in states is deeply unequal, that inequality will be reflected in the religion of state societies.   That may be hard to swallow; or you may find that it helps you understand things that have bothered you for years. For some, that can be a liberating experience.

With that said, we can examine religion as it functions in severely stratified societies. As in all societies, religion in states reflects the subsistence strategy. This is seen, for instance, in religious ceremonies to bless a harvest, people praying for a job, being expected to give money in church every Sunday, and the belief that it is immoral to break a contract. And as in other societies, religion in states deals with issues that people can't control, justifies the distribution of power, and acts as a tool of social control. These functions are so intertwined that we will talk about them all together.

RELIGION IN SUPPORT OF STRATIFICATION

First of all, a society's religion does not *cause* it to be structured in a particular way. That is putting the cart before the horse. Instead, as a society develops a particular social structure, its religion gradually begins to match the society. Once that happens, of course, people's religious beliefs help keep that structure going.

Generally speaking, religion does not cause a society to act in a certain way; instead it reflects and justifies the structure of a society.

For instance, the religious belief that women should obey their husbands, or that women cause evil, does not *cause* gender inequality; instead, if a system of gender inequality exists, then those beliefs can be used to convince both women and men that inequality is right. Religious beliefs about women, or about female pollution (such as Christian beliefs about the connection between Eve, evil, and suffering), may reinforce and reflect a society's separation of the sexes, gender inequality, and the sexual division of labor. In other words, religion plays important ideological functions in dealing with inequality and even with a subsistence strategy that depends on men and women playing very different roles. Believing that violating these roles will earn you the anger of the supernatural acts as a tool of social control. Some versions of Christianity believe that divorce is immoral. However, since religion tends to reflect the social structure, as divorce becomes more common, fewer and fewer churches say that divorce sends you to Hell. Or the belief that homosexuality is wrong reinforces heterosexuality, and in a society with gender inequality, it also reinforces patriarchy, giving women fewer options outside of life under the domination of a man. The gender inequality of a patriarchal society is then reflected in the religious institution itself: in patriarchal societies men hold almost all important functions and positions of religious authority. The implication is that men are truly closer to the gods and have special abilities that women don't have.

The dominant religion in all stratified societies justifies the power of the elite—both to the elite themselves and to commoners. For the elite, religion generally provides a formula that, if followed, guarantees that you are fulfilling God's will by carrying out your position of power properly. The elite are often expected to do a certain amount of redistribution through charity, or through funding the religious establishment, or through building or donating to churches, temples, mosques, or other religious symbols. They may fund institutions that provide some care for the destitute, the people who are most damaged by stratification. They may be expected to provide feasts for ordinary people during religious ceremonies. They may themselves be expected to perform particular religious rituals that are meant to ensure good crops or success in war. Religion thus justifies to the elite their position of power and privilege. They can see themselves as living up to the obligations of their position and have no need to feel guilty for exploitation and super-exploitation. They may be expected to see their wealth as a 'blessing' or as a sign of God's approval, and give thanks to God, rather than to the people whose work made their wealth.

The same religion can, at the same time, play a meaningful role for people in the subordinate group. It can justify the position of those in power and provide a sense of meaning and purpose for their own suffering as the work they do goes to enrich the elite but leaves little for themselves. They may believe that they are fulfilling the will of the gods in handing their surplus over to landowners and elite. Women dealing with severe gender inequality may feel more at peace with themselves and their situation if they believe they are fulfilling the will of the gods or pleasing the ancestors. The religion may teach that the nobility or upper castes are closer to the god, or gods, or that the king is a representative of God, as in Europe's divine right of kings, or that the king is necessary for functions that benefit you, such as performing rituals that bring back the sun at the winter solstice, or ensure good crops, or bring the favor of the gods. A religion may teach that a President or a king knows God's plan in time of war, making it appear that risking your life in a war that is conducted to benefit elites is actually the fulfillment of God's will. Such a belief can help assuage your guilt in participating in the devastation that war inevitably brings to the lives of ordinary people like you who have been defined as 'the enemy.' Religious explanations for war continue to play, as they have for centuries, a critical role in the arsenal of ideas that get ordinary people to agree to turn their lives over to the elite.

Accommodation
The process of adjusting oneself to difficult circumstances you are powerless to change. In particular, the term applies to situations of inequality, where the person with less power must somehow learn to live with the demands of more powerful people.*

Accommodation refers to the various ways people figure out to help themselves put up with a situation they don't like but also feel can't be changed. Examples include beliefs such as God has a reason for putting me in this position; the poor are more blessed than the rich, and will go to a heavenly reward but the rich will not, since it is easier for a camel to get through the eye of a needle than for a rich man to enter heaven. Hinduism gives religious support to India's caste system, and therefore to India's distribution of wealth, power, and prestige. The Christian beliefs that the poor will always be with us, that one should render unto Caesar that which is Caesar's, and that servants should be good has a similar message. These same ideas also can act as an instrument of social control. If you believe it is the will of the gods that you are suffering and your children are undernourished and must work even as little kids, then you are unlikely to join in a revolt. You may even think it is immoral to question the system at all.

Or another example: Hindu taboos on eating beef reinforce people's will to keep their cattle alive during periods of hunger (and even induce wealthier Hindus to let poor people's cattle graze on their land), just as our taboo on eating horse reinforced people's will to keep their horses alive during periods of hunger when horses were essential to our subsistence strategy. In both cases, your future welfare depends on not eating the animal on which you depend for survival.

Part of this accommodation is that religion can provide some sense of security and hope for the future. Religion may give a sense of hope, or it may define what is happening now as unimportant by stressing an afterlife, or it may give a sense that the gods approve of your behavior or are taking care of you. It may also give you a reason for giving tribute to a king, or for accepting your lack of power.

Prayer or the performance of various rituals may bring the feeling that God, or the spirits, or the ancestors have been brought onto your side—you have some influence over what happens to you by praying or performing rituals correctly. Without some feeling of control, (whether that control is real or not is less important for this reaction than the *belief* that you have some control) people are more likely to stop trying to accomplish something that they believe to be impossible. People with more power often blame the victim by calling this reaction 'apathy.' The belief that you can't accomplish something can act as a self-fulfilling prophecy. Be aware that this feeling of helplessness may be a perfectly reasonable result of being conquered or exploited. Maybe you truly can't accomplish your goal because the barriers built up around you by people with more power than you are truly insurmountable. The feeling of helplessness may be the result of a perfectly rational analysis of reality. But on the other hand, if you believe that you have the help of the supernatural, the self-fulfilling prophecy may actually make you more likely to succeed. Think of what nursing a sick child must have been like in the days before antibiotics: persistence day after day after day could make the difference between life and death for the child, and that persistence is easier if you believe that the supernatural is backing you. To outsiders your religious beliefs may appear irrational. However, it may be precisely those irrational elements that help to increase people's confidence in their success, so they may try harder, and actually succeed, or survive a period of extreme worry and stress. The sense of control or the sense that deities or spirits or the ancestors are on your side that religion often brings may be the source of your confidence.

> *If a society has a significant degree of inequality, then those people with less power may experience less control over their lives than do people with more power. As a result, they may be more consciously religious than people with more power.*

For instance, women may actually be able to control fewer of the things that happen to them than the men in their family and community can. In a stratified society some men will also have less control than others, as will people marked as belonging to an inferior category. For all of these people religion is likely to be particularly important. This depth of religious feeling as part of everyday life may not be as pervasive a pattern among the elite, although of course there will be exceptions.

Other aspects of religious organization also support the authority of elites. For instance, in complex chiefdoms and in states religious buildings may be designed to reinforce the structure of the society. The structure of religious buildings and lighting may be used to enhance the feeling of awe in the presence of the supernatural. An inner sanctum or a distant altar allows only a select group of people to see and know about secret rites that are performed there. Such esoteric knowledge gives elites an added religious aura.

Frequently ordinary people don't play an active role in many of their society's religious rituals. Rituals may be performed for their benefit, in which they are passive observers or minor performers. They may be more audience than participants. They are dependent on more powerful people for the performance of necessary rituals, such as the calendric rituals that bring the sun back at the winter solstice, and perhaps also for some crisis rituals and rites of passage. This dependence performs an ideological function in cementing those who have less power to those with more

• **Want more?** Try for pictures *Madurai Meenakshi Amman Temple* http://www.maduraimeenakshi.org/

power, and is particularly pronounced in complex chiefdoms and kingdoms.

In kingdoms and many other states the religious institution is financially supported by the state, and the religious specialists —imams, temple priests, preachers, popes, rabbis, ministers— are what anthropologists call priests, full-time religious specialists who are dependent on the good will of the king or state administrators for their job. In states without a state religion the religious specialists of the dominant religion are also priests, but are dependent on the good will of the local elite who provide much of the funding and much of the leadership. In either case, teaching religious views that are contrary to the views of the elite or that challenge the stratification system is hazardous.

Many states, especially ones without an effectively enforced state religion, have religious groups that function quite differently and are not under direct elite control. They are led by people who are more like shamans than like priests. Frequently such groups are found among the more exploited part of the population. Their religious specialists don't usually undergo extensive formal training, as priests do, and are not licensed to practice by a formal institution such as a university or seminary or board of other priests. They become religious leaders because they have talent and often serve an informal apprenticeship with another such practitioner. Often they feel that they have been 'called' to take this role. If others feel that they are truly good at getting in touch with the supernatural, they may be asked frequently to speak or conduct rituals. They may develop a group of regular followers. Such groups are rarely under the control of some wider governing body, and religious services or rituals are likely to be done in a more egalitarian manner, with everyone actively participating, rather than serving primarily as audience. Such groups can restore a sense of worth to people who, in the rest of their lives, are treated as if they are of little worth. In such groups all members at least have the potential to play parts that everyone acknowledges as important. The leader is one of themselves, not an outsider licensed or imposed by people in authority. This is a far more egalitarian structure than that found in religious organizations controlled by elites. Nevertheless, the message conveyed may be one of accommodation with the stratification system—the dominant version of religion.

RELIGION FIGHTING THE DENIAL OF RIGHTS

> *However, in most stratified societies the dominant version of religion is not the only one. People in the subordinate group may believe that stratification is wrong, that it is not the will of the gods that they be worked to death, or that their children should die of hunger or have to start working as little kids, while the elite experiences a very different kind of life. This version of religion often justifies a redistribution of power.*

Resistance
The refusal to accommodate (see accommodation) the exploitative demands of those with more power; the refusal to do something against one's will."

Liberation theology, for instance, emphasizes the religious obligation to work for real social justice based on a redistribution of resources. The non-dominant version of religion can provide religious backing for *resistance* and revolt. Like the dominant religion it gives a sense of security and hope, and of some control over the future—a feeling that what you do matters and can change the future. This helps to explain why people who are revolting against oppression often call on religion: it can be used to give back that lost feeling of control by convincing you that the supernatural will act on your side and help you win against frightening odds. In the U.S. the Civil Rights Movement provides an example: where do you get the courage to risk death, injury, or imprisonment by sitting at a forbidden lunch counter? Where do you get the determination to keep walking month after month instead of taking the bus because you refuse to sit in the back any longer?

Religion, but not in its dominant version, is one source of the courage it takes to challenge a powerful elite. Religion, in its dominant version, is one source of the belief that one should not challenge the elite and is a source of the strength it takes to make a life that somehow works at the bottom of a stratified society.

RESISTANCE AND REVOLT DESPITE IT ALL

> *But, and this is a very important 'but,' despite all the effort that elites and their helpers put into keeping their society stratified, people do regularly put their lives on the line to fight back, and if they can cross the wedge lines, including gender and race, that are meant to control them, they do sometimes succeed in improving their lives enormously.*

• **Want more?** Try
A Rebellion to Remember:
The Legacy of Nat Turner
http://docsouth.unc.edu/
highlights/turner.html

• **Want more?** Try
The Homestead Steel Strike
http://www.pbs.org/
wgbh/amex/carnegie/
peopleevents/
pande04.html
Or for a more recent
example try Photos:
Walmart Workers Arrested
http://thinkprogress.org/
economy/2014/10/16/
3580855/walmart-arrests-
photos/

• **Want more?** Try
The Fight for Women's
Suffrage http://
www.history.com/topics/
womens-history/the-fight-
for-womens-suffrage#

In the U.S. there have been many such examples of resistance and revolt by oppressed groups. Bacon's Rebellion was one; people who were enslaved revolted on numerous occasions—Stono, Denmark Vesey, the German Coast, Nat Turner—all were real revolts and terrorized Whites. Shay's Rebellion was a New England revolt of Revolutionary War veterans and farmers. During the Civil War so many enslaved Africans ran away to fight for the Union Army that by the end of the war it was one-tenth Black. Then there was the women's suffrage movement; children who worked 60 hours a week went on strike in Philadelphia for the right to go to school; women struck over the dangerous conditions in sewing factories; agricultural union wars in the Southwest and California, and coal mine unionization in Appalachia; the People's Party and the Tobacco Wars and the Civil Rights Movement, the on-going struggles of indigenous people around the world, as well as in the U.S., to prevent the destruction of the land on which they live—these are just a few of the revolts, although not all equally successful.

> *U.S. history as generally presented downplays or completely ignores the enormous and still ongoing dissent that has greeted stratification in this country.*

REFERENCES/SUGGESTED READING

Alexander, Michelle (2010) The New Jim Crow: Mass Incarceration in the Age of Colorblindness. New York: The New Press.

Allen, Theodore 1997 Invention of the White Race, vol. II, The Origin of Racial Oppression in Anglo-America. New York: Verso Press.

Anderson, Gary. Ethnic Cleansing and the Indian: The Crime That Should Haunt America. Norman: University of Oklahoma Press.

Buck, Pem Davidson 2001 Worked to the Bone: Race, Class, Power and Privilege in Kentucky. New York: Monthly Review Press.

Chomsky and Herman 2002 Manufacturing Consent:The Political Economy of the Mass Media. New York: Pantheon Books.

Feagin, Joe 2004 Toward an Integrated Theory of Systemic Racism. In The Changing Terrain of Race and Ethnicity. Maria Krysan and Amanda Lewis, eds. Pp.203-223. Russell Sage Foundation, NY.

Gallay, Alan 2014. 2002. The Indian Slave Trade: The Rise of the English Empire in the American South, 1670-1717. New Haven: Yale University Press.

Horne, Gerald. 2014. The Counter-Revolution of 1776. Slave Resistance and the Origins of the United States of America. New York: New York University Press.

Jackson, Antoinette 2012. Speaking for the Enslaved: Heritage Interpretation at Antebellum Plantation Sites. Walnut Creek, CA: Left Coast Press.

Mills, Charles 1997 The Racial Contract. Ithaca: Cornell University Press.

Mitrani, Sam. 2013. The Rise of the Chicago Police Department: Class and Conflict, 1850-1894. Urbana: University of Illinois Press.

Morgan, Jennifer. 2004. Laboring Women: Reproduction and Gender in New World Slavery. Philadelphia: University of Pennsylvania Press.

Roediger, David 1991 The Wages of Whiteness: Race and the Making of the American Working Class. London: Verso.

Waterston, Alisse 2006 Are Latinos Becoming 'White' Folk: And What That Still Says about Race in America. Transforming Anthropology 14(2):133-150.

Whitaker, Mark 2007 Learning Politics from Sivaram: The Life and Death of a Revolutionary Tamil Journalist in Sri Lanka. London: Pluto Press.

Zinn, Howard 2005 A People's History of the United States: 1492-Present (revised and updated). New York: Harper Perennial Classics.

On the role of the middle class

Buck, Pem Davidson 2008 Keeping the Collaborators on Board as the Ship Sinks: Toward a Theory of Fascism and the U.S. 'Middle Class.' Rethinking Marxism 20(1):68-90.

Hicks, Frederic 1999 The Middle Class in Ancient Central Mexico. Journal of Anthropological Research 55: 409-427.

On Liberation Theology

Farmer, Paul 2004 Pathologies of Power: Health, Human Rights, and the New War on the Poor. Berkeley: University of California Press.

On the social construction of race

Brodkin, Karen. 1998. How Jews Became White Folk and What That Says About Race in America. New Brunswick: Rutgers University Press.

Buck, Pem Davidson. 2012 Whither Whiteness? Empire, State, and the Re-Ordering of Whiteness. Transforming Anthropology 20(2): 105-117.

Goodman, Alan and Thomas Leatherman, eds. 1998. Building a New Biocultural Synthesis: Political-Economic Perspectives on Human Biology. Ann Arbor: University of Michigan Press.

Ignatiev, Noel. 1996. How the Irish Became White. New York: Routledge.

Race: Are We So Different? American Anthropological Association http://www.understandingrace.org/home.html

Race. A Project of the American Anthropological Association https://www.youtube.com/v/8aaTAUAEyho

Roediger, David 1991. The Wages of Whiteness: Race and the Making of the American Working Class. New York: Verso.

On BlackLivesMatter

Black Lives Matter: Eliminating Racial Inequity in the Criminal Justice System. 2015. The Sentencing Project. http://sentencingproject.org/doc/publications/ rd_Black_Lives_Matter.pdf

Burton, Orisanmi, 2015, Black Lives Matter: A Critique of Anthropology. Cultural Anthropology Hotspots. June 29. http:// www.culanth.org/fieldsights/691-black-lives-matter-a-critique-of-anthropology. Accessed Jan 11, 2016.

Williams, Bianca and Dana-Ain Davis, eds. 2015. Making Black Lives Matter: Reflections on the Declaration and Principles. Savage Mind Series. http://savageminds.org/2015/11/11/making-black-lives-matter-reflections-on-the-declaration-and-the-movement-introduction-part-i/

CHAPTER 8
GLOBALIZATION: THE RETURN OF EMPIRE

Globalization has led to some degree of similarity in local cultures around the world, such as the use of cell phones or the invoking of the concept of democracy to bolster claims to human and civil rights. This similarity is most noticeable among members of the professional managerial class. Anthropologists debate the degree to which this means the increasing homogenization of culture. Blue jeans may be worn by young men in India as dress clothes appropriate for attending a wedding, for instance. They may be the same blue jeans as those worn in the U.S.—and both made by underpaid workers in Guatemala who thus also participate in the culture of blue jeans—but the meanings of those pants, and people's relationship to them, is very different in the three contexts. Anthropologists—and local people—disagree about the extent to which the similarities that do exist amount to cultural imperialism, the almost forcible imposition of Western culture through the Global North's massive use of technologies such as advertising, internationally distributed movies, television, and the internet.

In this chapter, however, we will be looking at globalization and imperialism in quite a different way. Globalization in this sense is a rather neutral term for a modern form of imperialism that is organizing world wide inequality today. It continues the process of extracting cheap labor and cheap raw materials from exploitable people and places around the world, with consequences remarkably similar to those of colonialism.

• **Want more?**
For videos relating to many of the issues in this chapter try *Online University of the Left* http://ouleft.org/

In the Global North a large proportion of those most seriously exploited are immigrants from the Global South. In some countries they are formally denied rights by law. In others the resident population discriminates against them, denying them rights informally. In either case, except for those who arrive in the Global North from relatively privileged backgrounds with a good education, they serve as a source of cheap, unprotected labor. In the Global South transnational corporations frequently influence or control local governments to provide a 'good business climate,' where there is no labor unrest, people can't effectively protest the lack of welfare services, and natural resources can be extracted with minimal tax benefits to local people.

And now, with the 'War on Terror' and the occupation of Afghanistan and Iraq by the U.S. military, we are even seeing a revival of colonial style political and military control of other countries. As in the older version of imperialism, political and military control, perhaps disguised by installing a local puppet government, makes the country's resources available to the elites of the conquering country. And as in the older version, anthropological images, although often produced these days by journalists rather than anthropologists, play a critical ideological role, making occupation appear benevolent. A rash of internet images about the mistreatment of women in a particular country, for instance, is frequently a signal that occupation is immanent. Or the media may emphasize images and interpretations that make the local people appear incompetent and unable to govern themselves, while giving little attention to examples that demonstrate effective local organizing. These images are particularly effective when nation-building and the profits it produces are at stake.

Today empire is no longer a national enterprise. Instead, it is produced by transnational corporations working in conjunction with global institutions of governance and regulation and with the enforcing power of the armies of the dominant nations, those whose elites benefit from global apartheid. U.S. world hegemony has given way to the hegemony of transnational corporations, and even U.S. financial might is challenged by that of China.

The processes of globalization have been to some extent underway for several centuries; after all the slave trade was a global enterprise. Multinational corporations have also been in existence for generations; General Motors had factories in Germany producing trucks for the Nazi army during World War II, for instance. After World War II U.S.-based multinationals were able to operate on a much broader scale, and oil companies tightened their control of much of the world's energy supplies. *Maquiladoras*, U.S.-owned or contracted factories using almost exclusively cheap female labor, were set up just over the border in Mexico, and similar factories operated in the Philippines and elsewhere. These multinationals used the processes of neocolonialism to manage the local governments in the countries where they operated.

With the breakup of the USSR, however, the system began to change. Soviet power no longer restrained U.S. and other capitalist countries from engaging in direct imperial policies, and the power of multinationals grew exponentially. 'Multinational' was no longer an adequate adjective to describe them. They are no longer simply corporations that operate within the boundaries of a number of different countries. They are now referred to as transnational corporations: they have transcended the role of nations and national boundaries, and operate as if nations were merely administrative units within a larger empire. The budgets of the largest transnationals are larger than the budgets of most of the countries in the world, and they are once again able to use the military might of countries such as the U.S. for purposes of direct conquest. And despite the disapproval of a large majority of

Maquiladora
A factory established by a U.S. owned corporation just south of the border with Mexico in order to take advantage of the opportunity to make bigger profits than are possible in the U.S.; pays low wages by Mexican standards and extremely low wages by U.S. standards, and often gets favorable tax treatment and can lower safety and environmental standards.

Americans, in 2015 the U.S. military, although down-sized, still occupied Iraq, defending its puppet government and therefore the ability of that government to hand over oil rights to the transnationals. President Obama has intensified the occupation of Afghanistan, has intensified the use of secret drone attacks and secret bases around the world, and is now involved in Iran and Syria.

Under these conditions the indirect, and sometimes precarious, policies of neocolonialism are no longer necessary. Despite serious resistance, civil war, and tens of thousands of deaths in Iraq, for instance, transnational corporations now have contracts that give them de facto control of Iraq's oil.

George W. Bush declared his intent to ignore Congress should it attempt to curtail his use of the U.S. military as an occupying force or to curtail his right, should he so choose, to extend the war into Iran and Syria. Bush gradually increased the power of the executive branch and at the same time withdrew some of the rights that have historically accompanied full citizenship in the U.S. While rejecting some provisions of the Bush administration, Obama has largely allowed most of Bush's expansion of power to remain intact. Opposition in Congress to this expansion from either party has been feeble. While described as keeping Americans safe, it is actually the needs of the transnationals that dominate the U.S. government as well as the governments of conquered countries. Some analysts argue that the U.S., like other countries, has become another administrative unit within a larger empire.

Globalized empire today has been produced by both **neo-liberal** and **neoconservative** policies working in tandem. Neoliberalism tends to equate deregulation of business and of the market economy with freedom and the spread of democracy. The resulting free market has made it far easier for transnational corporations to operate without limitations imposed by the countries involved. Free markets and free trade generally work in the interests of those with power and to the detriment of those subject to exploitation and super-exploitation—those who need protection from the most severe consequences of life in a stratified world. The Neoliberal belief that corporations should not be regulated has also contributed to U.S intransigence in refusing to sign onto international agreements to cut greenhouse gases in order to slow climate change. The failure to regulate in the Global North and the inability to regulate in much of the Global South has also made it possible for global businesses to conduct many of their transactions illegally, operating under the radar to avoid taxes, tariffs, and safety inspections. Despite the fact that neoliberals and neoconservatives frequently disagree on policy, neoconservatism has also played its part in the construction of corporate global empire. Neoconservativism emphasizes the strategic necessity of maintaining U.S. world hegemony in the 21st century, and sees the use of military force as an acceptable method for doing so. Thus as

Neoliberalism
The political and economic philosophy that says that governments should not regulate private enterprise or intervene in the workings of the free market economy.

Neoconservative
The political and economic philosophy which emphasizes the role of military intervention and the promotion of U.S. corporate interests internationally, including the forcible imposition of democratic institutions.

• **Want more?**
For deregulation and jobs in the U.S. try *Workers on the Edge* http://prospect.org/article/workers-edge

U.S. economic hegemony has faltered, neoconservatives have provided the justification for the exercise of military muscle.

This use of the U.S. military has met with comparatively little resistance from U.S. citizens, at least partially because this is a volunteer army. There is no draft, and thus less anger. But there are also other factors in the lack of resistance. A significant portion of the military is immigrant and a significant portion of the danger is borne by private military contractors. The role of the military is described as nation-building and the media provides many images of soldiers helping children. No official accounting was made in the U.S. of the Iraqi and Afghanistani civilians—men, women, children—who have died of military action itself or of the inadequate nutrition or medical care that resulted from war. And while the number of U.S. military deaths was reported, little mention was made of the thousands who have been severely wounded, or who now live with PTSD.

Being the source of power for an empire has always meant suffering on the part of the working classes at the center of empire. That suffering was described as 'the White man's burden' under the British Empire, as 'manifest destiny' during the construction of the U.S. as a conquest state stretching from coast to coast, and now as 'sacrifice' to maintain our freedom and bring freedom to the people conquered and brought into transnational empire. That 'sacrifice' is borne almost entirely by the working class. It means the deaths of several thousand military personnel and the maiming of many thousands more, as well as a national debt that will hold the U.S. hostage to transnational financial institutions for at least a generation and will result in the under-funding of basic needs such as education, health care, roads, and even pay for military personnel. The result may turn out to be a de facto austerity program much like the austerity programs of structural adjustment imposed on indebted nations of the Global South, and more recently in Europe. The massive budget cuts demanded by many in Congress and by candidates running for nomination for president by the Republican Party in 2015, particularly those influenced by the Tea Party, would, if enacted wholesale, impose similar austerity measures in the U.S. The resulting hardship would, as elsewhere, be borne far more by the poor and working classes, and by women, children, and the elderly.

The sacrifice that austerity programs impose, however, is translating into soaring profits for transnationals in oil, but also for the corporations that produce tanks, trucks, ammunition—the supplies that are needed only in war, and need to be replaced only if they are destroyed in war. In the past decade a new market has opened up for military supplies with the arming of the border and militarized policy. Privatizing more and more military, policing, and military supply services provides an additional source of profits, sometimes even without the need to bid on a contract or to keep costs within the contract. The war machine carries consequences for all of us within the empire.

• **Want more?** Try *U.S. Military: A Growing Latino Army* http://nbclatino.com/2013/01/01/u-s-military-a-growing-latino-army/

• **Want more?** Try *The Great Austerity Shell Game* http://www.theguardian.com/commentisfree/2013/nov/04/great-austerity-shell-game

• **Want more?** Try *Ferguson's Police Got Free Military Gear Straight from the Pentagon* http://talkingpointsmemo.com/dc/ferguson-missouri-militarized-police-1033-program

LOSS OF NATIONAL AUTONOMY

National governance in the globalized world has to some extent been superseded by governance at the transnational level. Nations are no longer autonomous units, able to decide on their own policies. Instead, as administrative units within global empire, they are partially governed by their agreement to participate in such organizations as the World Bank, the International Monetary Fund, the World Trade Organization, and the numerous agreements, such as the General Agreement on Tariffs and Trade, that have spun off from these organizations. Participation in these organizations and agreements, in other words, denies the right of national sovereignty and conveys rights of governance to unelected bodies composed primarily of appointed members representing transnational corporations. These organizations work generally toward 'free trade,' which means that goods and services should be able to move around the globe unimpeded by national boundaries and by national laws that give an 'unfair' advantage to a particular country in selling its goods. So for instance, a free health care system in Mexico could be declared an unfair advantage, since then Mexican companies would not have to pay for insurance as (some) U.S. companies have to do. Since these institutions are controlled by the more powerful countries of the Global North, such declarations are generally made in their favor. In addition, the more powerful nations are more able to ignore the dictates of these organizations, but even Japan, for instance, has been forced to rescind its ban against importing beef from the U.S. in the wake of worries about mad cow disease and about feeding genetically altered corn to beef animals. The U.S. was able to ignore UN resolutions about the illegality of the war in Iraq while enforcing such resolutions against other countries when it has been in the interests of transnational corporations to do so.

Local elites and upper middle class families in the Global South have been able to benefit from this whole system, sometimes by their sale of land or other resources to transnationals, or by getting well-paid jobs with those corporations or in government bureaucracies. They are therefore likely to support participation by their governments, except when their control of resources is directly threatened.

To some extent the increasing misery caused by these policies, which local governments may no longer have the power to alleviate, is dealt with by Non-Governmental Organizations (NGOs). While these organizations may provide some relief, they are also frequently instruments of empire, providing governance and performing governmental functions under the control of outsiders, not of local people. The role of NGOs in failed states is particularly noticeable, and reflects a lack of national autonomy.

• **Want more?** Try *Seeds of Suicide and Slavery vs Seeds of Life and Freedom* http://www.aljazeera.com/indepth/opinion/2013/03/201332813553729250.html

RESISTING GLOBAL EMPIRE

Partially because of the loss of national sovereignty, and partially because capitalism is actually much more efficient in placing wealth in elite hands, socialist aspects of societies around the world are being undermined. True poverty—and real wealth for some—has been created in the countries of the former USSR and East Germany. China and Cuba are both experimenting with controlled and limited capitalism. Countries that have been slightly socialist in the recent past, like Canada and India and Western Europe, are seeing their socialist aspects undermined by capitalism. Even the minimal socialist aspects of the U.S., such as welfare, public schools, and Medicare and Social Security, are under siege, subject to austerity programs similar to those of structural adjustment in the Global South. In some cases public programs—roads, schools, prisons, military operations—are being turned over to capitalist enterprise and thus made available as sources of profit, governed by the imperatives of the market, rather than those of human welfare. Advocates of such policies believe that these two imperatives are not mutually exclusive, and that human welfare can be enhanced by adhering to the profit motive. Consequently socialist policies are declining as a result of the worldwide shift to an increasingly globalized capitalist economy and the imperialist effects of the New World Order.

> *At the same time, however, as the effects of globalized capitalism become more and more apparent, people, as usual, are not passively agreeing to their oppression.*

Individuals and families work out strategies to cope with their lives both as consumers and as producers. Pulling this off requires dealing with all the factors of inequality. How those factors affect you depends on your identity, since they impose far more difficulties on some than on others. People whose choices are most severely limited by the operation of these factors sometimes decide to work together, rather than as individuals, creating strength through organizing. Doing so may bring a sense of empowerment and sometimes brings real change. It is certainly the only possibility for change.

Some work to build or maintain non-capitalist community economies even within the context of globalized capitalism. One alternative being developed in some communities and groups around the world, is to opt out of the use of standard money. In parts of Europe and the U.S. there are time banks, where you can bank an hour's worth of work and use it to buy an hour's worth of someone else's work. So you could bank five hours of work by preparing someone's taxes. You could then spend those five hours having your house cleaned by some other member, who would

• **Want more?** Try *Food Stamp Cuts: A Bi-Partisan Scandal* http://www.thenation.com/article/food-stamp-cuts-bipartisan-scandal/

• **Want more?** Try *Time Banks Provide a New Way to 'Spend' an Hour* http://www.usnews.com/news/articles/2012/10/23/time-banks-provide-new-way-to-spend-an-hour

then have five hours to spend with some other member who repairs computers. Some hard-hit communities in Europe have created their own local currency, or even a virtual currency, avoiding use of the Euro.

Another option is a variety of worker cooperatives, in which workers themselves own the means of production and make the decisions regarding factory management and business policy, workplace issues, pay, and benefits. Sometimes this is done by direct vote and negotiation, sometimes it is done by elected worker representatives, sometimes a workers' council hires technical and management specialists. But in all these varieties, the bottom line is that people are all owners of the business, that they should all share in the profits from it, that no one should receive wages that are vastly higher than others, and that they should all have a say in the conditions that affect their lives. Generally those that have been successful have integrated themselves into their local communities: they are run by the workers, who are local, but in addition they have allied themselves with other groups that work for greater equality, and with other cooperatives. They often help to provide start-up funds for other cooperatives, and form umbrella organizations that provide support for all of them. Mondragon in Spain, with over 40,000 owner-members, is probably the most famous of these efforts. It has created a network of allied cooperatives, including everything from bakeries to health care, to education, to a grocery chain, as well as numerous small manufacturing plants. Its umbrella organization helps provide coordination—for instance if there is a slow down in one plant workers can be shifted to another one—and has a bank which uses the workers' mandatory savings from profits to distribute funds as needed to support public services such as health care and to fund start-ups and provide loans as needed. The mandatory savings then become the worker's retirement funds.

• **Want more?** Try searching for these videos: *The Mondragon Experiment* and *The Take.*

> *In essence the Mondragon network, started in the 1950s in a desperately poor section of Spain, became an alternative form of development—not the dependent development that typically creates poverty for huge numbers of people that we discussed in Chapter 2.*

Mondragon's products are sold world wide, so it is very much part of the globalized economy, but the Basque region where it is located, and Mondragon itself, seem to be surviving the current European economic crisis with far fewer problems than the rest of Spain. This supports the position of those social scientists who maintain, contrary to Neoliberal claims, that equality is actually good for the whole economy, not just for individuals.

• **Want more?**
Explore *Huffington Post
Alliance to Develop Power
Blog* http://
www.huffingtonpost.com
/alliance-to-develop-
power

• **Want more?**
Explore *Indigenous
Territory and Resource
Rights* http://
www.otherworldsarepossi
ble.org/indigenous-
territory-resource-rights

Commons
Land or resources held
jointly by an entire group
for the use of all.*

• **Want more?** Try
*Over One Million Voices to
European Parliament: Stop
Water Privatization* http:/
/
www.commondreams.org
/news/2014/02/17/over-
one-million-voices-
european-parliament-stop-
water-privatization

Around the world there are other organizations attempting to orient economies so that they produce greater equality (and remember the evidence that shows that even the well-to-do are better off in societies that are more egalitarian). Their efforts generally focus on making it possible for ordinary people to have a greater say in their own lives, and on supporting the non-capitalist forms of exchange and endeavor that are often done out of care and love and creativity (like the arts, childcare, gardening, the provision of affordable housing) that are basic to human happiness and well-being. The people of the city of Porto Alegre in Brazil build their city budget through a democratic process of local community financial prioritizing. The result has been a huge shift of funding to the needs of poor communities—streets, health care—all things that no individual is able to provide alone. Workers have taken over closed-down factories in Argentina and are running them successfully. A shrimp farming cooperative in Colombia is holding back the environmental and community destruction that would follow in the wake of dependent development by outside corporations. In western Massachusetts the Alliance to Develop Power, an umbrella cooperative organization, is fostering a Mondragon-like network of cooperatives, and Nuestras Raices (Our Roots), which started as a community gardening project, also in western Massachusetts, is now growing many offshoots. The Jackson Plan in Mississippi is likewise attempting to develop a community economy in the wake of the devastation left by Hurricane Katrina. And there are many others; most face at least some pressure from major corporations, many of whose owners and managers (and their support network) feel threatened or challenged by these examples of non-capitalist economic functioning.

Despite the difficulties, however, it is important to know that there are alternatives; our world is socially constructed, including our economy, and if we know there are people trying other ways, it helps us imagine change.

Many of these non-capitalist endeavors have been organized by indigenous people or people of color in neocolonial settings. They have been particularly concerned with developing a community economy that would provide food security—organizing land and production to provide local food for local people without being dependent on outside, and often undependable or unaffordable, sources. This means reclaiming possession of the land and rights that they have lost as a result of a long history of colonialism and discrimination. Many of them live in communities with traditions of communal or corporate landholding and sharing. Their ideas about control of their territory—including the land and the sea, their means of production—overlap with ideas about *"the commons,"* a concept that is now gaining some recognition in the Global North. This is the belief that the resources we all depend on should be held in common, as communal property for the good of all, as was the English village common at one time, where all had the right to graze their cattle. Thus water, for instance, would belong to all and would not be used up or contaminated for private profit. Water would be delivered to homes or communities by non-profit organizations, not by private companies that own water rights as private property.

Other forms of resistance to global empire include organizations, particularly women's organizations around the world, that have fought for years for their civil and human rights. In some areas the vote is being used. Recent democratic elections in Latin America, for instance, have placed in power governments expressing a commitment to the alleviation of poverty and the rejection of the dominance of the U.S. and of the organizations of global empire. Some have a clear socialist agenda. People around the world have come together in massive protests against the World Trade Organization, the International Monetary Fund, and the World Bank. By the end of the 1990s they were being joined by people from the Global North, who were finally beginning to see the effects of empire in their own lives. The largest anti-war protests the world has ever seen took place on a global scale as the U.S. invaded Iraq. And as the effects of the continuous war required to maintain empire became obvious, people in the U.S. resoundingly voted against the administration in 2008. In 2012 U.S. voters, in both the presidential election and in many state elections, appear to have rejected the Neoliberal policies that would create austerity for the majority of ordinary people. The unexpectedly strong support for Bernie Sanders in the run-up to the Democratic Primaries in 2015 would seem to indicate that same attitude.

The growing climate justice movement is led in large part by people from or in the Global South, with many Northern allies. It sees climate change as a global problem, to which only a globalized response is possible, but seeks to ensure that a fair share of the burden is borne by the Global North. After all, these are the countries that have created the global warming from which the Global South is bearing the first and most devastating consequences. Not only did colonialism and neocolonialism create much of the poverty in the Global South, making it far more vulnerable to high rates of death, homelessness, and suffering during violent climate events, but Global North policies bear significant responsibility for ongoing wars and the likelihood of resource wars in the future. And this all means that it is the poorer nations which bear the costs of Northern consumption, and yet they have the fewest resources with which to alleviate the suffering that climate change is bringing, and also have the least voice internationally in forcing a reduction of greenhouse emissions. Additionally there is the worry in the Global South that their right to development and to the consumer lifestyle of the North will be jeopar-

• **Want more?**
For differing opinions try
*The Paris Climate Accords
Will Cause the Planet to
Burn* http://
www.counterpunch.org/
2015/12/10/the-paris-
climate-accords-will-
cause-the-planet-to-burn/
and *Paris Means Climate
Change Science is Here to
Stay* http://
www.usnews.com/news/
blogs/at-the-edge/
articles/2015-12-14/paris-
climate-accords-what-do-
they-really-mean

• **Want more?** Try
The CO2 Coffee Project
http://www.scaa.org/
chronicle/2015/10/30/
the-co2-coffee-project-a-
new-model-for-
sustainability/ (other
examples are listed at the
end of the chapter).

• **Want more?** Try
*Robert Pollin Shows Us that
Greening the Global
Economy is Doable* https://
ourfuture.org/20151211/
robert-pollin-shows-us-
that-greening-the-global-
economy-is-
doable?utm_source=progr
essive_breakfast&utm_me
dium=email&utm_campai
gn=pbreak

dized by agreements that require equal reductions in greenhouse emissions from all nations.

The U.S. in particular has taken this position, arguing that the fastest rise in greenhouse emissions is in the industrializing Global South, while the Global North is cutting emissions (slightly). Global South nations argue that the only reason the North is cutting emissions is that it is shipping its industry South—so the South gets the blame for emissions that actually should be credited to the North and its extremely high rate of consumption of manufactured goods. Whether the Paris Climate Accords signed at the end of 2015, involving all nations and with leadership from Obama as well as others, will actually make a difference remains to be seen; analysts are divided, with many scientists and climate activists saying that even if fully implemented, its provisions are insufficient.

The climate justice movement is using the tools of globalization to make changes at the international level. And President Obama, at the end of his presidency, seems to be implementing policy changes that take the dangers of climate change seriously. At the same time there are many local initiatives, to reverse the consequences of climate change, such as agroforestry which has succeeded in raising ground water levels in areas that were about to become deserts. And there are local initiatives to cut greenhouse emissions. For instance, cities have voted to go green in the US, turning to wind, solar, and tidal generation of energy and the Povincial government in Ontario gives support for these sources, with the result that on hilltops in rural Ontario you are likely to see a couple wind turbines above small towns and hamlets.

There are ongoing arguments about whether climate change can be slowed—and whether climate justice can be achieved in the process—within a context of capitalism. There are strong arguments that say that capitalism depends on continuous growth and on exploitation of resources and people, and that capitalism is thus incompatible with climate change and global climate justice. Others argue that green capitalism can solve that problem, by substituting jobs and growth in green technologies for fossil fuels technologies. Others argue that the end of growth is imminent and must be carefully planned to transition the world to a society in which growth is not the indicator of economic prosperity, where we live within our resources rather than war over them, and that this transition does not have to mean the end of capitalism. Many of these arguments do not directly address the unequal vulnerability of people in the Global South, particularly those who are poor, and of those who are poor in parts of the Global North. Suffering is not equally distributed, and anthropologists concerned with climate change see this as the major issue which must be addressed in policy decisions about climate change.

> *Humans and their societies are not stuck in concrete. Because the world is socially constructed, it can also be changed.*

CONCLUSION: SEEING THROUGH DIFFERENT GLASSES

We are often blinded by the position of the U.S. in the global system. Global empire is organized so that wealth flows toward the U.S. U.S. and other Global North elites and upper middle classes do benefit financially from U.S. participation in this global empire. But some in the middle classes experience job loss, and the working class is definitely worse off. Nevertheless, since what is good for elite profits is portrayed as good for the country, we tend to think of the U.S. as being in control of this empire. We don't see ourselves as another administrative unit, but rather as the administrators. We identify with the transnational corporations headquartered in the U.S., and refer to ourselves and the elites together as 'we.' We have been taught *not* to see class differences, and we have been taught *to* see race differences. That 'we' should control 'them' thus seems natural; and thus many are willing to 'sacrifice' for the good of the empire, rather than joining with 'them' in resistance to an empire that uses us as tools and damages nearly all of us. We can learn to use new glasses.

> *In stratified societies there is a constant struggle between those who are exploited and those who exploit them. Those with power typically frame the terms of the debate as it is presented in the media, history books, and often in academic studies. Consequently, those who are most exploited rarely are able to make their voices heard by those who are less exploited and who learn about and see the super-exploited mainly through the framework given by the media and history books. So long as this framework stays in place, those who are less exploited—which includes some college students and their families—will be generally unable to see their own exploitation, and they will blame their problems on those who are most exploited. Divide and rule can then remain as an efficient means of assuring high profits, damaging all members of the working class, including those who are 'better-off.' It has been the goal of this book to encourage you to question the framework presented to you by the elite of a stratified society.*

REFERENCES/SUGGESTED READINGS

Globalization and resistance outside the U.S.

Comaroff, Jean and John Comaroff 2001 Millennial Capitalism: First Thoughts on a Second Coming. In Millennial Capitalism and the Culture of Neoliberalism, Jean Comaroff and John Comaroff, eds. Pp 1-56. Durham: Duke University Press.

Chomsky, Noam 2003 Hegemony or Survival: America's Quest for Global Dominance. New York: Henry Holt and Co.

Dawson, Ashley and Malini Johar Schueller, eds. 2007 Exceptional State: Contemporary U.S. Culture and the New Imperialism. Durham: Duke University Press.

Inda, Jonathan Xavier and Renato Rosaldo, eds. 2008 The Anthropology of Globalization: A Reader. 2nd ed. Malden MA: Blackwell Publishing.

Jameson, Frederic and Masao Miyoshi, eds. 1998 The Cultures of Globalization. Durham: Duke University Press.

Hardt, Michael and Antonio Negri 2000 Empire. Cambridge MA: Harvard University Press.

Klare, Michael 2001 Resource Wars:The New Landscape of Global Conflict. New York: Metropolitan.

Klein, Naomi 2007 The Shock Doctrine: The Rise of Disaster Capitalism. New York: Picador/Henry Holt and Company.

Moksnes, Heidi 2004 Militarized Democracies: The Neoliberal Mexican State and the Chiapas Uprising. In State, Sovereignty, War: Civil Violence in Emerging Global Realities. Bruce Kapferer, ed. Pp. 89-106. New York: Berghahn Books.

Nordstrom, Carolyn. 2007 Global Outlaws: Crime, Money, and Power in the Contemporary World. Oakland: University of California Press.

Reitman, Janet 2011 How the World Failed Haiti. Rolling Stone August 18. http://www.rollingstone.com/politics/news/how-the-world-failed-haiti-20110804

On the Importance of Female Labor to Globalized Industry

Gunewardena, Nandini and Ann Kingsolver, eds. 2008 The Gender of Globalization: Women Navigating Cultural and Economic Marginalities. Santa Fe, NM: School for Advanced Research.

On egalitarian or non-capitalist endeavors

Burridge, Tom 2012 Basque Cooperative Mondragon Defies Spain Slump. BBC News Europe, August 13. http://www.bbc.co.uk/news/world-europe-19213425.

Common Dreams staff. 2012 As Spain's Recession Darkens, Alternative Economies Rise. Common Dreams August 28. http://www.commondreams.org/headline/2012/08/28-6

Escobar, Arturo 2008 Territories of Difference: Place, Movements, Life, Redes. Durham: Duke University Press.

Gibson-Graham, J.K. 2006 A Postcapitalist Politics. Minneapolis: University of Minnesota Press.

Gibson-Graham, J.K, Jenny Cameron, and Stephen Healy. 2013. Take Back the Economy: An Ethical Guide for Transforming Our Communities. Minneapolis: University of Minnesota Press.

Graham, Julie and Janelle Cornwell n.d. Building Community Economies in Massachusetts: An Emerging Model of Economic Development? http://www.communityeconomies.org/site/assets/media/Janelle_Cornwell/Graham-and-Cornwell.pdf

Jackson Plan A Struggle for Self-Determination, Participatory Democracy, and Economic Justice.
http://mxgm.org/the-jackson-plan-a-struggle-for-self-determination-participatory-democracy-and-economic-justice.

Kurtzleben, Danielle 2012 Time Banks Provide New Way to 'Spend' an Hour. US News and World Report, October 23. http://www.usnews.com/news/articles/2012/10/23/time-banks-provide-new-way-to-spend-an-hour.

Poggioli, Sylvia 2012 Spain's Crisis Leads To Rise of Grass-Roots Groups. National Public Radio, December 10. http://www.npr.org/2012/12/10/166653449/spains-crisis-leads-to-rise-of-grass-roots-groups.

Wright, Erik 2010 Envisioning Real Utopias. New York: Verso.

On climate change, economic growth and local initiatives

American Anthropological Association Statememt on Humanity and Climate Change. 2015.
http://s3.amazonaws.com/rdcms-aaa/files/production/public/FileDownloads/pdfs/issues/press/upload/AAA-Statement-on-Humanity-and-Climate-Change-2.pdf

Baer, Hans and Merrill Singer. 2014 The Anthropology of Climate Change: An Integrated Critical Perspective. New York: Routledge.

Canadian Wind Energy Association. Nd. Wind Energy: Building a Stronger, Cleaner and More Affordable Power System in Ontario.
http://canwea.ca/wind-energy/ontario/

Heimberg, Richard, 2011. The End of Growth: Adapting to Our New Economic Reality. Gabriola Island, BC: New Society Publishers.

Holmes, Kassy. 2015. The CO2 Coffee Project: A New Model for Sustainability. The Specialty Coffee Chronicle.
http://www.scaa.org/chronicle/2015/10/30/the-co2-coffee-project-a-new-model-for-sustainability/

Jespersen, Lizzie. 2013. Climate Change: City Targets Zero Emissions.
http://www.austinchronicle.com/news/2014-05-23/climate-change-city-targets-zero-emissions/

Parenti, Christian. 2011 Tropic of Choas: Climate Change and the New Geography of Violence. New York: Nation Books.

Roberts, J. Timmons and Bradley Parks. 2007. A Climate of Injustice: Global Inequality, North-South Politics, and Climate Policy. Cambridge: MIT Press.

Seattle Climate Action Plan. 2013. http://www9.seattle.gov/environment/documents/Seattle_2013_CAP_for_web.pdf

Vaz, Patricia. 2000. Regenerative Analog Agroforestry in Brazil. Agricultures Network. http://www.agriculturesnetwork.org/magazines/global/farming-in-the-forest/regenerative-analog-agroforestry-in-brazil

GLOSSARY

Accommodation—The process of adjusting oneself to difficult circumstances you are powerless to change. In particular, the term applies to situations of inequality, where the person with less power must somehow learn to live with the demands of more powerful people. People who are poor and have little power may accommodate themselves to their lack of resources, believing for instance, that God will somehow take care of them. See also resistance, a very different response to oppression.

Accumulation (of surplus)—The producers in a society grow more or produce more goods than they need themselves, and this surplus can be somehow collected and stockpiled. This can be done by methods of preserving food, by transforming it into something else (for instance, feeding it to pigs, which turns it into meat), or by trading it for something else, or by turning it into money. If a society can accumulate a surplus, that surplus may be taken away from those who produced it, so that the surplus production of many producers can be accumulated in the hands of one person, or of an elite group (see also surplus).

Agriculture—Intensive cultivation of crops; this is a type of farming that uses various technologies, such as plowing or irrigation, to grow much more in a given area, generally using both human labor and energy supplied by animals or machines and generally meant to produce a large surplus (compare with horticulture).

Altered state of consciousness—A psychological/emotional state in which people feel they have transcended reality and have entered a state of consciousness beyond that of daily life.

Annual round—The pattern typically followed by a particular nomadic band as it travels each year within its territory, returning to the same places at the same time of year.

Anthropogenic—Caused by human activity.

Anthropology—The study of humans, past and present. Cultural anthropology focuses on how people in various parts of the world organize and govern themselves, and the meanings they create as they deal with the world they live in.

Apartheid—A legal policy of maintaining separation between racial or ethnic groups, with favorable working and living conditions and ownership of the means of production reserved for the group in power; the exploited group is forced to provide cheap labor to subsidize the lifestyle and profits of the group in power (see also segregation).

Aristocrats—In a ranking system, those people who are members of families or of linages that receive privileges by birth, have inherited rights to positions of power, and usually have control of the means of production.

Austerity program—A program pursued by a national government to reduce spending, usually by cutting programs and subsidies that benefit the poorer segment of a society; often instigated by international financial institution as a condition for loans to the national government.

Authority—The socially accepted right to tell other people what to do; people obey authority because they believe they have a religious or moral obligation to do so. Their compliance may be enforced by pressure from family and peers. In more stratified societies compliance may be more formally enforced through the exercise of coercive power.

Balanced reciprocity—The exchange of gifts or services between individuals who are keeping track of how much is given or when a return gift is to be made. The return gift is not made immediately, but must eventually be given and must be of equivalent value to the original gift (see reciprocity; compare with generalized reciprocity and with redistribution).

Band—A small kin-ordered egalitarian group that follows a foraging subsistence strategy. All band societies forage and are egalitarian; however not all foraging societies are egalitarian, and therefore are organized as tribes or chiefdoms, not as bands.

Barter—An exchange of goods or services in which people bargain and haggle over price, but do not actually use money to make the exchange. Barter may occur in an economy that uses market exchange, but without the use of money. Similar to balanced reciprocity in that the exchange is supposed to be of equivalent value, but the return is made at the same time as the original exchange. The value of the goods or services exchanged is often determined by market price.

Big Man—A leader in some tribal societies who has gained his position through competition with other men, primarily through giving away massive quantities of goods by becoming a center person in egalitarian redistribution. Big Men have much prestige but no power and give away all that they receive. Big Man status can not be inherited, and all men are eligible to compete (see also egalitarian redistribution).

Bilateral—Tracing descent from both parents, rather than being a member of only the father's or only the mother's family, lineage, or clan. A society using bilateral descent is neither patrilineal nor matrilineal.

Birthright—Rights that are conveyed to a person automatically at birth; such rights can include inherited position and privilege or rights of citizenship.

Blaming the victim—Claiming a bad situation is the result of the victim's own actions, thus avoiding the need to look for the social forces which might be causing the situation.

Boundary markers—Characteristics which are said to demonstrate or indicate membership in a particular group, often an ethnic group. These markers are often defined as much by more powerful groups as by the group itself, and frequently are said to indicate inferiority.

Bridewealth—Objects important for their prestige value that are given by the husband's group to the bride's group in order to validate a marriage.

Bureaucracy—An intermediate group between the elite and ordinary people. They do much of the actual work of governing or supervise and control workers.

Calendric ritual—A ritual performed on a regular schedule, such as Sunday church services, or Christmas mass, or Ramadan, or for good crops at the beginning of each planting season.

Capitalism (capitalist mode of production)—An economic/social/political system in which the means of production and distribution are privately owned by individuals (or by corporations legally acting as individuals) and operated for personal profit; land and labor are commodities that can be bought and sold.

Capitalist—A person who owns the means of production in the capitalist mode of production.

Carrying capacity—The sustainable number of people that can be supported on a particular area of land with a given technology, without destroying the environment and its productive capacity.

Cash crop—A crop grown for sale rather than to feed one's family directly; often a luxury crop such as sugar, flowers, or tobacco that is grown for export. In much of the world cash crops are associated with inadequate food supplies for local people.

Caste—A hereditary endogamous occupational social group in a society in which everyone is a member of such a group and the groups are arranged in a hierarchy of purity, prestige, and power.

Ceremonial valuable (or valuable)—Sometimes called wealth item. Non-money items used in ceremonial exchanges. The valuable generally has no use in itself, except to mark status of the giver and sometimes also of the receiver. A diamond ring is an example in our culture. These objects are valued by the people in the society because they are defined as conferring prestige on a person who gives them away and because of the prestige the recipient will eventually receive if he or she in turn gives it away in another exchange. Generally to be defined as a valuable an item must be scarce, difficult to get, or time consuming to make (see also status marker).

Chiefdom—A society with hereditary ranking but minimal stratification (most differences between people relate to their prestige and authority, rather than to their right to feed themselves), composed of a number of social groupings, and involving a much larger number of people than does a band or tribe.

Chief—The head of a system of ranked lineages, which form two or more local groups. The chief has real authority over resources and maintains position and influence by distributing resources to followers. People most closely related to the chief receive more benefits, are viewed as superior, and receive deference. The chief generally must be a member of the highest ranking lineage, and there are generally a number of other high ranked positions below that of chief.

Citizenship—A legal status conveying the rights and obligations of membership in a particular country. Citizenship is a birthright for people born within the territory of a country, although details vary from state to state for children born of non-citizen parents. Most states also have a system of naturalized citizenship for people immigrating to the country. Access to citizenship for immigrants may be very limited (see also civil rights).

Civil rights—The rights that belong to all full citizens of a state; for instance in the United States the right to vote and the right to trial by jury.

Clan—A descent group formed by all those who believe they are descended from a common ancestor, even if the exact connections can't be explained. The ancestor may have lived so long ago that connections are unclear, or the ancestor may be mythical. Clans are generally named and there will be several of them in a society that has clans. A clan is generally not a corporate group and is composed of a number of related lineages.

Class bias—The assumption that how one's own class sees the world and acts is the only natural, correct, and moral way; particularly the assumption that classes more exploited than one's own are irrational or stupid if they behave differently.

Class Consciousness—Awareness that one's difficulties are due to one's membership in a class that is oppressed, rather than to one's own bad luck, poor decisions, or inadequate effort. Can lead to class conflict, in which members of an oppressed class attempt to force the oppressing class to be less exploitative.

Classist—See class bias.

Class marker—Behavior, consumption patterns, and/or display of objects that identify someone as being a member of a particular class (see also status marker).

Class—A group of people who have the same relationship to the means of production. Class exists only in stratified societies where some people own the means of production, and the rest sell their labor to the people who own the means of production.

Climate Change—A process of change in overall regional or worldwide climate patterns, particularly referring to change resulting from global warming produced by the use of fossil fuels; this change includes for more rain and far more frequent and violent storms in some areas and droughts in others.

Collaborator—A member of a subordinate group who cooperates with the dominant group in maintaining control and/or extracting profits from the subordinate group.

Collaborator class—In a stratified society, a group of people whose function is to control ordinary people and to manage their production in order to extract wealth from them for the elite, with whom they are allied. They may be low-ranking aristocrats or commoners who have raised their status in a ranked society, or they may be employees in a capitalist society, often referred to as the professional/managerial class (see professional/managerial class).

Colonialism—The establishment of a relationship between two counties in which one country goes to another and reorganizes its culture, economy, and resource use so that the colonizing country can extract cheap labor and cheap resources from the colonized country. The difference between colonialism and dependent development (neocolonialism) is that in a colonial relationship the conquering country owns and politically controls the colony. In dependent development the country (often a former colony) is politically independent, but economic ties (often put in place during the colonial period) with economically more powerful nations have tremendous influence over political and economic processes in the country being dependently developed.

Commodity—A product or service that can be bought and sold through market exchange.

Commons—Land or resources held jointly by an entire group for the use of all; recently used by some ecologically oriented social justice groups and by some indigenous groups to emphasize that all humans should jointly use and conserve the resources of the earth, rather than allowing those resources to be used up for private profit.

Communal mode of production—All members of a specific group jointly control resources, to which all have rights. Group members may work together and share what is produced, or individual families in the group may produce for themselves using the group resources. Either way, all have equal rights; the resources are not privately owned by individuals, and members cannot be denied access.

Complex chiefdom—A ranked society that grants far more wealth, power, and prestige to high-ranking people than do chiefdoms; divided into many administrative sub-units. High-ranking people do not have absolute control of the means of production, as they do in kingdoms; however, tribute may be required to activate an individual's right to use land and other resources. Real inequality exists in complex chiefdoms (compare with chiefdom and kingdom).

Conquest state—A state formed by the forcible annexation of territory and people outside its former borders; the state's borders are expanded to include the new territory.

Core nation—According to world system theory, core nations are those that control the financial and investment centers of the world and often the final and most profitable aspects of manufacturing. They absorb raw materials and labor from the peripheral nations (see peripheral nation). Because of their economic dominance they heavily influence or virtually control the economies and governments of peripheral nations. This terminology, with its emphasis on individual nations and its implication that core nations are more important, has been to some extent replaced by referring instead to the Global North and Global South.

Corporate group—A group of people (such as the members of a lineage) who form a single legal entity in relation to outsiders. As a single legal entity the group as a whole controls property, usually land in the case of a lineage. This property is not the private property of any member; all members have equal rights to lineage property. This means that to outsiders all members of the lineage are the same, so that one member can stand in for another. So in the case of a debt, all members are responsible for repayment and are equally at fault if the debt is not repaid.

Crisis ritual—A ritual performed irregularly, as needed, such as weddings, prayers for rain, and healing ceremonies.

Cultural determination—The way in which human behavior is heavily influenced and to some degree controlled by the culture of the particular group in which a person lives.

Cultural universals—Human beings have certain basic needs that must be met by all cultures. Therefore all cultures have elements that deal with these universal needs, like childcare, getting food, having fun, and rules about sex (see cultural variation).

Cultural variation—Different cultures meet basic human universal needs (see cultural universals) in different ways. Cultural variation refers to those elements which make cultures different from each other.

Culture—The learned and shared behavior patterns of a group of people; includes all that the society produces, ideas as well as things. However, cultures are not cast in concrete; they change, individuals and groups may have different takes on their culture and, particularly in stratified societies, subordinate groups may actively reject some aspects of the culture as practiced by the dominant group.

Debt peonage—A system of involuntary servitude that allows employers to force people who owe them money to work for the employer until the debt is paid off. Charging exorbitant rates for room and board and paying low wages often allows the employer to keep the worker in debt indefinitely; no longer legal in the U.S.

Dependent development—See Neocolonialism.

Descent group—A kin group whose membership is based on a rule about how ancestry is to be traced to give you the right to be a member of the group. Matrilineal or patrilineal rules are the most common.

Deskilled—Tasks that have been deskilled have been organized so that they require less skill; this can be done by dividing the job into a number of smaller discrete operations that can be performed by people with relatively little training, or by using technology, such as cash registers that make it unnecessary for cashiers to know how to make change.

Deterritorialized—A culture, or significant aspect of that culture, is no longer associated only with the territory or geographical area in which it originated

Discrimination—Action that treats someone, usually based on their identity, differently from how a similarly qualified person of another group would be treated. Distinguish from prejudice, which has to do with attitudes, not actions.

Disposable labor—A term that implies that people are being treated like disposable paper plates: health and safety of workers is being ignored, and when workers are 'used up'—ill or disabled or dead—and therefore are no longer useful, they can be tossed aside and replaced.

Distribution—The assignment of goods and services to members of a society.

Divide and rule—The strategy of getting people to be controlled to fight each other rather than to fight those who are controlling them.

Division of labor—The performance of different tasks by different categories of people.

Division of labor by age—The assignment of a society's tasks according to age, so that the elderly, the middle-aged, and the young adults are expected to focus on different tasks.

Docile labor—People working for a company who cannot afford, either economically, politically, or socially to object to the policies of the company, or to the laws regulating company policies.

Domestication—The purposeful production and control of plants or animals to provide the major food supply.

Dominant group—-Those people in the category that includes the major power holders in a society, whether that group is based on race or class or gender.

Double vision—The ability, resulting from one's subordinate position in an unequal social structure, to interpret events both from a subordinate point of view and to some extent from the perspective of the dominant group.

Dowry—Wealth transferred from the bride's family to the bride, or more frequently to her husband or his family. In some societies this wealth is seen as giving the bride her share of the family property, transferred at marriage rather than as inheritance on the death of her parents.

Dying wages—Another term for super-exploitation, used only when super-exploitation is occurring in a capitalist economy where people are selling their labor, but for extremely low wages. The implication of the term is that in a community where lots of people are being paid dying wages, there will be a high death rate unless people have some other form of support.

Economic system—A society's organization for the production and distribution of goods and services.

Egalitarian redistribution—A form of redistribution in which the person at the center of the redistribution collects gifts of surplus produced by other people but then gives away everything received and does not keep anything for personal use; a system for gaining prestige in relatively egalitarian societies by giving away more than others and by repaying gifts by giving more than the original gift. Compare with balanced reciprocity in which no one individual plays a central role or tries to gain prestige by giving away more than others (see redistribution; also compare with stratified redistribution).

Egalitarian—A system of relationships in which everyone equally has access to needed resources. In the most egalitarian societies, no one can be denied access to the means of production. Leaders have no real power, their position is not passed on to their descendants, and they have no more material possessions or food than anyone else.

Elite—In a system of relationships based on inequality, the elite are the people who directly benefit from inequality and control the lives and labor of those who suffer from inequality. Usually refers to the people at the very top of a highly stratified society. They are considered to be better than other people and usually can pass their elite position on to their children.

Empire—Areas that are under the formal control of another state, but are not incorporated into the controlling state itself, although the empire is governed and exploited by the controlling state.

Endogamy—A pattern, preference, or requirement to marry a person who is a member of one's own social group or category.

Energy efficient (in food production)—The fewer calories of energy needed to produce a calorie of food, the more energy efficient that method is.

Esoteric knowledge—Information or activities which are known about by only a few people, who are expected to keep the knowledge secret from all except those who have the right to know it.

Ethnic group—A group of people within a larger society who are thought to share the same national or cultural heritage, which is different from that of other groups in the society; generally created in the context of conquest or migration.

Ethnocentrism (ethnocentric)—Judging the members of another culture or subculture by the standards of one's own culture, with the assumption that one's own culture is best and that it is the way all rational people would naturally choose to live.

Ethnography—A book, article, or film that makes an anthropological description or analysis of a particular culture. Ethnographies are generally based on fieldwork.

Ethnotourism—Tourism based on organizing tourist attractions by exhibiting the 'traditional' way of life of indigenous groups.

Exchange—The process of distributing goods and services by transferring them from one individual to another. In some societies money acts as a medium of exchange, and in others goods are exchanged directly (see also generalized and balanced reciprocity, redistribution, and market exchange).

Exogamy—A pattern, preference, or requirement to marry a person who is not a member of one's own social group or category.

Expansionism—A policy of trying to annex more territory, and the ideologies which get people to believe this is a good idea.

Exploitation—Using other people or their resources for your own benefit, without ensuring equal benefits to the people being exploited; possible only in situations of inequality.

Expropriation of value/Expropriation of labor/Expropriation of resources—The taking of profits or goods away from the people who produced them, or of resources from the people who have had the right to use them in the past. These terms are usually used in the context of colonization, internal colonization, or dependent development, and imply that the expropriation was possible because of extreme inequality or because of the use of force.

Extended family—A family consisting of three or more generations living together; may include several closely related nuclear families all functioning as a single economic unit.

Extensive cultivation—Cultivation which depends on using large amounts of land so that individual plots are not used heavily; depends on allowing the land to rest to restore nutrients. Also called horticulture.

Failed state—A state that is unable to enforce the state's monopoly on the use of force and thus cannot guarantee the right to private ownership of the means of production, control their infrastructure, or enforce control of its borders.

Fallow—Allowing land to rest without cultivation in order to restore nutrients; used heavily in extensive systems of cultivation.

False consciousness—The attitude of a person in a subordinate group who believes the ideologies that claim subordinate people are truly inferior or truly deserve to have limited access to resources or power. In a sense people with false consciousness are blaming the victim when they themselves are the victim.

Family—An intimate kin-based group, consisting, usually, of at least a woman and her children; forms the minimal social unit that cooperates economically and is responsible for the rearing of children. World-wide, most families include more than one adult; the adults are usually joined by a sexual relationship or by kinship or marriage (see also household).

Feudalism/Feudal mode of production—A form of the tributary mode of production. It is a system of social and economic organization where estates in land are held by conferred right (in fief) by members of a privileged class, who can then command the labor of serfs who are attached to the estate.

Fictive kinship—Building kinship rights and obligations by claiming an actually non-existent kinship relationship. Particularly important in kin-ordered societies for incorporating new members or visitors, thereby giving them a position in the social structure. In our own society fictive kinship is a way to legitimize good friends who act as kin.

Fieldwork—The process of studying the way of life of a particular group of people or of people in a particular situation by living with them, perhaps participating in their work and daily lives; fieldworkers learn from the people being studied, both through what people tell them and through face-to-face contact and observation. In the process the fieldworker learns to see the world from a new perspective; the same often happens to those people the fieldworker works with most closely. Fieldwork is a particularly important aspect of the methodology of anthropology.

Foraging—A subsistence strategy that is built around primary dependence on wild plants and animals. Often called hunting and gathering.

Fraternal polyandry—A form of polyandry in which the co-husbands are all brothers.

Gender—The learned behavior and attitudes associated with a particular sex in a particular society.

Gender diversity—The definition in some societies of multiple sexes and genders beyond the two typically regarded in the U.S. as natural and biological; includes also acknowledgement of transgendered, bi-sexual, lesbian and gay identities.

Gender equality—A relationship between the sexes in which men and women have equal degrees of control over their own lives and have equal access to the resources they need to live in their society. (Note that gender equality can exist when neither men nor women have much control over their lives or access to resources, as is sometimes the case with slavery.)

Generalized reciprocity—The exchange of gifts or services between people who are not keeping track of the exact amounts given or received, nor specifying when a return gift should be made. It is based on the assumption that people will make return gifts as they are able. This can mean that one person actually gives more than the other person, but that imbalance is not acknowledged. Generally carried out between individuals who are equals and have reason to trust each other and who are mutually dependent on each other. This is the basic form of exchange in egalitarian foraging societies (see also balanced reciprocity and reciprocity).

Global apartheid—A term used by some anthropologists to describe the relationship of powerful countries to less powerful countries as similar to that which existed under apartheid in South Africa. The implication is that the whole world is divided into two basic groups of nations, with the wealth of the powerful nations being created at least partially by the exploitation of the labor and resources of the less powerful nations.

Global North—A term which is used in place of terms such as First World or developed, which have positive implications, to refer to those parts of the world which exploit the rest of the world.

Global South—A term which is used in place of terms such as underdeveloped or third world, both of which have negative implications, to refer to those parts of the world which have been and continue to be exploited by more powerful nations—referred to as the Global North.

Globalization—The process by which the economies of the world are becoming increasingly interconnected, so that powerful (core) nations and transnational corporations control the economies of the rest of the world without necessarily directly controlling the governments of the world. This has been accomplished partially through the institution of free market economies, so that local governments cannot control investment and access to their resources by transnational corporations. It also means that the work force of the world is in direct competition with each other, since corporations can choose to use the labor of people all over the world.

Hegemony—The dominance of a set of ideas or of a power structure that is so powerful and so entrenched that it goes unchallenged and is rarely questioned; it appears natural and inevitable. The term is used to refer to the structure of a regional or world socioeconomic system as well as to the dominance of ideas that support that system.

Holism—An important aspect of anthropological method and perspective. In a holistic approach the anthropologist is attempting to understand the society as a whole, rather than just particular aspects of it, such as its economy. This approach assumes that all aspects of a society are interconnected and therefore cannot be understood in isolation.

Horticulture—A subsistence strategy that involves primary dependence on farming that involves cultivating plants without the use of non-human energy (no animals or machines used in cultivating) and without technologies such as irrigation to intensify production. Also referred to as extensive cultivation (compare with agriculture, which involves intensive cultivation).

Household—A group of people who live together in one house and are economically interdependent. It may consist of a family, it may include non-family members. If none of the people living in a household are kin, the degree of interdependence may be minimal (compare with family).

Human rights—Those rights that are believed for moral reasons to belong to all human beings. Access to the resources needed for a life beyond mere survival is seen by many as a human right. Such rights have been defined and redefined by the United Nations and by various activist groups, and are contested by other groups. These rights can include freedom from fear, freedom from abuse, freedom from hunger, and access to medical care.

Ideology—Belief systems that rationalize and legitimize the distribution of power. In stratified and ranked societies this means those ideas that justify systems of stratification and exploitation, making people feel this is natural and right.

Illegal force—The use of force that has not been legitimized by a society or by the legitimate authorities of a society. In our society for example, a woman who forcibly takes away another woman's child is using illegal force. But if the woman taking the child is a social worker or a police officer and is taking the child as a result of a court order, the use of force is legal.

Imperialism—The policy and practice of conquering areas outside the state, keeping them to some degree separate from the conquering state, and expropriating value from the conquered area for the benefit of the elite in the conquering state.

Indigenous Peoples—The descendants of the people who inhabited an area before conquest and now exist as minorities within the borders, or straddling the borders, of countries that are highly stratified.

Industrial agriculture—The factory-like production of crops or animals for slaughter, done on a huge scale, and highly mechanized. Examples would be agribusiness production of corn or producing eggs in enormous buildings where each hen is kept in a cage too small to turn around in, with feed provided in automatic feeders and eggs and manure dropping down onto conveyor belts.

Industrial—Producing goods using mechanization fueled by non-human and non-animal forms of energy, usually fossil fuel or nuclear energy.

Inequality—See social inequality.

Infant mortality rate—The number of children per thousand births who die before one year of age. A high rate means lots of children die.

Infanticide—The killing of infants, usually newborn. Female infanticide means killing baby girls.

Initiation—A rite of passage in which a person joins a new group; usually refers to children becoming adults or joining an older group.

Institutionalized—Built into the social organization and institutions of a society.

Intensive cultivation—Growing far more on a particular plot of land than in extensive cultivation. Depends on the use of fertilizers to restore nutrients to the soil and usually employs more complex technologies than extensive cultivation does. Also called agriculture.

Internal colonialism—Treating one section of a country or one group of people as if they were a part of a colony, so that what they produce goes to benefit outsiders; a form of dependent development that occurs within the borders of a particular country.

Kingdom—A state that employs the tributary mode of production, is ranked, is stratified, giving absolute control of the means of production to an elite, gives the legal right to use force to the king, and acknowledges no kinship between elite lineages and ordinary people (see complex chiefdom for comparison).

Kin-ordered mode of production—One form of the communal mode of production, where production work is organized by kinship, and as kin everyone jointly shares in the goods or food produced. This term is used to emphasize the fact that tasks are assigned and performed, goods are distributed, and decisions are made all according to how you are related to other people in the group.

Kinship—A way of defining a group of people with whom you have mutual rights and obligations due to shared ancestry; they are people defined as being 'related' to you by blood or marriage.

Labor importation—Acquiring workers, legally or illegally, from outside the borders of a state to work within the state, usually at very low wages and usually without granting them rights within the state.

Labor intensive—A crop or product that requires proportionately more hours of work than most others; for instance, tobacco is far more labor intensive than corn and making clothing in a factory is more labor intensive than making other products that can be made using automated processes.

Labor reserve area—A section of a colonized country where the traditional subsistence economy and related aspects of a culture are kept relatively unchanged. This policy is instituted by colonial administrations so that the traditional economy can feed the families of plantation and mine laborers. This means that the capitalist section of the economy (the plantations and mines designed to produce export goods to provide a profit) can pay its labor extremely low wages because those wages are not needed to support families. Most labor for the capitalist section of the economy is drawn from labor reserve areas. The term can also refer to an internal colony where traditional occupations or other means support large numbers of people who can be drawn into the capitalist economy as needed and pushed out again when no longer needed.

Language—The communication system that consists primarily of vocal sounds used as symbols to stand for ideas and objects, together with the rules such as grammar about how to organize those sounds into statements that are meaningful to other speakers of the same language.

Leader—In egalitarian societies, refers to a person whose opinions and actions have significant influence on the behavior of the group and on decision making within the group, but who has no power or authority to direct people's behavior.

Learned behavior—Behavior that is not built in genetically; it is behavior that is learned through contact with others and through experience. All behavior which makes up a culture is learned. Since humans have no instincts—no complex genetically programmed behavior—we are totally dependent on learned behavior.

Learned ignorance—A lack of knowledge which is fostered to protect the distribution of power in a society.

Legal force—The use of force that has been legitimized by the authorities of the institutions of a society and carried out by legitimate agents using specified types of force. A lynching is the use of illegal force; execution by the justice system is the legal use of force.

Legitimate—Seen by members of a group as correct, appropriate, and approved by people in positions of authority. To legitimize is to get people to agree that a particular situation is natural and normal and the way things ought to be, to define it as 'right.'

Leveling device—A means of minimizing differences in wealth, power, and prestige between people. In non-egalitarian societies leveling devices are sometimes used by people in an oppressed group on members of the group to keep them all more or less equal among themselves. In egalitarian societies, the device is one of many processes that help to keep everyone more or less equal.

Liberation theology—A religious doctrine and movement, primarily within Catholicism, but spreading beyond, that emphasizes justice and social activism on behalf of the oppressed. It refers to Jesus' role as he spoke against inequality and in defense of the poor; it sees oppressive social structures as wrong because they block the growth of the human spirit and because they are contrary to God's will.

Lineage—A group of matrilineal (in a matrilineage) or patrilineal (in a patrilineage) relatives all descended from a single known common ancestor, who act as a unit (they are a corporate group) and generally control property and land.

Maquiladora—A factory established by a U.S.-owned corporation just south of the border with Mexico in order to take advantage of the opportunity to make bigger profits than is possible in the U.S.; pays low wages by Mexican standards and extremely low wages by U.S standards, and often gets favorable tax treatment and can lower safety and environmental standards.

Magic—A set of beliefs and practices which are based on the idea that supernatural forces can be controlled or made to work to accomplish a particular objective.

Market economy—An economic system in which everything, including land and labor, can be exchanged through market exchange. A society can have market exchange without having a market economy. A feudal society, for instance, does not have a way of buying and selling land, and frequently no system for hiring people for a certain number of hours at a certain wage. So even though horses, jewelry, food, clothing and many other things are bought and sold, a feudal society does not have a full market economy.

Market exchange—A method of distribution in which commodities are bought and sold, generally using some form of money, without regard to the relationship between people, with the price set by market forces such as supply and demand.

Marriage—A socially recognized arrangement between two or more people that to some degree regulates sexual behavior and that creates a new set of rights and obligations between the members of the marriage themselves, between the members and the offspring of other members of the marriage, and between the members and the relatives of the other members. Exactly what those rights and obligations are varies enormously among societies, making it extremely difficult to come up with a cross-culturally valid definition of marriage.

Matrilineage—A lineage based on descent through the mother—a matrilineal lineage.

Matrilineal—Descent (who you are related to and what group you belong to) is traced through the female line only.

Matrilocal—Residence of a married couple with the wife's kin.

Means of production—The resources used in the process of production (tools, land, raw materials, etc.). People's work is not counted as part of the means of production; instead that is called labor (see also production; compare with mode of production and subsistence strategy).

Mechanized agriculture—Agriculture that depends on the heavy use of machinery, fossil fuels, and artificial fertilizer.

Military-Industrial complex—The economic and policy connections between defense contractors, the arms industry, the Pentagon, and the military; the term implies an undue influence of industrial corporations manufacturing and selling armaments and other military supplies over foreign and domestic policy, particularly as that influence promotes the likelihood of war rather than diplomacy.

Mode of production—The social and physical organization that is associated with producing food and other necessities in a particular society (see also production; compare with means of production and with subsistence strategy).

Money—Objects that have been assigned a standard value and serve as a medium of exchange in a wide variety of transfers. If the object is good for exchanging with only one or two other items, it is not money.

Monogamy—Marriage to only one spouse at a time.

Multinational corporation—A company with headquarters in one country (usually an industrialized one) and branches in many different countries around the world (see also transnational corporation).

Myth—A story that deals with fundamental questions concerning the human condition from that society's point of view (e.g. Christianity's explanation of evil by the myth about the Garden of Eden). A myth often tells about the deeds of supernatural powers in the past or about historical events, in both cases within a framework that explains and justifies the organization of society in the present.

Nation—A group of people who consider themselves to be 'one people,' that is sharing the same culture, history, language, and seeing themselves as different from people who are not part of the nation.

Nation-building—Can refer to the process of creating a single national identity among disparate groups in a newly formed state. More frequently today it refers to the process of foreign military, economic, and political intervention in a failed state or newly formed state in order to create governmental institutions that will ensure stability, will control the use of force by unauthorized groups, and will act in the interests of the intervening foreign state.

Nation-state—A state whose citizens are all members of the same nation, and ideally includes everyone within its borders who is a member of the nation.

Neocolonialism—Development in a country which is politically independent, but whose economy is dependent on other more powerful countries who guide the dependent country's development in such a way that they can continue the expropriation of labor and resources, much as they did during the colonial control of the dependent country (also see colonialism).

Neoconservative—The political and economic philosophy which emphasizes the role of military intervention and the promotion of U.S. corporate interests internationally, including the forcible imposition of democratic institutions.

Neoliberalism—The political and economic philosophy that says that governments should not regulate private enterprise or intervene in the workings of the free market economy.

NGO—Non-Governmental Organization; private or non-profit organizations frequently associated with development in failed states and in countries with a history of colonialism and neocolonialism. Often funded by organizations of the Global North

Nomadic—A way of life based on moving from place to place as resources become available for foraging or for pasturing herded animals; nomadic people do not have a permanent home base.

Norm—A formal or informal standard or guideline for appropriate behavior; specific norms vary from culture to culture.

Nuclear family—A family consisting only of parents and their children living together.

Origin myth—Religious and semi-religious explanations about the origins and values of a society and its place in the world (see also myth).

'Other' ('Othering')—Categories of people who are defined by you and your category as being so irrevocably different from you that they can't be understood or interacted with using the same standards you would use for people in your own category. They are seen as 'those other people, not part of us.' Generally a way of making people appear to deserve exploitation.

Ownership—The right to use and benefit from a particular item or resource and to prevent other people from using or benefiting from it without your permission; generally protected by law and the legal use of force. Generally includes the right to sell or otherwise dispose of the item or resource. Different from usufruct, or use right, which gives you the right to use and benefit from a resource, but does not give you the right to dispose of it, and often does not give you completely exclusive rights to control.

Paramount Chief—The highest ranking chief in a hierarchy of chiefs of sub-units within a complex chiefdom.

Participant observation—An anthropological research method in which researchers live among the people whose culture they are studying, being taught by them, observing them at close range and participating in their lives as much as possible (see also fieldwork).

Pastoralism—A subsistence strategy based on primary dependence on raising large herds of cattle, sheep, camels, goats, horses, or other animals, but not in the context of mechanized agriculture.

Patriarchy—A society in which some men have power over others, who in turn have power over women in their families and see themselves, and are treated as, superior to women in general. Conveying the right to control 'their' women to relatively powerless men is in some sense a payoff to powerless men in return for their submission to elite men.

Patrilineage—-A lineage based on descent through the father—a patrilineal lineage.

Patrilineal—Descent (who you are related to and what group you belong to) is traced through the male line only.

Patrilocal—Residence of a married couple with the husband's kin.

Peasant—A member of a farming category of people in a state who use non-mechanized agriculture to raise crops for their own subsistence and pay tax, rent, or tribute to the elites who control the land. Their payments may be specified to be in the form of crops, money, or labor.

Peripheral nation—World system theory analyzes the relationships between nations by dividing them between core nations (see core nation) and peripheral nations — those exploited nations (often former colonies) which supply labor and raw materials to the core nations. Semi-pheripheral nations were once peripheral but are now more industrialized and becoming influential in the globalized economy. They may at some future point gain enough power to push the present core nations into the semipheriphery. The term Global South has to some extent replaced this term.

Political system—A society's organization of the distribution of public power, and ultimately of access to resources. A society may have an egalitarian political system, such as a band or tribe, or it may have a political system that institutionalizes and legitimizes varying degrees of inequality, such as chiefdoms, kingdoms and other states.

Polyandry—Marriage of a woman to two or more men at one time; a form of polygamy.

Polygamy—Marriage to more than one spouse at a time.

Polygyny—Marriage of a man to two or more women at a time; a form of polygamy.

Population control—Forms of behavior which influence the rate at which a population grows; generally refers to limiting growth.

Population pressures—The difficulties a population experiences when it begins to come close to or exceed the carrying capacity of its territory.

Postpartum sex taboo—A rule or norm stating that a woman (and sometimes her husband also) should not have sex for a certain length of time after the birth of a baby; often reinforced by religious sanctions.

Poverty—The inability, due to lack of resources, to participate in a society as people in that society say people should.

Power—The ability to get other people to do as you want, even in the absence of their consent.

Precarity —A worker's perception that the conditions under which he/she is living are unpredictable, insecure, and full of risk.

Prestige—Deference or respect or other means of implying that one person is better or more important than other people.

Priest—A religious specialist who may or may not directly contact the supernatural; a priest may instead conduct the rituals which allow others to gain contact with the supernatural. Priests are full-time and may be paid or maintained by the group they work for, or they may be paid or maintained by the state or by a religious bureaucracy of which they are part. Priests are more common in stratified societies and are usually representatives of and certified by the dominant religion in that society (compare with shaman).

Primogeniture—Literally 'first born;' a society that follows rules of primogeniture requires that an estate and the rights that go with it go to the oldest child. Usually it actually means the oldest male child. Other children do not share in the inheritance, or share only in a very limited fashion. Various societies have different methods of dealing with the situation if there are no boys.

Production—Taking raw materials from nature and making them into goods that are useful to humans (see also mode of production and means of production).

Professional/managerial class—In a capitalist economy, the section of the working class that performs professional services and/or managerial services for the capitalist class by managing, training, and controlling the rest of the working class. Like the rest of the working class, this class does not own the means of production and are paid wages by their capitalist class employers or by the government. Their wages are in some cases very high, as CEOs or lawyers, but in others, for instance as social workers, their wages may be not much higher than those of the rest of the working class (see also collaborator class).

Psychological wages—W.E.B. Du Bois' term for 'compensating' people psychologically for accepting inferiority by giving them someone over whom they can feel superior.

Purdah—The isolation of women from men in public (Arabic term); in some societies this means that women live their lives almost entirely within the household.

Purification—A spiritual cleansing, sometimes symbolized by physical cleaning, in preparation for contact with the supernatural or entrance into the sacred realm.

Race—An artificial grouping of people invented to fill ideological needs in situations of massive inequality. The claim is made that different groups have biological differences which are said to be important and are passed on from one generation to the next. In reality, however, there have never been isolated groups of people for long enough to establish biologically distinct categories of people. Instead, traits which are more common in the subordinate group than in the dominant group are given arbitrary importance. For instance, Americans claim that skin color is important, but not hair color, in determining race. However, we used to claim that hair color was important, because red hair was said to indicate Irish ancestry, and the Irish were a separate race, said to be lazy, short-tempered, irresponsible, and inclined to drink too much. People of English and German ancestry in the U.S. discriminated against the Irish, sometimes even killing them. Since we no longer discriminate against the Irish, we no longer think hair color is very important, and we no longer distinguish them as a separate race. 'Race' in other words, is socially constructed, and is not real biologically. Although race is not real biologically, however, the organization of societies on the basis of race has very real consequences (see Thomas Theorem).

Racialization—The ideological process of designating certain categories of people as biologically separate and different from the dominant group. This process of race-making generally occurs to justify and enable super-exploitation.

Racism—The belief that members of another 'race' are inferior and that unequal treatment is therefore justified and natural. Racist policies are ones that protect the power and privilege of the dominant race and lead to unequal consequences for members of different 'races' even when the people enforcing the policies are not personally racist and don't realize the racist implications of the policy.

Rank—A ranked society is one in which certain formal, prestigious offices belong to certain lineages, and must be held by someone who is a member of that lineage. The lineages themselves are ranked, so that some have more prestige and power than others. Ranking is often associated with chiefdoms.

Reciprocity—The exchange of gifts and/or services between individuals, in which the goods and services given and received are expected to be approximately equal. This form of exchange is most common among people who consider themselves to be equals; it is therefore most common in egalitarian societies. Does not involve using money as a medium of exchange.

Redistribution—A method of exchanging goods in which the surplus produced by many people is given to a central person or institution who then redistributes it to group members and other people. The Big Man system is based on redistribution; so is the use of taxes for education and other public services (see also egalitarian redistribution and stratified redistribution).

Religion—The cultural assumption that there are supernatural forces or beings outside of human life and the physical world. Religion generally includes specifications about interaction with these beings and forces. It involves myths and rituals and is found in all cultures.

Religious specialists—People who are felt to be particularly good at getting in touch with or dealing with the supernatural. Shamans are part-time specialists; priests are full-time specialists.

Republic—A state which is not a ranked society; positions of political and economic power are not directly assigned by ancestry or inheritance (compare with kingdom).

Reserve labor force—Those people in a capitalist society who do not have a job but would take one if it were available, or who work part-time but would work full time if a job were available.

Resistance—The refusal to accommodate (see accommodation) the exploitative demands of those with more power; the refusal to do something against one's will. Organized resistance is the attempt of oppressed people to jointly refuse the demands of those with power (for instance by striking or boycotting).

Resources—See means of production.

Revitalization movement—A social movement, frequently religious or with strong religious aspects, that attempts either to bring new life to a society which has been conquered or otherwise damaged, or to bring to life a new society in its place. Such movements generally incorporate aspects of the old society as well as aspects of the conquering society, reinterpreting both in order to deal with life in the new and generally more powerless situation.

Revolt—An organized attempt to overthrow established power relations.

Rite of passage—A ritual dramatizing the transition from one social state or phase of life to another; for instance, weddings, funerals, and initiations.

Ritual—A highly stylized, repetitive behavior at a set time and place; it provides access to or interaction with the supernatural.

Sacred realm—A place or state of consciousness outside of daily life, where ultimate or supernatural beings or forces in the universe are accessible; the sacred realm involves a feeling of religious significance.

Secular—Not having to do with religion.

Sedentary—A way of life built around staying in one place year-round, for many years at a time; the opposite of nomadic.

Sedentary foragers—People who live by foraging in an area so rich in resources that they do not need to move regularly to avoid exceeding the carrying capacity of their land.

Segregation—The legal separation of two or more segments of a population, based on an ideology claiming that certain kinds of contact with a subordinate group is damaging or demeaning to the dominant group, effective as an instrument of divide and rule (see also apartheid).

Self-fulfilling prophesy—A prediction that comes true because people believe the prediction and act in ways that make the prediction come true. For instance, a teacher telling you that you have no talent for math may cause you to quit trying and your family to quit pushing you, with the result that you don't do well and the statement that you have no talent for math appears to be true.

Sexism—The assumption that the way one's own sex lives and works and thinks is the natural and correct way, and that members of the other sex are actually inferior, so that unequal treatment is justified. Sexist policies are ones which protect the power and privilege of the dominant sex and lead to unequal consequences for members of the other sex even when the people enforcing the policies are not personally sexist and don't realize the sexist implications of the policy.

Sexual division of labor—The assignment of a society's tasks according to sex. In some societies the division between the work that men do and the work that women do is very clear. In others there is considerable overlap.

Shaman—Part-time religious practitioner who is believed to have the power to contact supernatural forces directly, on behalf of individuals or groups. They are usually paid or given gifts by the individuals they help; however, they make their living in the same way as other people. Shamans are more common in fairly egalitarian societies. In stratified societies they are more common among groups that are being exploited, and may be in competition with priests (see priests for comparison).

Sharecropping—A social and economic arrangement in which non-landowners farm land, often under the direction of the owner, and give the owner a portion of the crop, usually half.

Shun—An informal type of social control, in which members of a group refuse to acknowledge the existence of an individual who has seriously offended the group's sense of appropriate behavior. Typically people in the group do not speak to or even look at a person who is being shunned until the person changes his or her behavior.

Slavery—A system of forced labor in which people's ability to work, and in some cases their entire bodies, including their ability to reproduce, no longer belong to them. The value of the work they do is taken from them with no compensation at all.

Social construction of reality—A way of understanding the world and human life which recognizes that people make what is real in our world; there is very little about being human which exists naturally; most situations and relationships and ways of thinking and doing and treating other people are made by humans (e.g. there is nothing built into humans which makes it part of nature that most diapers in the U.S. are changed by women; our systems of diaper-changing are organized by our social relationships with the people around us and by our entire socio-economic system).

Social control—Those processes, both formal and informal, in a society which lead most people most of the time to act according to the norms of their culture or subculture.

Social inequality—A system whereby certain individuals can gain more power, prestige, influence, or wealth than others. Social inequality becomes stratified when people who gain wealth, power, or prestige through their own efforts gain control of the means of production and can then pass their advantages on to their children. Egalitarian redistribution involves some social inequality, but no stratification; ranking systems involve more social inequality and some degree of stratification. States have great social inequality and are highly stratified.

Social security—A system by which a society as a whole takes some degree of responsibility for the basic well-being of its members. Such systems work on the presumption that it is impossible for all individuals to provide entirely for themselves. Frequently systems of social security are used to partially offset inequality in a society.

Socialism—A socio-economic system in a state society in which, unlike capitalism, all or some of the means of production are owned by the state as representative of the members of the society. Production and distribution is legitimated by appeal to the needs of people, rather than by the appeal to the need to make a profit.

Socialist republic—A republic whose political and economic system is based on socialism.

Society—A group of people who are relatively separated from surrounding populations, occupy a specific territory, and share a common culture (complex societies may have various subcultures within them).

Sororal polygyny—A form of polygyny in which the co-wives are all sisters.

Sovereignty—The supreme authority within a recognized territory; the right to govern that territory and the people in it without outside interference.

Specialization—A detailed division of labor in which some people specialize in producing one good or service, while other people produce different goods or services; these are then exchanged. This contrasts with a society in which people produce everything or almost everything they need for themselves. Specialization on a large scale is usually associated with systems of market exchange.

State—A political entity that exercises sovereign rights over a territory, has a monopoly on the use of force within that territory, and exercises power through centralized, hierarchical bureaucracies to enforce control of the means of production, collect revenue in taxes or tribute, and enforce laws and norms about members' duties and rights. States are stratified societies in which some groups monopolize wealth, power, and prestige.

Status marker—an object or activity that indicates the status of a person. As the term is generally used it refers to the indication of wealth or high rank (as in the royal purple or owning a Mercedes driven by a chauffeur, or playing polo rather than basketball). However, driving a beat up pick-up also marks status, but not high status. Used in a different sense, wearing a wedding ring is also a status marker indicating your status as a married person (see also ceremonial valuable and class marker).

Stratification—A system which enables one group to maintain control of the means of production and use the labor of those who don't; a stratification system shifts surplus into the hands of those who control the means of production. This means particular groups have greater access to wealth, power, and prestige than others and are able to pass their position to their children. Such groups include ones based on rank or on class, 'race,' or gender (see also class and social inequality).

Stratified redistribution—A form of redistribution practiced in ranked and stratified societies in which people at the center of redistribution do not give away all that they receive, and they and their lineage are better off than other people, since they are able to benefit from the labor of other people. They are able to use the redistribution system to create wealth for themselves. Generally only people of high rank can act as central people (see redistribution; compare with egalitarian redistribution).

Structural adjustment—The imposition of austerity measures to cut government spending, mainly on social welfare and social justice programs, thus adjusting the structure of a society so that poorer people have fewer options and will work for less or will be more docile, and making it possible for the government to spend more on repaying loans from other countries or from international organizations such as the World Bank.

Structural violence—Violence that is not a result of individuals or the state taking direct action to harm others. Structural violence generally results from inequality built into the social structure and results in deaths, maimings, malnutrition among those most seriously exploited. A death resulting from a society's refusal to commit adequate tax money to care for the poor is an example of structural violence. A death caused by murder is not.

Studying up—In studying up, the anthropologist consciously decides to focus on the people who hold power in an exploitative situation, with the hope that the knowledge they gain will give clues about how to change the situation.

Subordinate group— Those people in the category that is excluded from most positions of power in a society, whether that group is based on race, class, gender or ethnicity.

Subsistence strategy—The methods used by a group of people to get food and other resources, such as foraging or horticulture. Do not confuse with mode of production or means of production.

Super-exploitation—People are left with so little of what they produce, or are paid so little for the work they do and the value that they produce, that they cannot pay for the cost of raising the next generation, or of maintaining themselves as workers. If super-exploitation is occurring through the use of wages, you can also refer to this situation as being paid dying wages. In a group that is being super-exploited, on average people actually die younger and have more of their children die, which is where the expression dying wages comes from.

Supernatural—Forces or beings that are not part of physical nature but believed to exist by members of a particular religion.

Surplus—Production beyond the subsistence needs of the producers (see also accumulation of a surplus).

Surplus labor—Work beyond what is needed to provide for yourself and family and therefore can be allocated to other uses, including non-necessities for yourself or to provide profit or other benefits for someone who has a claim on your labor, such as an employer or landlord or lord.

Terrorism—The systematic use of violence designed to terrify an entire population or group within a population into submission. Typically violence carried out by a state in the context of a declared war is not called terrorism, nor is violence carried out by authorized police action within a state. However, definition of terrorism is difficult because one group's freedom fighters may be defined by their conqueror or government as terrorists (as in Palestinian or Iraqi use of violence), while violence carried out by the more powerful group or conquerors is defined as justice or as legitimate violence (as in lynching and racially imbalanced jailing and execution during segregation in the U.S. South; or as in the massive death toll of civilians in Afghanistan and Iraq at the hands of the U.S. military at the behest of the U.S president as legitimated commander in chief).

Thomas Theorem—The Thomas Theorem states that if enough people believe something is real, the belief can have real consequences for people's lives, even if the belief is false. Thomas was a sociologist.

Trading partners—A system of carrying out (usually) balanced reciprocity between members of distant hostile groups. Partners on opposite sides vouch for and protect each other when one group or the other makes an expedition to the other for purposes of exchange; such partnerships are sometimes passed on from generation to generation.

Transnational corporation—A term now used for multinational corporations that have become so powerful that they transcend the power of most nations.

Tribe—A pastoral or horticultural group organized through kinship and lead by people who gain their position by ability, rather than by birth. Such leaders are frequently heads of lineages who act as central organizers of egalitarian redistribution and are sometimes known as Big Men. There is considerable ambiguity about the use of the term (see also Big Man).

Tributary mode of production—An economic/political/social system in which low-ranking people activate their hereditary right to use the means of production by giving tribute in wealth, surplus, or labor to an individual of higher rank who has hereditary authority over the land or other resources that low ranking people use. The giving of tribute can be enforced by political or military means.

Universals—See cultural universals.

Usufruct (Use right)—A traditional right to the produce of a certain piece of land (to use the fruits of the land), generally in a society that does not have a system of private property. For instance, a lineage may grant usufruct rights on its corporate lands to members of the lineage. Also used to indicate a traditional right to the use of a piece of land which must be validated by some service or small payment in kind to a higher ranking land-holder. This system is most likely to be found in areas where land itself has relatively little value or cannot easily be sold.

Valuables—See ceremonial valuable.

Variation—See cultural variation.

Wage—Compensation in the form of money for selling labor in a system of market exchange.

Wage labor—Selling your labor to someone who owns the means of production.

War—-War involves the purposeful gathering together and organizing, usually under the direction of a leader with some degree of authority, of a group of men (and occasionally women), who are seen as legitimately authorized by their group and the institutions of their society to steal resources from, and if necessary kill, members of another group. Revenge is frequently cited as the justification for aggressive war.

Wealth—Items which can be owned and have money value or and exchange value (see also ceremonial valuable).

INDEX

and class 147, 150
and inequality 166
and market economy 156
and ownership of means of production 156
Inequality 4
as basic to understanding societies 22
see also gender, birthright, rank, caste, race, class, social inequality
Infant mortality 8
and inequality 51
and socialism 55
in egalitarian societies 88
Inheritance
and birthright 137
and polyandry 125
in patrilineal societies 132, 134, 136
of birthright 130–131
see also privilege
Institutionalized 88
Internal colonialism 68, 218
and Appalachia 37
and benefits to elite 36
creation of 38
defined 36
ideology about 37, 39
International Monetary Fund 5, 52, 201, 205
Iraq 33, 59, 109, 197, 199, 201, 205, 225
Irish people 9, 61, 153, 185, 222
and potato famine 51
Islam 4, 17, 26, 57, 145, 178
U.S.attitudes about used for divide and rule 184

J

Japan and empire 41
Justice system 152, 185
illegal 152, 162, 183, 186
legal 152, 177, 180, 185

K

Katrina 8
Kentucky 38, 179
Kingdom 99, 131
aristocrats' kinship with others 96, 130
compared to republic 100
defined 96
problems with concept 99
Kin-ordered mod 97
Kin-ordered mode of production 78, 96, 129
in tribes 128
Kinship 75, 78
Kinship obligations 78, 81, 95, 129, 132
Knowledge
false 17
incomplete 17

see also anthropological knowledge, learned ignorance, esoteric knowledge
Ku Klux Klan 152, 162

L

Labor force
and caste 146
and women 58, 125, 136, 139, 198
control of 183
creation of 45–46, 51, 124, 143
in kingdom 96
see also reserve labor force, labor reserve
unfree in U.S. 155
Labor importation 32, 157
and bracero program 36
and denial of rights 36
and guest worker 36
and illegal immigrants 36
defined 35
slavery as 35
Labor reserve 32, 43, 50, 218
defined 43
organization of 43
Lakota 63
Land redistribution 44, 54, 146, 182
Latino/a 153
and racialization 185
and unfree labor 34
history in U.S. 33, 160
removal 34
Leader 83
Learned behavior 9
Learned ignorance 18, 21, 23–24, 48–49, 51, 61, 207
Least industrialized 47
Legitmate use of force 104, 108
Leveling device 83, 87, 219
Liberation theology 57, 193, 219
Lineage 7, 75, 77–78, 81, 93–96, 106, 120–123, 125, 128–132, 212, 219, 221–222, 225–226
and origin myth 104
and right to title 93
aristocratic 93–95, 131
commoner 94
conveying rights 77, 128
in chiefdoms 130
Living wage 165–166, 174
Low-paying jobs 167
and gender 166, 174
and race 166
Lynching 16, 152, 162, 183, 186, 219, 225

M

Magic 86

N

of paramount chief 96
Powhatans 180
Precarity 11, 111
Prestige 74
Priest 85, 104, 192, 221
    and dominant religion 192
    and justification of power 104, 146, 192
Priest, defined 104
Prisoners
    as unfree labor 155, 157, 180
    creation of 180–181
Privatization 111, 200, 204
Privilege 132
    and birthright 130
    see also inheritance, gender inequality-male priv-
    ilege, white privilege, white supremacy, rank
Production 79
Professional/managerial class 14–15, 59, 148, 150,
213
    and illegal use of force 186
    and promotion of ideology 174, 183
    elite control of 37, 49, 172
    ideology of 37, 172, 174
    providing supervision and control 149, 155,
    172–173
    see also middle class
Profit
    and capitalist mode of production 148
    and socialism 54
Progress
    ideas about 20, 73
Providing labor
    and caste 146
    and class 148
    and race 152
Psychological wage 182
PTSD 200
Puerto Rico 33, 47
Purdah 138

R

Race 151
    and behavior 9
    and capitalist mode of production 151
    and creation of cheap labor force 151
    defined 151
    explanation of physical difference 179
    interracial cooperation 39, 181–182, 186
    lack of 'racial' distinction between workers in co-
    lonial Virginia 181
    not real biologically 179, 185
    social construction of 60, 179, 181
    uses of by elite 185
Racialization 37, 39, 60, 179–182, 185
    defined 185
Racism 15, 18

and control of labor force 184
    elite promotion of 183–184
Racist 13
Rank 92
    and birthright 130
Ranked societies
    and use of others' labor 94
    comparison of types 99
    defined 93
Rape 66, 138, 140, 162, 177
Reciprocity 79, 102
Reconstruction after the U.S. Civil War 151, 162
Redistribution 82, 84, 86–87, 94–95
Religion 5, 27, 32, 57, 61, 85–86, 103–104, 111,
138, 150, 160, 163, 172, 174, 178, 185–193
    and accommodation 190, 192
    and critical but uncontrollable issues 190–191
    and elite 189
    and esoteric knowledge 191
    and gender inequality 188–189
    and hope 190–191
    and magic 86
    and non-elite 189
    and patriarchy 188
    and social control 104, 153, 188–190
    and subordinate group 192
    and subsistence strategy 188
    and war 108, 189
    as a wedge issue 61, 178
    dominant version 174, 193
    in complex chiefdoms 104
    in stratified societies 187
    justifying distribution of power 57, 85–86, 103–
    104, 146, 172, 187–188, 191–192
    non-dominant version 57, 193
Republic 101
    capitalist 101, 147
    compared to kingdom 100
    defined 101
    democratic compared to dictatorship 101
Reserve labor force 39, 50–51, 54, 153, 156, 164
    creation of 157
Resistance 19, 25, 31, 45, 53–57, 64–65, 67, 161,
164, 169, 177, 182, 193–194, 199–200, 205, 207–
208, 211, 223
    and empire 202
Resources
    control of 132, 150, 201
    see also means of production, access to means of
    production
Reverse discrimination 178
Revitalization 57
Revitalization movement 57
Revolt 39, 46, 54–56, 151, 173
    examples in U.S. 53, 186, 194
    preventing 40, 42, 167, 171–173, 175
    preventing through force 185
    preventing through patriarchy 175
    preventing through race 177, 182–183

Subsistence strategy See foraging, horticulture, pastoral, agriculture, industrial
Super-exploitation 38, 61, 152–155, 162–163, 189, 215, 225
    and racialization 61
    see also dying wages
Supernatural 86
Surplus 72, 91
    accumulation of 95–96, 102, 143
    and egalitarian redistribution 81
    and inequality 91, 172
    and marriage 123
    and slavery 107
    and stratified redistribution 94
    and war 105
Surplus labor 91–92, 95
Syria 112, 199
Syrian refugee crisis 112
System of exchange See reciprocity, egalitarian redistribution, stratified redistribution, market exchange

T

Taxation
    and stratified redistribution 102
    in capitalist states 102
Tea Party 200
Terrorism 152, 162, 183, 186, 225
    state terrorism in U.S. 182
Third World 47
Thomas theorem 225
    see social construction of reality
Tobacco Wars 194
Trading partners 102
Trail of Tears 42
Transnational corporations 49, 200, 207
    and domestic policy 199, 201
    and empire 198
    and foreign policy 199
    and local elites 201
    and professional/managerial class 201
    and use of military 199
    defined 198
Tribe 76, 81
    and war captives 107
    problems with concept 60
Tributary mode of production 96–97, 99–100, 147, 216, 218
    and patriarchy 175
    basic characteristic 172
    defined 97
Tribute 32, 41, 44–46, 95–98, 103–104, 107, 160, 173, 176, 190, 214, 221, 224
    in an empire 40
    limitations of 41
Trickle up 154, 167
Trickle-down 48

Truth 12, 14–16
    see also perspective, anthropology and perspective problems

U

UN 201
Underdeveloped 47
Unfree labor
    see also Labor force-unfree, women, immigrants, prisoners, welfare, encomienda, hacienda, indentured servants, debt peonage
    state provision of 157, 160–161, 180–181
Unions 38, 49, 52, 54, 165, 186, 194
Universal health care 178, 184
Use of force 173
    and dependent development 49
    and gender inequality 177
    and white supremacy 34, 162, 181
    elite control of 186
    illegal 186
    in capitalist states 148
    in kingdoms 99
    legal 185
    see also justice system
    to maintain stratification 185
    to prevent movement toward equality 54
Use of others' labor
    by elite 99
    in bands 84
    in chiefdoms 94
    in egalitarian societies 75
Use of others' labor
    and gender equality 127
    and marriage 124
    in matrilineal societies 133
USSR 55, 198, 202
Usufruct 162, 221

V

Vagrancy 33, 162, 180
Violence 31, 34, 66, 72, 111, 113, 117, 151–152, 183–187
Vote 23, 33–35, 53, 101, 151, 182–183, 205, 213

W

Wall Street 55
War 4, 20, 33–34, 38, 44–45, 47–48, 54–55, 57, 59, 62, 66–67, 82, 85, 95, 104–109, 111–113, 117, 129, 132, 136, 151, 156, 160–161, 177–178, 180, 184, 187, 189, 194, 197–199, 205–206, 208, 226
    and benefit to corporations 198, 200

and empire 205
and gender inequality 59, 129, 132
and inequality between men 106
and religion 189
and theft 105
in bands 105
in chiefdoms 106
in ranked societies 132
in tribes 106
making it appear reasonable 108, 200
reason for 105
reasons for 106
War captives 95
War machine 109, 140, 200
War on Terror 178, 184, 197
and denial of rights 35, 199
Water 39, 50, 58, 65, 72, 105, 111, 140, 158, 181, 204—206
Wealth 71
in capitalism 143
in feudalism 143
source of 154, 167
Wedge issues 178, 194
Weiner, Annette 17
Welfare 11—13, 28, 53, 156—157, 174, 202
and socialism 166
and stratified redistribution 102
and unfree labor 156
attitudes about 11
for corporations 47, 52—53
reform 13, 178
Western Europe 202
White man's burden 200
White men
and jobs 166
anger of 166—167
elite control of 166
White privilege 181
White supremacy 182
and terrorism 162
ideology of 34, 60, 183, 200
Whiteness 182—183
and divide and rule 181—182
as used to control whites 182
invention of 181—182
non-existence of idea in colonial Virginia 181
psychological wage of 182
Women
and dependent development 53, 59
and unfree labor 155
Hindu 146
in government 59
Muslim 26
see also control of, gender equality, gender inequality, gender roles
Working class
and empire 200, 207
and Europe 165
and family structure 136

compared to slaves, serfs 148
defined 148
in fast food 14
see also labor force
world-wide 50
World Bank 5, 52, 201, 205
World Trade Organization 201, 205
World War II 33—34, 47, 136, 165, 198

Y

Yousafzai, Malala 56